The Open University

D103 SOCIETY AND SOCIAL SCIENCE: A FOUNDATION COURSE

BLOCK 5
IDENTITIES AND INTERACTION

THE OPEN UNIVERSITY

D103 PRODUCTION TEAM

John Allen
James Anderson (Chairperson)
Robert Bocock
Peter Bradshaw
Vivienne Brown
Linda Clark (Course Secretary)
David Coates
Allan Cochrane
Jeremy Cooper (BBC)
Neil Costello
Clare Falkner (BBC)
Stuart Hall
Sue Himmelweit
Jack Leathem (BBC)
Richard Maidment
Doreen Massey
Gregor McLennan
Andrew Northedge
Kay Pole
Marilyn Ricci (Course Manager)
Paul Smith
Richard Stevens
Elaine Storkey
Kenneth Thompson
Diane Watson
Margaret Wetherell

External Consultants
Tom Burden
David Deacon
David Denver
Caroline Dumonteil
Owen Hartley
Tom Hulley
Robert Looker
Angela Phillips
Colm Regan
Richard Sanders
Neil Thompson
Patrick Wright

Tutor Assessors
Alan Brown
Lyn Brennan
Mona Clark
Ian Crosher
Donna Dickenson
Brian Graham
Philip Markey
Norma Sherratt
Jan Vance

Tom Hunter, Chris Wooldridge, David Wilson, Robert Cookson, Nigel Draper, David Scott-Macnab (Editors); Paul Smith (Librarian); Alison George (Graphic Artist); Jane Sheppard (Designer); Sue Rippon (Project Control); Robin Thornton (Summer School Manager); John Hunt (Summer School IT); John Bennett ; and others.

External Academic Assessors
Professor Anthony Giddens, Cambridge University (Overall Assessor)
Dr Geoffrey Harcourt, Cambridge University (Block III)
Dr Patrick Dunleavy, London School of Economics (Block IV)
Dr Halla Beloff, Edinburgh University (Block V)
Professor Brian Robson, Manchester University (Block VI)

The Open University,
Walton Hall, Milton Keynes,
MK7 6AA

First published 1991. Reprinted 1992, 1993, 1994, 1995 Copyright © 1991 The Open University

Designed by the Graphic Design Group of the Open University

Typeset by The Open University and printed in the United Kingdom by The Alden Press, Oxford.

ISBN 0 7492 0041 3

For general availability of supporting material referred to in this text, please write to Open University Educational Enterprises Limited, 12 Cofferidge Close, Stony Stratford, Milton Keynes, MK11 1BY, United Kingdom.

Further information on Open University Courses may be obtained from the Admissions Office, The Open University, P. O. Box 48, Walton Hall, Milton Keynes, MK7 6AB.

1.6

2264C/D103u19i1.6

BLOCK INTRODUCTION AND STUDY GUIDE

Prepared for the Course Team by Margaret Wetherell

1 IDENTITY AND INTERACTION

You are now more than half-way through D103. And the course has come a long way since the terms 'social' and 'social science' were first introduced. Block by block we have tried to build up your understanding of some of the major processes and structures of UK society. You have progressed from the study of social structures and social divisions to economics, and then to politics. In all these subjects the focus of the course has been on large-scale trends affecting masses of people.

However, towards the end of Block IV — in Unit 17 — some different kinds of issues became more prominent: issues concerning people's beliefs and ideologies, their perceptions and representations. Block V continues to explore these areas, turning from the study of the large-scale to the study of people as individuals and their relationships in daily life.

Block V develops two topics in detail: the study of *identity* and of *social interaction*. The term 'social interaction' covers the processes involved in acting jointly in social situations, in relating to other people, in mutual reaction and influence. 'Identity', however, is more difficult to define. It is one of those words which appear all over the place but which are difficult to pin down precisely.

The term 'identity' is a recent one in social scientists' vocabulary, appearing first only in the 1950s. We talk about ethnic identity, about national identity, about people having lost their sense of identity, about having a crisis of identity. Roughly, these issues all seem to concern a person's possible answer to the question: 'Who are you?', or 'What kind of person do you see yourself as, and how do you define yourself?'

ACTIVITY 1

Before going any further, take a pen and paper and write some ten to fifteen adjectives or phrases in answer to the question 'Who are you?' What words would you use to describe yourself?

The answers you gave in Activity 1 tell you something about how you see yourself. It is not so much any one characteristic which constitutes identity; but rather a number of characteristics make up a particular pattern. These characteristics comprise both a sense of personal continuity and of distinctiveness which set us apart, and also the shared characteristics and common experiences which bind us to others.

Take a look at the list of characteristics below. These are descriptions which different people have given in answer to the question 'Who are you?'

aggressive	16 years old	a socialist
a good dresser	Scottish	athletic
human	Susan	skin-problem sufferer
black	quite nice looking	communications engineer
blind	a lazy sod	gay
fabulous, glamourous grandmother	a mobile set of chemical reactions	a complex arrangement of abstract thoughts
full of life	not British	good with my hands
spiritually growing	vulnerable	mature
a strong-willed person	quite shy	

These descriptions fall into different categories. There are some which stress social characteristics — political affiliation, gender, occupation, national origins and so on. But other characteristics seem more personal, pointing to personality traits, styles of behaviour, physical features, and private experiences.

To be comprehensive, our discussion of identity, which takes place in the first two units of the block, will need to reflect all these different aspects. Unit 19 will take up the more personal dimensions of identity by looking at subjective or private experience, at the influence of time and development through life, and at how physical characteristics, our bodies and biology, might be influential. Unit 20 will then take up the social dimensions of identity and ask how our sense of identity — our sense of who we are — might be moulded by the kind of society we live in.

Although Block V does involve a change in focus from previous blocks, as we move from what is sometimes called the 'macro-social' to the 'micro-social', you will see that there are still strong links between our discussion of identity and the study of UK politics, economics, and social structures. In one way or another you have done quite a bit of work on identity already. Think back, for example, to Unit 10 where the importance of work as a source of identity was stressed. Unit 20 will come back to this issue. Think, too, of the discussion in Unit 8 and in associated Reader chapters about the biological basis of gender. Unit 19 will give you an opportunity to explore this question in more depth.

One identity characteristic I haven't mentioned so far is people's sense of place, of belonging to a particular locality. In the examples above, for instance, one person felt that being 'not British' was something significant about her/his identity, another that being Scottish should be pretty high on his/her list. When British people meet abroad one of the first questions they ask each other is 'What part of the UK are you from?' One of the television programmes associated with Block V (TV 10) will look at people's feelings about national identity. D103 hasn't yet considered substantially the contribution of geography, and the impact of the regions on life in the UK — that's the task of Block VI — but clearly the study of identity raises questions about our sense of place which can be carried forward into Block VI.

Block V does not claim that there can be any one single answer to the basic issues about human nature raised by the study of identity and interaction. You will find many answers which will be compared and contrasted with each other. Units 19 and 20 describe four very different perspectives on identity. The social dimensions described in Unit 20 make up one perspective while the personal dimensions described in Unit 19 break down into three other perspectives — the 'phenomenological' (the study of personal experience), the 'developmental' or 'psychoanalytic' (the study of changes through life), and the 'biological'. It may seem daunting to look at one topic from four different angles in this way but this is necessary if we are to begin to understand the different facets of identity and the factors on which it depends. It is also good practice to compare and contrast different answers to controversial questions.

Unit 21 moves from the study of identity to the study of social interaction. The four perspectives discussed in Units 19 and 20, particularly the social and the biological perspectives, also structure the study of this topic. Once again you will find links with previous blocks. You have spent time studying social relations on a broad front; now comes the opportunity to look at social relationships between two, three, or four people, and between people in small groups: the conversations, friendships and actions which constitute our experience of everyday social life.

One of the advantages of studying topics from several perspectives is that it is possible to see how different points of view encourage different kinds of research methodology. The way in which advocates of contrasting perspectives go about actually doing social science depends on their very different assumptions about what they are researching. Unit 22 will not only review Block V but will also add this theme of methodology to the work on theory you have been doing in the other theory-review units of D103.

Your work on identity and interaction will not end with Unit 22 but will continue with a module on these topics at Summer School. Your thoughts are probably already beginning to turn to Summer School and the effect that the summer period generally might have on your pattern of work. Be sure to look at the *Preparing for the D103 Summer School* booklet before you go to Summer School.

What about the course themes in Block V? What, for example, is *public* and *private* about the study of identity and interaction? How can the theme of the public and the private be used? The private will be defined here as the personal, inner world of the individual, consisting of private thoughts, motives, attitudes and so on. The public will be defined as the faces that people present to the world, and as the social context in which identities and interactions are played out. Global processes will be important too. Ethnicity is an important aspect of self-definition, for instance, yet the context for ethnic identity in any one locality depends on international movements of people and historical patterns of colonization.

The theme of *representation and reality* will also feature substantially. If you think back to the list of terms that people used in describing themselves, it is clear that these descriptions of identity reflect these people's representations of themselves: what characteristics they select as important and how they interpret these. Identity is very much about representation, about our capacity to make sense of the social world and our place in it. But different representations of identity do not just arise because of *what* we see; they arise also from *how* we see what we do see. The reason this course has avoided trying to define identity too precisely is that any definition would itself be a representation. It would depend on assumptions about such things as the best way to study and make sense of identity. To define identity too precisely at this point would be to bias the discussion towards one or other perspective. We want you, for the moment, to keep an open mind.

2   COMPONENTS AND STUDY GUIDE

2.1   COURSE READER

At various points in the units of Block V you will, as usual, be directed to the Reader, specifically to Chapters 15–18. These follow a different format from other sections of the Reader. You will find eight readings, for instance, rather than three longer pieces. We want to present you with a wide range of material, including pieces of people's autobiographies and more literary accounts, to show you the sheer diversity of views on identity and interaction. So note that you'll use the Reader more frequently than usual, particularly in relation to Unit 20.

You will also be asked to complete your reading of Chapter 22 on traditions of social thought in this block. The remaining section is Section 3, entitled 'The presence of the traditions in the study of society', and this is to be read along-side Unit 20.

2.2   STUDY SKILLS

There is one hour set aside in this block for further reading of *The Good Study Guide*. You should focus on Chapter 6, Sections 6 and 7. In addition there is a study skills section attached to Unit 21 which looks at the process of developing arguments in essays, and is intended to develop your essay-writing skills further. This section works through the kind of essay question you might get for Unit 21 and you should find it useful, therefore, for both exam revision and when doing TMA 05.

2.3   AUDIO-VISUAL COMPONENT

There are two television programmes, two radio programmes and one cassette associated with this block, together with some related activities and material in the *Media Booklet*.

The two television programmes take up two central aspects of identity: nationality, which is dealt with in the first programme, and ageing or the transitions people go through in life, which is dealt with in the second programme. TV 10, on national identity, is linked to the social perspective developed in Unit 20. You will watch TV 11 on age and identity in the week that you study Unit 22, and the emphasis in this programme will be on investigating the social and biological changes in identity that occur as we grow older along with changes in people's personal experiences. Audio-cassette 5 is divided into three parts which are linked to Units 19, 20 and 21. Among other things, it deals with the questions raised by sociobiology and the issues involved in the comparison of multiple perspectives, while Radio 09 questions further the concept of identity. The remaining radio programme (Radio 10) will help you with TMA 05.

2.4   RESOURCE FILE

If you have been compiling a file throughout the course you'll find plenty of material on identity and interaction to add to it, as these topics are continually discussed in newspapers and magazines. You might like to collect material on two particular areas.

First, there are the different representations of identity found in magazines and other sources. Many magazines, for instance, have quick personality questionnaires in which you are asked to answer some questions and then add up the scores to discover if you are a good friend, an aggressive person, or whatever. Ask yourself what assumptions are being made about identity in these different materials and what perspective in the units these relate to. You could look, too, at advice in 'agony aunt' columns, at child-rearing advice, at articles on biology and identity, and at articles on the effects of the different roles that people play — for example, the stresses of being a working mother. Novels are a further good source of different views on human nature and relationships. In each case try to identify the assumptions being made and the identity concepts being used; and, analyse and criticize the representation, looking for parallels with the perspectives examined in the various units of this block.

A second area in which you can collect material is your own life story. You might like to collect some autobiographical materials — family history, material from any diaries you have kept, your short description in answer to the question 'Who are you?' in Activity 1. Again, you could use this material to question yourself about your theory of your own identity and patterns of interaction. How do you conceptualize or make sense of yourself, and what do you think helps to make you the kind of person you are?

As always, you are welcome to introduce material from your resource file into your TMA answers, provided it is relevant to the question, but don't work on the file at the expense of time you should spend on the units and other components of the block.

2.5   STUDY TIME ALLOCATIONS

The following study guide will enable you to plan roughly what proportion of your available time to devote to each component.

Block components	Approximate study time (hours)
Block Introduction and Study Guide	$\frac{1}{2}$
Unit 19: Personal Identity	7
Reader: Chapter 15	$2\frac{1}{2}$
Radio 09	$\frac{1}{2}$
Tape 5: Part One	$\frac{1}{2}$
Total	11
Unit 20: Social Identity	6
Reader: Chapters 16 and 17	$2\frac{1}{2}$
Reader: Chapter 22, Section 3	1
TV10: 'National identity' (and D103 *Media Booklet*)	2
Tape 5: Part Two	$\frac{1}{2}$
Total	12
Unit 21: Social Interaction	6
Study Skills Section: Good Writing 2	2
Reader: Chapter 18	2
The Good Study Guide: Chapter 6, Sections 6 and 7	1
Tape 5: Part Three	$\frac{1}{2}$
Radio 10	$\frac{1}{2}$
Total	12
Unit 22: Investigative Methods	4
TV 11: 'Age and identity' (and D103 *Media Booklet*)	2
TMA 05	6
Total	12

UNIT 19   PERSONAL IDENTITY

Prepared for the Course Team by Richard Stevens

CONTENTS

1   INTRODUCTION — WHO AM I?

So far, the emphasis in the course has been on social processes and the significance of larger social groupings of which we are part, such as class, ethnic origin and gender. Such differences as there are between people have largely been attributed to this. But, of course, we find much individual variation in behaviour and personal style among members of any one of these groups: two people from exactly the same background can have quite different identities.

We tend to think of each person as having an *identity* which is particular to her or him. Take any group of people you know — the staff at work, children in a class-room, the locals at your pub or club, even your family. You will probably have no difficulty in seeing them as distinct 'individuals', each with their own character, style and way of looking at the world — i.e. her or his identity.

In this unit we are going to consider the topic of personal identity from three perspectives — the phenomenological, the psychoanalytic and the biological.

1   *The phenomenological perspective.* The unit begins (Section 2) by exploring identity from the standpoint of a person's own experience. What does it feel like to be you? What broader features seem to be involved in this *personal experience* of identity? This kind of approach is called *phenomenological* for it focuses on the 'phenomena' of experience (i.e. that which we can perceive or are aware of).

2   *The psychoanalytic perspective.* The second perspective takes up the idea that we live in *time*. Identity develops throughout life, and experiences change from one age to another. What are the implications of this for understanding the nature and origins of personal identity? As an example of a theory which takes such a developmental perspective, the ideas and methods of *psychoanalysis* are introduced. Psychoanalysts try to go below the surface of what we experience and to look for the ways in which our unconscious minds also help to make us what we are.

3   *The biological perspective.* Personal identity has an 'embodied' quality in the sense that each of us inhabits a particular *body*, designated by a particular name, context and personal history. It is probably hard to imagine yourself as existing totally independently of your body (it is for me!). But in what specific ways does the body contribute to our identity? This question of the *biological* basis of identity is considered in Section 4. There is also a Reader article on 'sociobiology' which adds the dimension of time to the biological perspective. Sociobiology observes that our present condition is the outcome of millions of years of evolution, and asks whether this process has generated an inheritance which influences our personal identities and social behaviour today. Not an easy question to answer, as we shall see, but one which merits consideration.

Three perspectives on personal identity will be explored in this unit then: the *phenomenological*, the *psychoanalytic* and the *biological*. As indicated in the Block Introduction, there is also a fourth perspective to be considered and this will occupy the whole of Unit 20. This concerns the way our identity is rooted in the *social*: how it emerges from and is sustained by relationships and comparisons with others and the ideological representations of the culture in which we live.

There are several theories in psychology and social science that are relevant to understanding personal identity. These particular perspectives have been selected because, taken together, they give us insights into different but fundamental facets of being a person — subjective experience, personal development, biological inheritance and social influence. They require you to look at identity in very different ways, thus enriching your understanding. As also noted in the Block Introduction, they use very different methods and approaches. These will extend your knowledge of the kinds of method which are used in social science for investigating social behaviour and their respective advantages and problems.

Looking at identity in this multi-perspective way does, however, raise the difficult issue of how we interrelate these different views. Can they be fitted together or are they, at least in some ways, in fundamental opposition? As with methods, this issue will be looked at as we proceed. Both topics will be discussed more explicitly in the final section of this unit and taken up again in the next.

2 A SENSE OF SELF: THE PHENOMENOLOGICAL PERSPECTIVE

Let us begin by considering personal identity from the standpoint of subjective experience. When we make statements like 'I am feeling much better today', 'I went down to the shops', 'I am managing to complete my assignments more easily now', then we are talking from the standpoint of subjective experience. So what is it like to be an 'I'?

First of all, the experience of identity depends on the capacity to be aware, to be conscious of the world about and of ourselves as part of that world. Think, for a moment, of the importance of language in such awareness. We have words and concepts ('symbols') which denote various aspects of our experience. Often, these refer to perceivable objects such as a house or a table. But, equally, they may refer to abstractions (e.g. justice) or feelings (e.g. happiness) which are not specifically related to particular objects in our world. Words and concepts also carry with them connotations. Words like 'happy', 'pleasant', 'nationalist', 'prejudice' etc. carry positive or negative value. As we saw in Unit 17, giving particular connotations to the words we use is a means by which ideologies help to structure the ways in which we see our world.

Language and thought enable us to go beyond the actual situations we are physically in. Stop for a moment and think of where you were last on holiday. Think of your parents. Although neither of these may be physically present at the moment and, indeed, your parents may now no longer be alive, you are nevertheless able to be aware of them. The capacity for conscious thought enables us, in a sense, to transcend time and space — to think about what has happened in the past and what may happen in the future, of places and people not actually present, and of possibilities which, in fact, may or may never be.

I shall use the word 'self' to designate the core of identity — the sense of 'I' which is reflected in statements like those above (e.g. 'I am a bit worried about getting that TMA completed in time'). This sense of self depends on a highly developed capacity for 'symbolic' thought — the ability to monitor and reflect on our own actions, as well as think about the world around us. We may call such self-awareness *reflexive awareness* in that we are turning awareness back upon ourselves. Self-awareness is, then, 'the human capacity to be aware of one's self as being a particular person distinct from all others, and to reflect on the experience of being that person and who that person is' (Stevens, 1985).

There is another ingredient which is an intrinsic part of our sense of self. This is a feeling of *continuity*. There is a sense in which the self I experienced yesterday or last year or even when I was a child of five goes on existing now in the person I am at the moment. I am clearly different now than when I was five but there is still some sense of connection, of continuity.

A third ingredient of the sense of self is awareness of *agency*. An 'agent' is someone who produces an effect. By 'personal agency' we refer to our power as persons to produce effects. Through our actions we can bring things about and initiate change both in ourselves and others (e.g. 'I am going to put the kettle on'; 'I am going to persuade her to try harder').

I am suggesting, then, that there are three core ingredients in a sense of self: (i) the ability to be aware of our own actions and feelings, (ii) a sense of continuity, and (iii) awareness of being an 'agent'. There is every reason to suppose that this sense of self, which with its three aspects comprises the core of personal identity, is uniquely human. (Although there is evidence that some apes (e.g. chimpanzees) may possess a rudimentary capacity for awareness of themselves as distinct from others, without the symbolic flexibility given by the human capacity for language, this is only likely to be at a very basic level.)

2.1 SOME IMPLICATIONS OF THE HUMAN CAPACITY FOR SELF-AWARENESS

This sense of self carries with it some fascinating and powerful implications. It means, for example, that we are aware of our own mortality and our capacity for choice.

Mortality We experience ourselves as existing now; but, because we are capable of anticipating the future and can see ourselves as a person like any other, we know that at some point we too will die; and our personal identity, at least in its present form, will cease to exist. It is identity, rather than physical survival, that is the issue here. Identity is as precious as life itself: mere existence, for example on a life-support machine, as a vegetable without awareness or agency, is to most people tantamount to death.

Some people can more or less comfortably accept eventual non-being as a fact of existence. For others, such a realization can be deeply disturbing. Most cultures and many people resolve the issue by assuming some kind of spiritual after-life, so that, although the body dies, they believe that they will continue to exist. Perhaps most people in our secular society try to avoid the issue for as long as they can and immerse themselves in the immediacies of everyday life. One way of dealing with the prospect of eventual non-being is to leave what we might call an 'identity legacy'. This is to create something which, indirectly at least, is an expression of one's identity and which will live on after one's death. So by deeds which have impact on others — perhaps by having children, or by creating a house or garden, a painting or poem — we can ensure at least some continuity of our identity, if only in the thoughts and feelings of other people.

--- ACTIVITY 1 ---

Think for a moment if there are ways in which you are already involved in creating such an 'identity legacy', perhaps without being aware of it. Or do you feel that at some time in the future you might wish to do so. If so, what kind of 'legacy' would you choose to create to leave behind?

Choice   The ability to conceptualize possibilities, coupled with the power of agency, creates the human capacity for *choice*. To a greater or lesser extent, we have the sense that we are 'free beings': that, ultimately, it is up to us to make the choices we do. Certainly the legal sphere presumes this: To plead in court that an offence was the result of an unconscious impulse, an instinct, or one's class background is unlikely, except in the most extreme cases, to carry much weight. The law assumes, as a general rule, that we are responsible and accountable for our actions. And this probably accords with most people's view of themselves. We have to eat to live, and are constrained by the money in our purses and the availability of goods on the shelves; but, within these limits, most of us feel that it is *we* who choose what to buy. In order to stay fit, we may even choose to resist the desire to eat. There is a sense of the self as a selector, initiator and controller of actions.

What has been suggested, then, is that awareness of our own mortality and the capacity for choice are two issues which arise from the self-awareness and sense of agency made possible by the human capacity for symbolic thought. These are sometimes described as 'existential issues' because they are intrinsic to the experience of being an existing human being. They are issues for which there are no solutions. We cannot, for example, avoid dying or *not* choose (the act of not choosing being a choice in itself). Yet they demand from us a response, even if that response is only to ignore that they constitute a problem.

Erich Fromm (1960) has argued that self-awareness and personal agency — what he calls 'individuation' — are not present from the beginning, but emerge in the course of childhood development. He also points to the double-edged nature of the development of individuation. On one side, it represents increasing autonomy and self-strength. On the other, it represents growing aloneness, an awareness of being cut off from the primary ties of early childhood — a time free from concern about personal choice and any sense of separateness.

--- ACTIVITY 2 ---

Do you have any recollections of becoming aware, as a child, of your own identity. If you know children of different ages, it might be an interesting exercise to get them to talk about 'What it's like to be me'. Can you detect any development of self-awareness and sense of personal agency as they get older?

2.2   IDENTITY: A SELF OR SOCIAL CONSTRUCTION?

If self-awareness and self-monitoring, choice and the capacity to consider alternatives are all intrinsic to the human condition, this strongly suggests that we can *self-create*: i.e. play a part in constructing our own individual identities.

Glover (1988) has argued that, '... shaping ourselves is a more important aspect of us than is usually supposed. It should be given a central place in our thinking about social and political issues' (Glover, 1988, p.110). The process of creating our own identity is not necessarily, he argues, a question of a grand design or a directing life-plan, but emerges from the everyday decisions we make about choices of job, of partner and where we live. It comes from taking decisions for oneself about what television programmes to watch, which newspapers to read, what clothes to wear. All these help to influence, if only in small ways, the kind of person we each become.

> To varying degrees we take charge of our lives. Through controlling our actions by our own plans, we become active rather than passive. We may hardly notice changes taking place in ourselves, through being absorbed in what we are doing. But sometimes we are more self-conscious, and this starts to change us. We form pictures of the sort of person we want to be. Someone may want to be braver, more tolerant, more independent or less lazy. Consciously shaping our own characteristics is self-creation.
>
> (Glover, 1988, p.131)

Like no other aspect of our world, our identity is shaped by the way we think. A most potent source of our identity, Glover argues, resides in the beliefs we have about ourselves, and the stories we tell (to ourselves and others) about how we came to be the kind of person we are.

> Self-creation depends on the beliefs we have about what we are now like: on the stories we tell about ourselves. We tell other people what to expect of us, or else we send signals by actions or style. The stories vary. Applying for a job, we tell a story about our competence and energy, about how we have cared more about Quantity Surveying than about anything else in the world. To our family and our friends we tell stories ranging over more of our life. But we also tell ourselves a story about ourselves. This is our inner story. It stretches back as far as we can remember. We think of it as the truth from which other stories may deviate a bit.
>
> (Glover, 1988, p.139)

We can edit and change these stories. Looking back on our past, we may tell a very different story from the one we told at the time. Much of psychotherapy involves reflecting on and modifying the stories we tell about ourselves. But, even allowing for self-deception, there are limits to what we can believe about ourselves — to the representations of identity that we can adopt. And because we cannot believe just anything we want about ourselves, there are limits also to the self-creation possible in this way.

The overall pattern of choices and decisions we make and ways we behave (which Glover attributes to 'a mixture of natural development and conscious choices') constitutes our distinctive individual 'style'. We may feel this to be a deep expression of our inner identity. It carries an emotional charge, so that we may experience any criticism of our style — our taste, the choices we have made — as an attack on the kind of person we feel ourselves to be.

—————————————— ACTIVITY 3 ——————————————

How far do you agree with Glover's idea that we play a part in creating our own identity? Can you think of objections, perhaps from your reading of earlier units in the course, which might give you cause to disagree?

(Hint — try to remember back to Unit 3, Part II 'The shaping of consumption'; Block II, *Social structures and divisions*; or Unit 17, *The power of ideology.*)

1 One objection which might be raised is — how far are our decisions and choices themselves determined by what we are? In other words, the idea that we create our identity is to put the cart before the horse. Rather, it is the other way round. Our identity determines the decisions and choices we make. This kind of argument will be taken up in the psychoanalytic and biological perspectives discussed in the following sections of this unit.

2 A second objection was raised in Unit 17. There it was pointed out that the representations and images we use as the raw material from which we shape identities and beliefs and stories about ourselves — that these are themselves part of the ideologies and belief systems of our culture. We may assume our 'style' to be a very personal thing but on reflection it may seem, rather, to be dictated by the trends and fashion of the time. These give us models and scripts for the kinds of person we might seek to become. Is it being a yuppie, for example, or a new age vegetarian that strikes a chord for you and provides an image to guide the development of your style? The fact that an expression of style requires someone else to recognize and appreciate it also opens us up to being shaped by the images and representations of our time and culture.

That which is most private within us may have its source in the public domain. Among the deepest beliefs of some people is their religious faith. For my friend Lydia, her faith as a Jehovah's Witness plays a radical role in determining how she lives her life and the choices she makes. Her religious faith lies at the heart of her identity. We assimilate such a faith from the culture or group in which we live. This complex interplay between self-image and cultural context is taken up in the next unit.

3 Another objection which might be raised, on the basis of the discussion of ideology in Unit 17, is that the very notion of an autonomous self engaged in the construction of its own identity may itself be merely the product of liberal ideology, rather than a statement about a universal existential reality. Not only, might it be argued, does ideology shape identity, but a particular ideology (liberalism) generates the myth that the influence of culture can be transcended — that we are capable of creating ourselves.

4 A more muted form of this objection is that which questions whether belief in an autonomous self is found globally in all cultures and historical times, or only arises as a result of certain social conditions. Following Weber, Erich Fromm has argued that it emerged with, or at least was accentuated by, capitalism.

> Significant changes in the *psychological atmosphere* accompanied the economic development of capitalism ... One outstanding consequence of the economic changes affected everyone. The medieval social system was destroyed and with it the stability and relative security it had offered the individual. Now with the beginning of capitalism all classes of society started to move. There ceased to be a fixed place in the economic order which could be considered a natural, an unquestionable

one. *The individual was left alone; everything depended on his own effort, not on the security of his traditional status.*

(Fromm, 1960, pp.49–50)

So it appears that we have opposing arguments. The phenomenological position argues for our power as individuals to create, at least partially, our own identity. The opposing sides suggest in different ways that this is a subjective myth; that what appears to be an active process of personal construction is guided by forces beyond our control: forces such as biology, or early development, or society which already make us what we are.

Are these arguments in fundamental opposition or is some reconciliation possible? The phenomenological view may seem to fit the way we experience our lives but the opposing positions are supported by cogent arguments. One clue to resolving their opposition may lie in the idea of *ideological dilemmas or contradictions* mooted in Section 1.7 of Unit 17. In the UK today, we do not live in a culture with a single, monolithic ideology. We are exposed to different ways of representing and making sense of the world. And because we are able to choose, at least between the alternatives offered, the situation becomes a two-way interaction between ourselves and social contexts in which we live.

In the modern world there is not only ideological pluralism but also a pluralism of individual experience. In other words, each of us lives in multiple worlds (Luckmann, 1970). There may be home and family, for example, and circles of acquaintances and friends, as well as work, hobbies and perhaps clubs or societies to which we belong. As we participate in any one world, there are always facets of ourselves (related to the other worlds) which will not be involved. It is this experience of never being entirely part of any sphere in which we engage which generates, according to Luckmann, a sense of individual identity.

One effect of such pluralisms of ideology and experience, the phenomenological perspective would suggest, is to force us to *search for meaning*. (We can add this as a third existential issue to the two others — mortality and choice — which were discussed earlier.) We seek for meaning to make sense of the variety of belief systems and representations which surround us, to get some coherence and direction in our lives. For some, like my friend Lydia, this may be achieved by taking up a faith. But within the modern UK, it is probably more common for people to find such meaning by creating everyday projects related to work and family (Cottrell, 1979).

This raises the idea of *individual differences*. If our beliefs do help to make us what we are, it would not be surprising that beliefs make a crucial difference to how actively a person participates in the process of creating his or her identity and how far he/she allows that identity to be created by the prevailing orthodoxies of fashion and ideology. In line with this idea, Bandura (1989) claims that the factor most relevant to personal agency is 'perceived self-efficacy', i.e. how capable we see ourselves of achieving what we want to do. This acts like a self-fulfilling prophecy in the sense that the more we believe we are capable of initiating events and bringing about change, the more we are likely to try. Bandura has found wide individual differences in this respect. People with high perceived self-efficacy are more likely to believe that abilities are acquired rather than fixed. Making errors is for them therefore less of a threat to self-esteem, and they can learn more easily from their mistakes. Perceived self-efficacy (and, therefore, the capacity to play a part in creating one's own identity) is something which Bandura believes can be developed.

2.3   MULTIPLE IDENTITY

So far in this discussion we have treated identity as a coherent pattern — we have assumed that a person has one distinctive identity. But is this the most appropriate way to look at it? In the previous section, it was suggested that in modern society each of us lives in multiple worlds. There is a sense in which the identity we present depends on the situation. Different contexts bring out different aspects of ourselves. Although he may always appear to be the same person, Jim the worker in the factory canteen does not have quite the same identity as Jim the father at home, or Jim the amateur disc jockey at his local club. Very different aspects of our identity may be drawn out also in the different relationships we have: when the same woman is, for example, mother, wife, daughter and lover.

An extreme version of multiple identity occurs when people lead double lives (as spies or bigamists, for example, usually do), where different aspects of themselves are systematically concealed and revealed in the separated compartments of their lives.

In a study of doctors at the Auschwitz concentration camp, Lifton (1982) has argued that where situations require radically different emotional responses or identities a psychological barrier may be erected between them. The identity of 'doctor' is that of a healer, not a killer. The only way an Auschwitz doctor could handle the contradictions of his position was by developing two relatively separated identities, a process which Lifton calls 'doubling'.

A celebrated literary example of one life lived through two identities is Robert Louis Stevenson's story of Jekyll and Hyde — of the eminent and curious Dr

*'I haven't even got dressed yet. I can't decide
which me I want to be'*

Jekyll who turns into the monstrous and violent Mr Hyde at night. Although it is relatively rare, there have been several well-documented case histories of such 'hysterical dissociation', as it is called. One girl (reported in a study by Thigpen and Cleckley, 1957) had two main identities: one she called Eve White — demure, shy and living a quiet life — her usual self; the other, Eve Black — mischievous, flirtatious and promiscuous — who 'came out' occasionally, especially at night. Eve Black knew of Eve White's existence and regarded her disparagingly. Eve White apparently had no knowledge (before she underwent psychotherapy) of her other self.

In a more ordinary and less extreme way, this phenomenon of 'sub-identities' is familiar to many people. Do you feel, for example, that you have different identities or different sides of yourself which emerge at different times, and not necessarily as a function of the situation? Under the influence of one identity, we can find ourselves doing things which another side later regrets; looking back, we might say we got 'carried away'. The two sides represent different 'stories' we can tell about who we are.

Given the complexity of our experience and our personal development over time and in the context of different relationships and situations, a degree of such fragmentation is perhaps not surprising. A new mother, for example, may find herself in a situation requiring responses and behaviours quite unlike those she has experienced before. She may be isolated from her friends at work and the busy social events which may have been a central part of her life. The new circumstances demand a degree of identity transition.

What is being suggested here, then, is that identity does not remain static, nor is it necessarily unified. One way of thinking of a person is as a set of identities rather than as a single, coherent self. The issues of how identities change with time, and the complex and often conflicting nature of our inner life, will be taken further in the next section.

SUMMARY

- The first perspective we have taken in this exploration of personal identity is a *phenomenological* approach which focuses on *subjective experience*.

- The experience of personal identity depends on self-awareness, a sense of personal continuity and a sense of agency.

- Such self-awareness generates existential issues, such as awareness of our own mortality, choice and the need for meaning.

- The core question raised by this phenomenological perspective is: Does it make sense to say that we play a part in creating our own identities? We saw that there are three possible answers. One is that our sense of self-awareness does play a key, if inevitably limited, role. An opposing position is that the idea of an autonomous self is a subjective myth, and one fostered, in particular, by a liberal ideology. A third response is to suggest that we are dealing here with a complex interplay between the processes of personal and social construction. There may also be differences between individuals in the degree to which they exert their capacity to self-create.

- The section ended by raising the issue of the multiple nature of personal identity, pointing out that identity rarely exists in unified, simple form.

2.4   REFLECTIONS

You may have been struck by differences in the mode of analysis and methods used here, compared with much of what has gone before in the course. There was no presentation of evidence or data. Rather, you were invited to reflect on and reason about the nature of your own experience. In doing so, perhaps your attention was drawn to characteristics which you may have been aware of already but not thought about in quite the same way before. This process is intended, hopefully, to deepen your understanding and to raise questions. The discussion also invited you to carry out 'thought experiments': for example, to consider whether the idea of multiple aspects of identity makes sense in terms of your own experience.

The approach used here is a form of philosophical investigation. It has a place in psychological and social science enquiry also, especially where the reader, as in this case, has direct access to the phenomena in question (the subjective experience of identity), and where this is essentially a qualitative subject-matter that can be effectively described only in terms of meanings and qualities rather than measurements. Would it be possible or desirable to try to *measure* the experience of identity? From the phenomenological perspective, the answer is 'No'. (The opposing case — that measurement is appropriate — will be discussed in Section 4.)

In terms of course themes, the one most relevant to this discussion is that of *representations*. The experience of identity is essentially a representation in itself, and, as was argued, we are capable of creating this in different ways — of telling different stories about ourself. We have also noted how what can seem to be the most intimate and *private* aspects of our identity can have their origin in the *public* images and ideologies of our culture.

The account of personal identity from the perspective of subjective experience emphasizes identity as an open, autonomous, self-creating system. And we have seen that the validity of this idea is open to question. We go on now to probe a little deeper, to raise questions about the here-and-now experience of identity. Each of us has a personal history in the course of which we change and develop, and so the next section places the self in the context of time. It introduces a new perspective on identity — psychoanalysis — which raises questions about the limits of awareness and autonomy, for it suggests that much of our identity may be unconscious and governed by influences from the past of which we may be unaware.

3   THE SELF IN TIME: THE PSYCHOANALYTIC PERSPECTIVE

Sigmund Freud (1856–1939) has been by no means the only theorist to concern himself with childhood development and its influence on adult identity. (You will be looking in the next unit at the work of G.H. Mead who had a similar focus of interest.) But Freud is the primary theorist to emphasize: (i) that the past of his patients affected their present identity; and (ii) that such an influence was very often unconscious, i.e. one of which the patient was unaware. So the psychoanalytic perspective, which Freud originated, is a good one to use to explore identity in time: to consider the influence of the past on present identity, and to raise questions about the limits of trying to understand identity solely from the perspective of conscious experience, as we did in the last section.

Sigmund Freud

(It is worth noting in passing that Freud himself did not use the word 'identity', though some of his followers did. As the Block Introduction points out, this is a relatively recent term in social science. Psychoanalysis is usually described as a theory of *personality*. But this term, which refers to the ways in which a person feels and behaves, overlaps to all intents and purposes with our broad usage of the term 'identity'.)

3.1 PSYCHOANALYSIS

Psychoanalysis is both a method of therapy and a theory, but it is only the theory that will concern us here. To understand how psychoanalysis sees identity as influenced by the past, we need to get an idea of the three core ideas which form its heart: these are *psychosexual development*, *psychodynamics* and *the unconscious*. Each is discussed in turn in the sections which follow.

PSYCHOSEXUAL DEVELOPMENT

While a student of science and medicine, Freud read Charles Darwin, whose book *The Origin of Species* had been published in 1859, three years after Freud's birth. Later, Freud spent six years on physiological research, much of it dissecting fish and the sex organs of river eels. Not surprisingly, his studies in biology influenced his concept of the person, and the idea of biologically based drives as the underlying motivating force in human behaviour is central to his theory.

The drive which Freud considers of greatest significance psychologically is sexuality or *libido*. This term is used to denote sexuality in its widest sense — any kind of body stimulation which produces pleasure. According to Freud (1905), during the first five years of life, the source and nature of the stimulation which is most pleasurable to the child changes as a result of biological development. For the very young infant, the mouth is the source and pleasure is derived initially from sucking and, later, as teeth develop, from biting (the oral stage). (You may have noticed how, once children begin to be able to handle objects, everything is held to the mouth.) At some time, usually in the second year, excretion is likely to become the focus of attention, pleasurable stimulation being derived from the retention and elimination of faeces (the anal stage). Still later, perhaps in about the fourth year, the focus of interest shifts to the genitals. This is reflected in curiosity about sex differences and pleasure in masturbation and physical stimulation from rough-and-tumble play (the phallic stage). From about the age of five until adolescence, there is a 'latency period', during which attention shifts to the world of school, to learning skills and developing peer relationships. At adolescence, according to Freud, sexuality becomes directed outwards and, instead of the child's own body being the primary source of gratification, becomes focused (if only in fantasy) on another partner. The 'pre-genital' modes of childhood sexuality will be incorporated into this. Thus, oral stimulation, for example in the form of kissing, is usually involved in sexual relations.

What, then, is the significance of these ideas for the development of identity? Each developmental stage, as we have noted, involves not only a particular body *zone* but a *mode* of activity. Thus the oral phase involves sucking and biting. They also each involve a characteristic *psychological quality*, reflecting the nature of the predominant relationship at that time (which is why it is described as a theory of *psycho*sexual development). The oral stage, for example, comes at a time when the child is entirely dependent on others for the satisfaction of its comfort, contact and sustenance needs. Psychoanalysts (e.g. Erikson, 1950) have argued that if these needs are met, the result is a general optimism, a sense of the world as a positive place; if they are not, this lays the basis for a generally pessimistic emotional orientation.

The anal phase is the prototype for relationships with authority. For the first time perhaps, demands may be made on the child for some kind of control of body functions. In other words, the child has to control her/his impulsivity and desires in response to the demands of others.

Freud associates the phallic phase in boys with *Oedipal* conflict (named after the Greek story of Oedipus who unknowingly killed his father and married his own mother). Because the erogenous zone of stimulation at this stage is the penis, the close affection a boy is likely to feel for his mother becomes 'sexualized'. With his growing awareness of the relationships of others, the boy comes to see his father as a rival for his mother's affections. This can result in increased hostility towards his father and perhaps also fear of him. According to Freud, the usual way this conflict is resolved is through increased identification with the father, taking on his role and characteristics, and 'introjecting' or assimilating his perceived values and attributes.

Bear in mind when thinking about Freud's ideas here, that young children's thought (as many psychological studies have demonstrated) is not based on principles of logic and causality like that of most adults, but is much more a world of fantasy and imagination. Freud believed, for example, that because of the boy's focus on his penis at the time of Oedipal conflict, the fear of his father is likely to be experienced as anxiety over losing it ('castration anxiety'). If this idea may seem odd, it is worth considering the powerful appeal of fairy stories which involve themes that are strange, to say the least, unless they are regarded as fantasies relating to psychosexual stages (see Bettelheim, 1976). For example, characters are often eaten, heads are cut off, and a beanstalk soars magically into the sky until it is cut down to destroy a threatening giant.

How is this relevant to understanding adult identity? A key concept here is the general notion of *transference*. This is the idea that the emotional feelings which characterized an early relationship stay with us and, at least on an

Oedipus Complex

unconscious level, are 'transferred' into relationships in adult life. If the response to parental pressure at the anal phase, for example, was overly submissive or rebellious, this may carry over into later relationships with authority. Or, to take another example, one way of handling Oedipal conflict may be to split feelings of affection towards the mother from sexual feelings. This may result in an adult man who has difficulty in integrating sexuality and affection; who uses one woman as a sexual partner but who puts another on a pedestal as a potential wife.

Another key notion in psychoanalytic theory is *fixation*. Fixation can occur if a child is *either* overstimulated *or* deprived at one or other of the three stages. This may result in an overemphasis in later life on the characteristics or satisfactions associated with this phase. Thus, we can see that, according to psychoanalysis, the basis for many aspects of identity is laid in childhood.

———————————————————— ACTIVITY 4 ————————————————————

For each of the following, indicate at what stage (oral, anal, phallic) the person is most likely to be fixated, according to Freud's theory of psychosexual development.

1   Someone who can't stop chewing sweets.

2   An obsessively tidy person.

3   Someone who is over-dependent on others.

4   A very creative person.

5   A miserly person.

6   Someone who talks excessively.

(Answers at the back)

The theme of Freud's psychosexual theory, then, is that the child is the 'parent of the person'. It is interesting, in view of the fact that the majority of his patients were women, that Freud has relatively little to say about the develop-

Penis Envy

ment of girls. Perhaps this is a reflection of his dependence on self-analysis as a source of ideas. He believed that for the little girl the crucial issue equivalent to the Oedipal conflict in boys is the realization that she has no penis. This is experienced as a sense of loss which leads her to devalue women and turns her towards her father. Later she will come to identify with her mother because she is in the same position, but her underlying emotional desire to possess a penis will remain. This may be manifested in a wish for a baby. The whole notion of *penis envy* has been criticized as being 'phallocentric', and other accounts of girls' development have been put forward by later writers. Chodorow, for example, has emphasized 'the importance of the mother-daughter relationship and the crucial role it has in transmitting … qualities of nurturing' (Eardley, 1985, p.103). She considers that masculine development is the harder route in that it involves boys *differentiating* from their mother and thus suppressing their nurturing qualities. It is this, she believes, that results in the tendency of adult males to suppress emotional feelings.

Criticism of Freud's account of male sexual development has come also from another quarter. Instead of the Oedipus complex being universal as Freud supposed, some critics have suggested that it is unique to a particular kind of family structure where the father remains dominant and aloof — as in the patriarchal Jewish family in which Freud himself was reared.

Freud acknowledged other drives besides sexuality, such as those concerned with the preservation of the individual, like the needs for food and sleep. But sexuality carries the most significant implications for identity because it does not *have* to be satisfied, and can be satisfied in many ways. With the impact of the First World War, Freud began also to consider the possibility of a 'death' instinct. In his later papers, he suggested that the experience of guilt comes from destructive impulses being turned in upon the 'I' or *ego* (these terms are explained below). But the death instinct has never become a fully accepted part of psychoanalytic theory.

PSYCHODYNAMICS

A second core area for understanding psychoanalytic ideas about the nature of identity is psychodynamics. Freud gradually came to regard *conflict* within the self (intrapsychic conflict) as being of central importance to understanding personality. He conceptualized the self as having three aspects. First, there is the drive for the satisfaction of biological needs. Because it is rooted in the body, Freud described this aspect as the 'It' (*das Es*). As the child grows older, perceptual and logical capacities develop, bringing increasing understanding of the world around. The goal of pleasure is tempered by the demands of realities. This reality-testing, perceptual aspect of the self, Freud designated the 'I' (*das Ich*), denoting that it includes consciousness and is concerned with integrating the different aspects of self. As we noted in the context of the Oedipus conflict, children, as they grow older, may introject or assimilate values and attitudes through identification with the adults who care for them. This is the basis for the development of the third aspect, the 'Above-I' (*das Über-Ich*) as Freud called it to indicate its moral, regulatory power. It is worth noting in passing that such assimilation of values is one way in which the ideological beliefs of the prevailing culture may begin to be taken in by the growing child.

(In the standard translation of Freud's works, the 'It', the 'I' and the 'Above-I' are translated as *id*, *ego* and *superego*, respectively. However, it is perhaps preferable to use literal English translations of Freud's original words as these convey better that they refer to *aspects* of the self rather than actual parts of the mind. As Bettelheim (1989) notes, the translators' use of Latin terms rather than everyday words gives them a spurious scientific character, and the ultimate effect has been to reify (or 'make a thing of') the concepts and thus do a disservice to our understanding of Freud's ideas.)

These aspects may come into conflict with each other. For example, sexual desire, say the desire to masturbate, (the drive for pleasure of the It or *id*) may be countered either by a fear that this may lead to punishment (the concern of the I or *ego* for the consequences of reality) or by guilt that it is wrong (the introjected inhibitions of the Above-I or *superego*). Psychodynamics refers to the conflicting forces of these different aspects of the psyche and explores the ways in which conflict may be played out.

The conflict creates anxiety. The anxiety may be alleviated by reducing conflict by means of various defensive devices. In the case above, one way of doing this would be to *repress* the sexual desire from consciousness. This defence might be supplemented by *projecting* repressed desire onto others so that *they* are seen as being sexually motivated (even though they may not in fact be so). Or it may be *displaced*, as when repressed aggression is directed at another target: when anger at the boss, for example, is discharged by kicking the cat. Another more productive way of alleviating conflict would be to *sublimate* the repressed desire: for example, when sexual feelings are converted into warm friendliness and concern for others, or into creative effort. Repression, projection, displacement and sublimation, then, are all examples of ego 'defence mechanisms' which lead to desires being expressed in an indirect or distorted way. In his later writings, Freud, and also his daughter Anna amongst others, described a number of these.

Becoming aware of the different ways in which underlying motivations may be distorted by defence processes can provide useful insights into identity. For example, a major American study of anti-Semitism (Adorno *et al.*, 1950) used this principle to make sense of prejudiced attitudes. By means of attitude scales, the researchers found that anti-Semitic people were likely to be prejudiced also against other minority groups and to be aggressively patriotic.

Repression

Intensive study of the most and least prejudiced subjects suggested that such prejudice is an expression of repressed aggressive feelings from childhood. The highly prejudiced were more likely to have come from homes where they have been forced to repress hostility against parents for fear of punishment. The researchers concluded that the repressed hostility was being displaced and projected, in this case in the form of prejudice, onto the 'safe' targets of minority groups, and in an exaggerated respect for authority.

THE SIGNIFICANCE OF THE UNCONSCIOUS

The central core of the psychoanalytic approach is that much of what constitutes our personality and identity is not conscious. When we approach identity solely from the standpoint of conscious experience as we did in Section 2, we concern ourselves directly only with the I or *ego*, not with the unconscious aspects which Freud regards as the essential basis of personality. We may feel aggression or affection towards a particular person and be unaware of the source of this feeling: perhaps a displacement or transference from our past. Beliefs, desires, dislikes, attitudes, even our behaviour — all may have their origin in unconscious conflict and desires. We may *think* we know why we feel and do as we do, but the reasons we ascribe may merely be rationalizations and the underlying motivations may be quite different. Thus, according to psychoanalysis, excessive concern with religion *may* reflect unconscious submissiveness to the father; patriotic convictions *may* represent early identification with authority figures. Many of our actions and feelings as adults are deemed to be unconscious residues of childhood experiences. So, according to psychoanalytic theory, there is an unconscious basis for identity which emerges from the nature of our childhood experience and the defences we characteristically use to deal with inner conflict.

3.2   IMPLICATIONS FOR IDENTITY

If we accept psychoanalytic theory, it deepens our understanding of identity in three ways.

1   First, it draws attention to the idea that much of our identity reflects unconscious motivations and conflicts, and that our conscious insights may be only rationalizations.

2   Secondly, it emphasizes that the basis of many aspects of identity are laid down in the relationships and development of childhood.

3   Thirdly, it supports the idea put forward in Section 2.3 that a person's identity is not necessarily a unity. The I or *ego* may attempt to integrate the various aspects of personality but these may lead us to act and feel in conflicting ways.

According to psychoanalytic theory, an important source of identity in childhood is the assimilation of perceived, parental values through identification with parents. Some later psychoanalysts have suggested that this can lead to the development of an *ideal self* — an unrealistic, idealized image always urging us on to what we *should* do, or *should* be like (Horney, 1950). According to Horney, a major source of neurosis is the failure to reconcile the different aspects of self: the self as experienced, for example, and the 'ideal self' one 'should be'. Much of psychotherapy, even outside the psychoanalytic tradition, is concerned with encouraging patients to realize the unrealistic nature of such *shoulds* and exploring their origin in childhood. Carl Rogers' non-directive counselling, for example, is directed at getting his 'clients' (as he calls them) to distinguish between what they *should* feel (i.e. what they have been told they should feel by parents and other people in the past) and what their real feelings (i.e. those which arise from their own actual experience) are.

Psychoanalytic theory also bears on the question we asked in the previous section: To what extent does each of us actively create his or her own identity?

From your reading about psychoanalysis, what kind of answer to this question do you think it suggests?

In fact, the answer that psychoanalysis gives is not entirely clear. On one hand, the three core ideas you have just read about suggest little, if any, scope for self-creation, and they imply a *determinist* position: that is, that our identity is created by factors (like the pattern of our psychosexual development and unconscious conflict) over which we ultimately have no control. However, the aim of psychoanalytic therapy is, in fact, to gain insight into the unconscious sources of our feelings and behaviour and, in so doing, to enable us to begin to participate (admittedly with help and in only a very partial way) in our own development.

3.3   THE NATURE OF PSYCHOANALYTIC IDEAS AND METHODS

The value of the insights into identity which psychoanalysis offers depends, of course, on how far we can accept its ideas as valid. Psychoanalytic ideas have been very influential and, in a general sense, pervade the way of thinking of our culture. But what evidence is there to support them? Freud and his followers were more interested in generating ideas about the way the mind works than in assessing their validity. But subsequently many studies have tried to do just that. Some evidence has been found, for example, to substantiate the notion of an anal syndrome (i.e. the particular and otherwise rather unlikely combination of characteristics associated with this phase), and for the idea that unconscious meanings can influence our responses. (For a review see Kline, 1981 or Stevens, 1983). But the results have been patchy.

There are several problems in establishing to what extent the ideas of psychoanalysis hold up. For an example, look back to Activity 4 in this unit (p.22). The characteristics described in items 2, 4 and 5 are very different but all are supposed to be characteristics of an anal fixation. If anal fixation can result in such diverse characteristics, then you can see that it is going to be very difficult to establish a clear-cut connection between any one of them and its origins in the anal phase. It is equally unclear which particular characteristic is most likely to result from the fixation. There is also a probabilistic quality about it all in that the causal connections claimed are only probable or possible, not definite. If we also remember that fixation may result from either over-indulgence or deprivation, the propositions begin to take on the character of 'heads I win, tails you lose' — they can't fail! This is not to say that psychoanalytic theory is necessarily wrong, but what it does make clear is that the propositions are difficult, and in some cases impossible, to establish (or reject) conclusively.

Another problem can be illustrated by the discussion of defence mechanisms (see under 'Psychodynamics' above). Given the distortions these create, understanding behaviour inevitably becomes a matter of interpretation. An act of charity, for example, may result from genuine concern or as a reaction to strongly repressed aggressive feelings. Such explanations are in terms of theoretical concepts (e.g. repression), not in terms of events we can observe. The outcome of such problems is to render much of psychoanalytic theory *unfalsifiable*; in other words, we cannot test it to find out if it works or not.

There are those (e.g. Eysenck, 1985) who would reject psychoanalysis on this count; but are they right to do so? The problem is that interpretation may be the only way to understand human action and society. For these depend on meanings — the ways in which we make sense of the world and ourselves. As discussed at the beginning of Section 2, this is a 'symbolic' world of concepts rather than a world of physical objects. The psychological and the social are intrinsically *conceptual*. Ideologies, for example, are not tangible. They demand interpretation. Such interpretations can never be unquestionably validated. But a good case for a particular interpretation may be made all the same: for example, they can be compared to see which makes best sense of the phenomenon in question, as you will have been doing in this course with the theories you have encountered.

In spite of the problems his theory poses, Freud's great achievement was to recognize the importance of meanings (both conscious and unconscious). If meanings constitute the core of human experience and understanding, identity inevitably becomes a matter of interpretation with all its attendant difficulties. And, in this respect, psychoanalytic theory is no different from most other theorizing in social science.

The *methods* Freud used to develop his ideas are varied. They include observing the behaviour of his patients in psychotherapy and listening to their accounts and 'stories' of their experiences. He also developed special techniques for trying to uncover unconscious meanings. One way to do this, for example, is to analyse the transference of childhood feelings in the patient's relationship with the analyst.* (One reason why analysts traditionally remain neutral and interact little with their patients is so as not to interfere with this process.) Another much-used technique is 'free association', where the patient is encouraged to say everything and anything which comes into mind — the idea being that this train of thought may lead to unconscious preoccupations.

Freud regarded dreams as a 'royal road' to the unconscious. In sleep the conscious mind is relaxed, and he believed that unconscious meanings are reflected in dreams, although in distorted form. The analyst's task is to work through the distortions in the dream as reported to get at the underlying or 'latent' meaning. Here is an example reported by Ferenczi, a pupil of Freud's.

---

* Transference is described under 'Psychosexual development' above.

One of his patients saw herself in a dream strangling a little white dog. Free association suggested a link between the dog and her sister-in-law. She not only had a notably pale complexion but the dreamer recalled a row which they had had a few days earlier in which she had accused her sister-in-law of being 'a dog who bites'. Using another colloquial phrase, she told Ferenczi that her annoyance stemmed from the fact that her sister-in-law was trying to come between her husband and herself 'like a tame dove'. The patient had previously associated the action of strangling the dog with wringing the neck of a chicken which she was occasionally obliged to do. To express her hostility directly in the form of a dream in which she killed her sister-in-law would be too disturbing. So, according to Ferenczi's interpretation, the underlying wish was displaced on to a disguised representation of the sister-in-law — the dog.

(Stevens, 1983, p.32)

Over and above these specialized techniques designed to get at unconscious material, Freud also relied on introspection and analysis of his own experience in a way analogous to the phenomenological form of enquiry we used in Section 2. A major source of his ideas was also his own synthesis of the broad understanding of human nature he derived from his knowledge not only of biology but of languages, history, philosophy and literature.

SUMMARY: PSYCHOANALYTIC THEORY AND IDENTITY

- There are *three core ideas* of psychoanalytic theory:

  Psychosexual development. (a) Children develop through oral, anal and phallic stages. (b) Fixation at any one may influence later adult identity. (c) The emotional feelings of childhood may later reassert themselves in adult life (transference).

  Psychodynamics. Identity will also be shaped by the way intrapsychic conflicts are handled and the defensive strategies used to deal with the anxiety such conflict creates. (Some types of prejudice have been explained in this way.)

  Much of motivation and the underlying basis of identity remain at an *unconscious* level.

- Psychoanalytic theory implies: (a) that much of identity is unconscious and not open to conscious introspection; (b) its basis is laid down in childhood; (c) it may encompass conflicting tendencies; (d) identification with parents may lead to the development of an *ideal self* difficult to reconcile with the self as experienced.

- Although it is determinist, psychoanalysis encourages clients to increase their capacity for self direction.

- The validity of psychoanalytic ideas is difficult to establish. This is largely because, like many ideas in social science, they are concerned with meanings and these inevitably require interpretation.

- Freud's basic method was the analysis of introspections and observations. He also developed special techniques such as the analysis of transference, free association and dream interpretation aimed at uncovering unconscious meanings.

3.4   THE DEVELOPMENT OF IDENTITY THROUGHOUT LIFE

Freud's developmental theory stops at adolescence. But some of his followers, notably Erik Erikson, have interested themselves in the ways in which identity develops and changes throughout life. Erikson's idea is of a series of stages during which different aspects of identity development assume importance. The first three of his 'eight ages' map closely on to Freud's theory and we have already noted Erikson's idea that the dependency of the oral stage lays the basis for the identity characteristics of optimism or pessimism. Beyond childhood, the stages which are of particular relevance to identity development are times of radical change, such as the transition at adolescence from being a child to becoming a young adult.

Erikson sees dramatic personal changes happening at *adolescence* which force young people to confront their identity. Bodily changes sensitize them to their body images and how people see them. The nature of the process of identity development itself changes. It is no longer just a matter of identifications with others, and inner conflicts and resolutions, but a more conscious and active search and experimentation about the kind of person they want to become. Erikson sees much of the typical phenomena of adolescence — for example, the need for teenage idols and clannish groups — as being part of this exploration. Even the intensity of young love he sees as the attempt to share one's deepest feelings with another person in order to become more aware of one's own identity. This is why 'so much of young love is conversation'.

Different aspects of identity are involved. Erikson regards the need to establish some sense of occupational identity as perhaps most important. But so also are ideology (what kind of beliefs and attitudes about the world do I hold?) and relationships (what other people do I identify with, whom do I reject?). Erikson sees identity as reflecting the interplay of opposites or 'polarities'. So, for example, adolescence is a time of intensive belonging within chosen groups and also of isolation.

Although Erikson trained and practiced as a psychoanalyst (his first supervising analyst was Freud's daughter Anna), his approach goes beyond that of tradi-

Erik Erikson

tional psychoanalysis. His concern with how people make sense of their experience and the world about them, for example, is not dissimilar to a phenomenological perspective and, in his analysis of individual development, he particularly focuses on the way personal experience interrelates with the social context. The relationship Freud postulated between the individual and society was essentially an oppositional one. Society requires individuals to control and repress their instinctual needs. A very different view has been put forward by Erikson and other Neo-Freudians. This label refers to later psychoanalysts, such as Erikson, Fromm and Horney, who have modified Freudian theory to take more into account the role of social structure and culture in shaping individual identity. Interestingly, almost all of the Neo-Freudians moved to America in the 1930s to escape from Nazi Germany. Through their experience as emigrés and analysts, they have had the opportunity to observe at first hand the influence of different cultures. So Erikson regards identity as intrinsically *psychosocial*: 'We deal with a process "located" *in the core of the individual* and yet also *in the core of his [or her] communal culture*' (Erikson, 1968, p.22). The search for identity is therefore a *psychosocial* process, requiring the individual to match his or her awareness of inner experience (the kind of person I feel I am) with the prototypes and opportunities offered by society.

Another time of major transition is *mid-life*, perhaps just after the age of forty when the realization comes that 'one has stopped growing up and begun to grow old'. For many people this is a time of reflection and re-appraisal; a time when they search for meaning and consciously attempt to reformulate their identity. Tolstoy records in his *Confessions* how, in his forties, questions began to torment him: 'Why should I live? Why should I wish for anything or do anything? Or to put it still differently: Is there any meaning in my life that will not be destroyed by my inevitably approaching death?' (Tolstoy, 1983, p.35).

=== READER ===

Read now the extract by Daniel Levinson on 'The mid-life transition' in Chapter 15 of the Course Reader, together with the commentary that follows below.

Over a period of seven years, Levinson and a team of co-workers carried out an intensive interview study of forty men of different ages. Their aim was to chart the changing pattern of identity development in men between the ages of twenty and fifty. Their results were published as a book, *The Seasons of a Man's Life* (Levinson et al., 1978), from which this extract is taken. As the respondents were men, it is worth considering how far the basic experiences described here apply also to women. Levinson seems to assume that in large part they do. (Indeed, he includes in his account a quote from a woman playwright — Lillian Helman.) If you have a tutorial or self-help group which includes both men and women, you might like to discuss this issue.

In his account of the mid-life transition, Levinson, like Erikson, focuses on the notion of *polarity* in the sense of the interplay between opposing needs and characteristics. He suggests that there are four polarities which are particularly important in mid-life — young/old, destruction/creation, masculine/feminine and attachment/separateness. The polarity which is discussed in detail in the extract is the need at mid-life to resolve the shift from the experience of being young to that of being old.

The account Levinson gives is a distillation of the understanding which he gleaned from the interviews with men at this phase of their lives, combined with reflections on his own experience (Levinson was forty-six when he started

the study). It is worth noting how he uses poetry to try to get at some of the deeper meanings involved. This raises the difficult question of how far it is possible to fully represent meanings and feelings in words and communicate them to others.

The extract also prompts thoughts about how far it is possible to generalize from accounts such as this that are based on a relatively small sample of people from a particular society and historical period. In the course of both adolescence and mid-life, there are changes occurring which are universal to all humankind — for adolescents, for example, physical changes and initiation into adult society; for those at mid-life, the experience of encroaching age and increasing proximity to death. But how far can we assume that the kinds of experience which Levinson describes would apply to someone from a different time or culture? Or is an interactive position most likely: i.e. that although the surface forms of the transitions may vary depending on cultural models, their underlying, 'existential' qualities of searching for identity and confronting polarities will remain?

TV 11, *Age and Identity*, will look at the way identity changes with age for people in the UK today and at how we might explain this.

3.5   TOOLS TO THINK WITH

We have now briefly considered two life transitions — adolescence and mid-life — as examples of the way in which identity may be reworked and developed during the course of life. We have noted the psychosocial nature of such development: how it emerges from a complex interaction between individual and social process.

The methods which you have encountered in this section might broadly be described as *clinical*. The ideas of Erikson and other Neo-Freudians, like those of Freud, emerged, in part at least, from their experience with patients and therapy. (Erikson spent much of his life as a child psychologist, hence his particular interest in youth and adolescence.) The accounts by Erikson of adolescence and by Levinson of the mid-life transition represent personal syntheses based on clinical experience, interviews and introspections.

All of these approaches involve interpretation, and the problems of validating interpretation were discussed earlier in this section. Because of such problems we must regard their analyses with caution. They are intended to stimulate your thinking about identity rather than to present a definitive account. (Erikson calls his ideas 'tools to think with'.) You might apply them to your recollections or observations of adolescence. Or, if you have reached or passed the mid-life transition, you might like to consider how well Levinson's account applies to you. It may serve to deepen your understanding of your experience, drawing your attention to features which you may have been aware of but not thought about in quite that way before. In this kind of way, social science methods such as these can have the effect of 'heightening awareness' even if they do not necessarily present a conclusive account of the way things are.

Looking at the self in time, we see even more clearly the significance of *narrative*. Our identity forms a set of stories about how we have lived our life and what makes us what we are. These stories change in the telling as we grow older and as the experience of our past becomes reworked in the light of our experience in the present.

Erikson has described his approach as 'triple book-keeping'. By this, he means that to understand personal identity and what is significant for a person at particular stages of life, we need to take into account biological, social and developmental aspects, and consider each in relation to the other. We have added to our exploration of the *experience* of identity by considering the self in time — the *developmental* basis of identity. In so doing, we have also touched briefly on its *psychosocial* nature and this will be taken up in more depth in the next unit. We now turn in the next section to the relevance of the *body and biological processes* for personal identity.

SUMMARY: THE DEVELOPMENT OF IDENTITY BEYOND CHILDHOOD

- Erikson sees adolescence as a crucial phase for the development of identity, and argues that identity development is a psychosocial process.
- Levinson suggests that the mid-life transition is concerned with coming to terms with polarities such as the shift from youth to middle-age.
- Social science methods are as much about providing tools to think with and to heighten awareness as for presenting conclusive analyses of the way things are.

4 THE EMBODIED SELF: THE BIOLOGICAL PERSPECTIVE

Among the responses to the *Who am I?* exercise that we looked at in the Block Introduction, there were several which made direct reference to the body and physical appearance: 'I am … red-haired', 'a skin problems sufferer', 'athletic', 'quite nice-looking', 'a good dresser', even 'a mobile set of chemical reactions'. Freud emphasized the body as a focus of pleasure and fears; he also pointed out the significance for later identity of biological maturation during childhood. Erikson's account of adolescence notes the young person's concern with physical appearance and the significance of bodily changes for a sense of self. These all suggest that we need to look more closely at the relationship between the body — its physical characteristics and biological processes — and personal identity.

4.1 IS MY BODY ME?

Even on the face of it, it would seem the body has a good deal to do with identity. The body is its 'home'. Its boundaries are the boundaries also of identity. My body is always with me. It is mine for life. I cannot exchange it for another, nor effectively get outside it. When it dies so too, presumably, does my present sense of self.

It is through our body (if only through movements of the eyes or lips) that we engage with the world. Our body makes actions possible and is the instrument of desire. If a body becomes infirm, through disability or age for example, this may circumscribe the form that such engagement can take. Physical vulnerability too can limit our actions, inhibit relationships. If a woman cannot go out alone at night for fear of attack, then her scope for choice, for self-creation, becomes more circumscribed.

When you think of the different people you know, it is perhaps almost impossible to think of them without some sense of the way they appear — the shapes of

The disabled author Christie Brown at work on his typewriter

their faces, the style or colour of their hair, or the sound of their voices. Even with pen friends, photos are likely to be exchanged so that some sense of physical presence can be registered. There are exceptions: you may feel you 'know' the author of a book or poem even though you have never seen or heard her or him in person. But even here, such acquaintance seems limited without some awareness of what they are physically like. Most biographies will include at least a picture or two of the subject in question. And even some of the units in this course include, like this one, a photo of a theorist under discussion.

My contact with you as a person is through your body — the sound of your voice, the look in your eyes. When two people become lovers, it is through their bodies, their hands, and their lips that they express and explore their togetherness. If my body is treated as unlovable then so also, I may all too easily feel, am I myself.

So, while the body may be social as was argued in Unit 6, the social and psychological are also physical in that relationships and personal identities are intrinsically rooted in the experience of a body self.

4.2   BODY AWARENESS

There are several ways in which we are aware of our bodily identity.

1   We have intrinsic knowledge of *what our body feels like* in its changing states; in times of energy, fatigue, pain or ecstasy.

> Consider the nude body self in the dark or suddenly exposed in the light; consider the clothed self among friends or in the company of higher-ups or lower-downs; consider the just awakened drowsy self or the one stepping refreshed out of the surf or the one overcome by retching and fainting; the body self in sexual excitement or in a rage; the competent self and the impotent one; the one on horseback, the one in the dentist's chair, and the one chained and tortured — by men who also say 'I'.
>
> (Erikson, 1968, p.217)

If the body is in pain, so too is the self. In extreme cases, the pain of the body can overwhelm the experience of self. When the body is tortured, identity is violated: the assault is psychological as well as physical.

2   Another kind of body awareness comes from feeling how my body moves and *how effective an instrument it is*; from sensing the ease or difficulty with which I walk or run, or execute the actions I intend. This is particularly true when something goes wrong. In his book *A Leg to Stand On*, Oliver Sacks describes, for example, how his sense of self was radically undermined by the effects of a broken leg.

3   We have some notion also of our *body image* in the eyes of others. We may see ourselves, for example, in a mirror or even on video. We know also that our appearance will influence people's attitudes and behaviour towards us, especially if they do not know us well.

> To see someone is to see a body. And bodies tell us a lot about people. We learn about their age, their sex, and perhaps their race, something about their strength, their state of health and their weight. We learn about their attractiveness, and we can see something of how they think of themselves and how they want to be seen. From their posture and from their style of bodily movement we may get an impression of their mood or even of their job.
>
> (Glover, 1988, p.70)

People's attitudes and behaviour towards us, influenced by our appearance, in turn affect how we think about ourselves. In this way our appearance also becomes an influence on the kind of person we think we are.

Even with regard to our body, we have some scope to self-create. We can to some extent manipulate our image, by the clothes we wear, or the way we smile or do our hair. Major industries support our desire to present ourselves in appropriate ways. Through effective presentation, we can get others to confirm, by the way they respond to us, the identity we would like to be.

There are definite limits, however, to the extent to which other people's reactions to us can override how we feel ourselves. We may be slow to fully appreciate how our appearance might have changed — for example as a result of ageing. While others see us as old, we may feel as young as ever (see TV 11, *Age and Identity*). Unless undermined by an inner sense of bodily deterioration, older people often believe that they look younger than they do. The disjunction between experienced identity and that attributed by others can also be a major problem for the physically disabled. Other people can sometimes generalize from what they see and treat the disabled as if their identity was impaired, while a disabled person remains only too aware of his or her normal sense of self.

4.3   PHYSIOLOGICAL EFFECTS ON BEHAVIOUR AND MENTAL STATES

One has only to drink a few glasses of whisky to realize how dependent is one's sense of self on the biochemical balance of the body. While habitual depression or high spirits feel like a part of our identity, such mental states are closely tied to the balance of chemical substances in the brain. An imbalance of certain chemicals is known to influence the transmission of neural impulses in the brain and has been fairly clearly established to relate to depression. Depression arises from a complicated interaction between biological processes and life events. But it seems certain that a particular biochemical imbalance can make us more prone to despair at times of stress. Hormonal changes (for example at puberty) also influence patterns of sexual desire and aggressiveness (e.g. Olweus, 1988). Brain deterioration, as in the senile dementia which affects some old people, can also precipitate dramatic changes in the experience of self and identity as perceived by others.

All these examples indicate the interactive relationship (albeit a complex one) between biological functioning and aspects of personal identity. In order to examine this relationship in more detail we are going to look at two very different ways of studying it: first, at the theory and research which the British psychologist Hans Eysenck has been working on for the last forty or so years; and secondly, using an article in the Reader, at an approach to understanding the evolutionary origins of social behaviour called 'sociobiology'. While both of these represent a biological perspective on behaviour and identity, and both stress the significance of genetic inheritance, they are quite different in approach. Whereas Eysenck is concerned with personality characteristics which make one person different from another, sociobiology is focused on the social behaviour of humans as a species and how this has evolved.

Both theories are interesting in that, in different ways, they present a marked contrast in method and approach from the perspectives we have considered in the preceding sections. Eysenck, for example, purports to go about his investigations in an essentially *scientific* way (i.e. by following the procedures of a

Hans Eysenck

natural science like physics). How far this makes his ideas any more useful and valid than the perspectives we have looked at so far is a question which will be discussed later. In order to convey at least something of the flavour of Eysenck's approach, it is necessary to introduce one or two technical terms and statistical concepts. These will be at a very basic level and you will only need to grasp their general principles. But if you should want more help with these do ask your tutor either at home or summer school.

4.4 DIMENSIONS OF PERSONALITY

The focus of Eysenck's work is to explore the nature of 'personality' and its biological basis. By 'personality', he means 'more or less stable internal factors that make one person's behaviour consistent from one time to another, and different from the behaviour other people would manifest in comparable situations' (Child, 1968). As this notion of personality encompasses both the pattern of the ways in which we feel and act and the continuity of that pattern over time, it is clearly closely related to what we have been calling 'identity'.

—————————————————— ACTIVITY 5 ——————————————————

Read the following descriptions.

A

You are sociable, like parties, have many friends, need to have people to talk to, and do not particularly like reading or studying by yourself. You crave excitement, take chances, often stick your neck out, act on the spur of the moment and are generally an impulsive individual. You are fond of practical jokes, always have a ready answer, and generally like change; you are carefree, optimistic, and like to 'laugh and be merry'. You prefer to keep moving and doing things, tend to be aggressive, and lose your temper quickly. Altogether your feelings are not kept under tight control, and you are not always a reliable person.

B

You are a quiet, retiring sort of person, introspective, fond of books rather than people; you are reserved and distant except with intimate friends. You tend to plan ahead, to 'look before you leap', and distrust the impulse of the moment. You do not like excitement, take matters of everyday life with proper seriousness, and like a well-ordered mode of life. You keep your feelings under close control, seldom behave in an aggressive manner, and do not lose your temper easily. You are reliable, somewhat pessimistic, and place great value on ethical standards.

How far do these descriptions fit you? Place a √ in one of the five boxes on the scale below to indicate your verdict.

most like A	
somewhat like A	
not like either A or B	
somewhat like B	
most like B	

These two descriptions are how Eysenck conceptualizes extraversion and introversion respectively. Note, however, that, as our scale implies, he sees these as forming a continuous dimension, running from extreme extraversion at one end to extreme introversion at the other. Any person, he believes, can be located somewhere along this dimension. For example, someone who is neither particularly extravert nor particularly introvert would be placed around the middle.

You may have found Activity 5 a difficult task to do because of all the different characteristics which were clustered together in the two descriptions. If you were actually doing Eysenck's personality test (known as the 'Eysenck Personality Inventory'), you would answer separate questions relating to each characteristic mentioned in the descriptions, and others as well. But Eysenck does claim, on the basis of his research, that the characteristics grouped within each description (i.e. A or B) tend to go together or 'inter-correlate'. For example, a person who is very sociable is also, more often than not, likely to be impulsive and fond of practical jokes.

There are many thousands of words in English which describe 'personality traits' or characteristics. Eysenck and his colleagues began by devising questions and tasks of skill which would reflect or measure a wide variety of these. They then collected responses from a large number of people (about 10,000). What Eysenck was interested in was how these different measures 'correlate' together. In other words, if a person scores high (or low) on one kind of item, is it more likely that he/she will also score high (or low) on certain other ones?

Eysenck believes that, as with any natural science such as physics or chemistry, one of the first essentials is to find a way of measuring what it is you are interested in. So he assigned numerical scores to indicate the responses given by his subjects (i.e. the people he tested) to the questionnaire items and tests which he gave them. (Thus, for example, the responses to the question at the end of Activity 5 might be assigned scores from 0 to 4, 'most like A' being given, say, a score of 4 and 'most like B' a score of 0.) One advantage of using such quantitative data is that the subjects' responses can then be analysed statistically. In this way, the researcher can discover, for example, in what ways responses on different tests and questions cluster together. On the basis of his research, Eysenck claims that extraversion–introversion is one of the core factors or dimensions which underlie surface traits, i.e. the specific characteristics (like those in descriptions A and B) which we observe in our own or others' behaviour.

A second core dimension of personality, Eysenck claims is the degree to which a person is emotional (or neurotic) or stable. These qualities can be measured on

Eysenck's N scale, which runs from high emotionality at one end, to stability at the other. A person who scores high on this scale (i.e. at the emotional/neurotic end) would tend to answer 'yes' to the following questions (taken from the Eysenck Personality Inventory or EPI):

1 Do you sometimes feel happy, sometimes depressed, without any apparent reason?

2 Do you have frequent ups and downs in mood, either with or without apparent cause?

3 Are you inclined to be moody?

4 Does your mind often wander while you are trying to concentrate?

5 Are you frequently 'lost in thought' even when supposed to be taking part in a conversation?

(Eysenck's later research also revealed a third dimension, P — psychoticism or tough-mindedness — but we will not consider this here.)

People's scores on questionnaires assessing these dimensions fall into the pattern of a 'normal distribution'. As with height and weight, most people tend to be average on the scales of E and N, neither strongly at one end nor the other, with successively fewer people as you approach either extreme.

--- ACTIVITY 6 ---

The graph in Figure 1 shows a normal distribution. It represents a hypothetical set of extraversion scores (on a scale ranging from 0 to 10) from 162 people. As you can see from the graph, the score which the largest number (40) of people gets is 5. As the scores get progressively higher and lower than 5, so fewer people get scores at those levels.

How many people in this distribution get an extraversion score of 7?

(Answer at back)

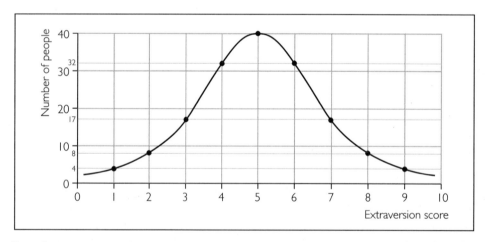

Figure 1

E and N, the main personality dimensions which have come out of Eysenck's research, are 'independent'. In other words, there is no relationship between being extravert and being emotional: an extravert (or an introvert) might equally well be high or low on the N scale. One way of expressing this independence is to place the two dimensions on a graph at right angles to each other. In this way any person's scores on both can then be plotted at one particular point on the two-dimensional graph.

—————————————— ACTIVITY 7 ——————————————

Study the graph in Figure 2. As you will see, the two personality dimensions E and N have been placed at right angles to each other.

Point X on the graph marks the N and E scores of a certain person. What are these scores, and what do they indicate about this person?

(Answer at back)

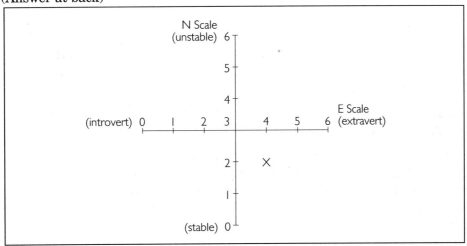

Figure 2

—————————————— ACTIVITY 8 ——————————————

In Figure 3, you can see the kinds of traits which Eysenck claims people are likely to show according to their position on the two dimensions of E and N.

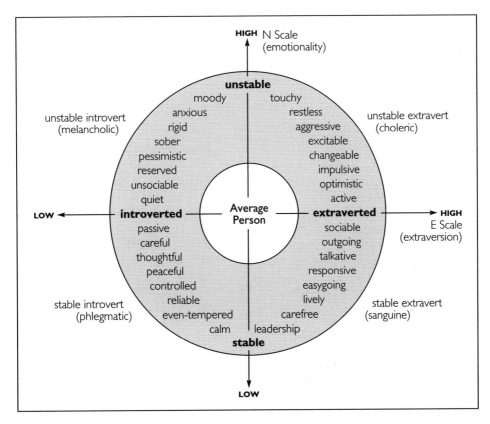

Figure 3

We can see from Figure 3 that someone who is moderately high on both extraversion (E) and emotionality (N) might be described as excitable and changeable. What kinds of traits would you expect in someone who is moderately high on extraversion (E) but moderately *low* on emotionality (N)?

(Answer at back)

Taken together, the two dimensions yield, as you can see in Figure 3, four extreme types: stable introvert, unstable introvert, stable extravert, unstable extravert. (Interestingly, Eysenck notes that these four types, which he discovered through his research, are very similar to the four types used in a system of categorizing people that dates back to the Greeks: these are, respectively, phlegmatic (meaning 'slow and persistent, calm, not very outgoing'), melancholic ('anxious and worried'), sanguine ('carefree and optimistic'), and choleric ('hot-headed and irritable').)

4.5   THE BIOLOGICAL BASIS OF PERSONALITY DIMENSIONS

Why should characteristics cluster together in this way? Why, for example, should someone who is pessimistic also be more likely to be anxious, or someone who is optimistic also be more likely to be impulsive? Why are E and N basic dimensions underlying personality? Eysenck considers that a fundamental reason for this is the nature of the biological processes which he claims underlie our behaviour and experience. Let us take the stability–emotionality (N) dimension first. He explains this in terms of a special part of the nervous system called the *autonomic nervous system*. Among other functions which it serves, this system comes into action in emergencies, in situations of sudden fear or anger for example. It ensures that breathing and heart rate increase and that hormones are secreted which are appropriate for effective and energetic action. Essentially, Eysenck considers that the N or emotionality measure reflects the constitutional or inherent degree of 'lability' (i.e. changeability) in this system. In the case of people who get higher scores on the N scale (i.e. who are more emotional), their autonomic nervous systems are called into action more easily.

And what of introversion–extraversion (E)? Eysenck relates this to the functioning of a particular part of the brain called the *ascending reticular activating system*. This controls arousal level — for example our sleep and wakefulness — serving rather like an amplifying or dampening system for the stimulation we are exposed to. If we are highly aroused, we feel stimulated. With low arousal level, a person can feel bored and desire stimulation. At any point in time, there is a preferred or optimal arousal level. Eysenck's theory is that extraverts have a constitutionally low arousal level and thus are more likely to seek out stimulating activities and experiences in order to compensate for this. By the same argument, introverts are already near or above the optimal level and therefore are more likely to want to avoid over-stimulation.

Arousal level, Eysenck believes, can influence behaviour in a number of important ways. For example, there is some evidence that it is related, in the case of some behaviours, to conditioning. Conditioning is where particular behaviours are made more likely in future because they have been 'reinforced' by being associated with rewards or desired experiences in the past. A child might learn to smile when talking with adults, for example, because it is a behaviour which has been reinforced by parental approval in the past. Eysenck claims that people with higher levels of arousal (i.e. introverts) can, in some cases, condition more easily (i.e. their behaviours are more easily shaped by reinforcements.) He also claims that extraverts, because of their low arousal level and consequently their greater need for stimulation, will get bored and fatigue more easily. Because of such 'built-in' biases, degrees of extraversion (E) or emotionality (N), according to Eysenck, can influence the way a person will learn and the impact that environmental events will have on her or him. The long-term influence on identity of E and N is therefore likely to be substantial.

IS PERSONALITY INHERITED?

If extraversion (E) and emotionality (N) have a biological basis, as Eysenck proposes, it is not unreasonable to suppose, as he does, that aspects of identity are constitutional or inherited. It is clear that genes (the units of inheritance passed to us in equal measure by our two parents) do play a major role in controlling the development of physical characteristics such as height, eye colour and predisposition to certain diseases. Although the connection between heredity and human behaviour is very difficult to establish, such a link has been demonstrated in other species, for example in the complex nest-building and courtship behaviours of many birds. And rats have been selectively bred for patterns of response such as emotionality (Broadhurst, 1958).

In the case of humans, methods for trying to study the hereditability of behaviour are necessarily more indirect. One way is the study of separated twins. Bear in mind that each conception involves the mixing of an enormous number of genes contributed by the two parents. This is why every child is genetically unique. The only exception is identical twins. These result from the splitting of the same fertilized egg. They have, therefore, identical sets of genes. Very occasionally, such twins are separated at birth and brought up in separate families. It can be argued that, in such cases, any special similarities are likely to be due to their genetic affinity. Some studies have claimed to find extraordinary consistencies in cases of this kind. For example, two brothers located by Bouchard (1981) who had not met or known each other since being separated shortly after birth, are reported to have followed the same career as security officers, to have the same hobby — carpentry — and to dress similarly. (Even the names of each of their two wives (both had been married twice) were identical; though quite how this could have been influenced by inheritance is hard to imagine!)

Eysenck's claims are less dramatic. In one study (Shields, 1976), the E and N scores of identical twins brought up separately were found to be very similar. Their scores were significantly closer than those of separated *fraternal* twins. (Fraternal twins have no more genetic similarity than brothers or sisters because they result from two eggs which happened to be fertilized at the same time.) Other studies have shown some tendency for E and N scores of different family members to resemble each other according to how close a genetic relationship they have.

As Kamin (1974) has argued, however, such claims from twin studies have to be treated with caution. The separated twins could, for example, have been placed in two families of a similar type. So that even though the twins were separated, their environments may have been similar and the similarities between them could be due to this rather than to common genes. This would not, however, explain the greater similarity that exists between identical as compared with fraternal twins. Moreover, studies of foster parents and adopted children show no indication that a shared family environment has any lasting effect on E or N scores (Eaves *et al.*, 1989).

The twin brothers described by Bouchard, each seen in front of his white seat built round a tree in the garden, and in his basement workshop. They had actually been given the same name (Jim) by their different sets of adoptive parents, even though these had no knowledge of each other.

4.6 EYSENCK'S THEORY AND PERSONAL IDENTITY

So what has this to do with personal identity? E and N scores would seem to relate to the ways in which people interact with each other and respond to experiences and events. Eysenck has broadened his analysis to try to show that they are also implicated in a range of social behaviour, from crime to political attitudes. For example, several large-scale studies have compared the E and N scores of prisoners with those of other males of similar age and background who had not been in prison (MacLean; see Eysenck, 1977). They found that the prisoners had significantly higher scores than the control group on both E and N. (Eysenck points out that the analysis is complicated by the different kinds of crime involved. Relative to other categories, for example, those convicted of crimes of violence or theft are lower on N and violent offenders are likely to be particularly high on E.) It should be pointed out though that some studies have failed to find that prisoners score higher on E, though they still confirm the N difference. It should also be remembered that the fact of living in prison might itself have an influence on responses to N scale items (for examples of these items see the EPI questions listed in Section 4.5).

One reason why extraversion (E) is implicated in crime, Eysenck argues, is because of its association with poor conditionability. An extravert's behaviour would not therefore have been so easily shaped in a law-abiding direction. There is also the fact that crime can offer stimulation and excitement, which are particularly appealing to the chronically under-aroused extravert. As one ex-criminal has put it, 'Crime made life ... dangerous, dramatic, illegal, demanding and always exhilarating. I loved it' (McVicar, 1973). Of course, excitement can be found in many ways. The fact that crime is selected will be a function of the particular opportunities and models offered by the social context in which that individual lives. Eysenck is not in any way seeking to deny the importance of environmental factors. Whether or not a person becomes labelled as a criminal depends on the interaction of many factors: from whether he or she is caught and the attitudes of the judiciary to what is defined by law as a crime. But biologically determined personality, Eysenck claims, is one factor which may also be involved.

SUMMARY

- The body is an intrinsic part of identity. It is through the body that we relate to other people and the world about us.

- We become aware of our bodily identity through (a) what the body feels like in different states; (b) how effective it is in its action; and (c) the reactions of others.

- Mental states (e.g. depression), and therefore associated aspects of identity, depend on biochemical and brain processes as well as life events.

- In his research on personality, Eysenck has analysed statistically the way specific traits go together. In this way, he claims to have identified underlying personality dimensions, two of the most important of which are E and N. Eysenck's model of personality is hierarchical in that he considers that these dimensions are the underlying factors which produce the pattern of surface traits as well as the continuity of identity.

- Eysenck claims that the personality dimensions E and N are related to arousal level and the autonomic nervous system. In other words, personality has a biological basis. Through their influence on conditionability, the need for stimulation, and emotionality, these can play a major role in the development of identity.

- According to Eysenck's theory, therefore, personality traits or characteristics develop out of the interaction between biologically-based underlying dispositions and the experiences and situations which a person is exposed to.

- Eysenck claims that his studies offer some evidence that E and N dimensions are inherited. If we accept Eysenck's findings, they would indicate that some aspects of identity at least, and some forms of behaviour — such as involvement in crime — are based partly on inherited, physiological characteristics.

4.7 HOW USEFUL IS A 'SCIENCE OF PERSONALITY'?

In terms of method and approach, Eysenck's work presents a complete contrast to both the phenomenological analysis of subjective experience (Section 2) and psychoanalysis (Section 3). Eysenck claims to take a 'scientific' approach to investigating personality.

What do you suppose a scientific approach to personality involves?

Eysenck's scientific approach means that he tries to apply to psychology the kinds of method which have been successful in sciences such as physics and chemistry. This involves:

1 *Measurement*. Although biologically oriented, Eysenck is essentially behaviourist in his approach to psychological research. In other words, he believes that the only thing worth studying is behaviour which we can see and observe. (Compare, for example, psychoanalytic concepts such as repression and sublimation: to what extent can you actually see and measure these?) So Eysenck's research is based either on questions to which people can answer 'Yes' or 'No' or indicate their response on, say, a five-point scale, or on measurements of behaviour (e.g. how quickly a person can press a buzzer when a light is flashed).

2 *Statistical analysis*. Because such methods produce *quantitative* data rather than qualitative or descriptive accounts (compare, for example, the analysis of the experience of self in Section 2), the results can be compared and analysed statistically.

3 *Experiments*. By confining his research to that which he can observe and measure, Eysenck can set up experiments to investigate the relationship between, say, personality measures and behaviour (e.g. do people with high E scores press a button more quickly in response to a light signal than those with low E scores?).

Eysenck asserts that such a scientific approach is essential if we are to begin to understand personality. He is scathing of approaches such as psychoanalysis where these features do not apply. 'Psychoanalysts, unfortunately, are unlikely to understand the insistence on factual evidence which is so characteristic of the scientist; they prefer to float on clouds of interpretation based nebulously on imaginary fantasies. Not in this way is a science constructed!' (Eysenck, 1985, p.192).

Although, on the face of it, Eysenck's attempt to adopt a scientific approach of this kind seems admirable, does it, in fact, actually help to increase our understanding of personal identity?

First of all, it would be wrong to suppose that such an approach is objective and without controversy. Eysenck's results, for example, depend on the kinds of questionnaire items he used and the forms of behaviour he chose to measure; also on the type of statistical procedures he adopted. Other researchers following a similar approach but using different procedures have come up with somewhat different personality dimensions to those of Eysenck. Also, as we noted earlier in relation to prisoners' E scores, even when the same test is applied to the same kind of subjects, researchers may come up with different results.

But the essential question here is: are such methods appropriate for investigating a topic like personal identity? How far is it possible, for example, to *measure* important aspects of identity? Look back at the questions from the EPI that are listed in Section 4.4. Do you consider that the answers 'yes' or 'no' to questions such as these would tell you much about the person responding? The problem, as we have seen in Sections 2 and 3, is that most of what we call identity is conceptual; i.e. it is constituted by the meanings we and others ascribe to feelings and actions. And it could be argued that it is difficult to render these meanings — except in their most trivial aspects — into measurable, observable forms. As Erikson has put it, 'man, the subject of psycho-social science ... will not hold still enough to be divided into categories both measurable and relevant' (Erikson, 1968, p.43).

Eysenck's theory also assumes that we are dealing with fixed personal traits. This takes no account of the arguments presented earlier that each of us has a multiple identity which depends on situations and relationships. In one of these, we may be more sociable than in another, for example. Nor does Eysenck's theory allow sufficiently for the possibility that identity may be both personally and socially created.

Taking a 'scientific' (i.e. natural science) approach in an area such as this is as open to question as any other perspective in social science. This account of Eysenck's theory, however, does serve to illustrate the kind of relationship that there *may* be between identity and the body, and how identity may depend partly on inherited characteristics. It also provides us with a useful comparison of the very different methods which may be applied in investigating identity and in social science.

The human body is, of course, the outcome of millions of years of evolution. If identity depends, at least in part, on biological process and the genes we inherit, can we dig deeper still and gain further insight into identity by exploring the implications for human behaviour of evolutionary development itself? This question is taken up in the article by Stevens in Chapter 15 of the Reader entitled *The evolutionary origins of identity*. This provides our second example of a biological perspective on identity. You will find though that, although sociobiology also considers that much of social behaviour depends on inherited predispositions, it comes at this issue from a very different angle and with very different methods than Eysenck. Sociobiologists are interested in social behaviour as it evolved for humans as a species rather than the nature and basis of personality differences between individuals.

==================== **READER** ====================

You should read this article now, noting (i) the main points of the sociobiological argument, (ii) the ways in which these may be applied to specific aspects of behaviour and identity, and (iii) the evaluation made of the sociobiological position.

==================== **AUDIO-CASSETTE** ====================

Once you have read this article you should at some point listen to Part I of Audio-cassette 5 which reviews and discusses the sociobiological approach.

SUMMARY

- Eysenck insists on a natural science approach to personality research which involves measurement, statistical analysis of quantitative data and experiments.

- Results based on this approach are not to be regarded as objective, unquestionable facts.

- The central question is whether such an approach is appropriate for investigating identity (or personality) which, it might be argued, is constituted by meanings.

- Sociobiology (see the Reader article) provides another approach to studying the biological bases of identity. While sociobiologists also accept the idea that behavioural predispositions can be inherited, they focus on the social behaviour of humans as a species and on the evolutionary origins of this behaviour rather than on differences between individuals.

5   STAND UP THE 'REAL ME'!

5.1   PERSPECTIVES ON IDENTITY

We seem to have come a long way. Starting from a simple question 'who am I?' we have ended up in the distant past. We have moved from the world of immediate experience to biological processes and speculations about our origins: from personal concerns to universal principles. In this journey we have encountered three very different perspectives or stories about personal identity. The first, which we might call the phenomenologist's tale, explored the nature of our *experience of self*. The second, the psychoanalyst's story, looked at identity as it changes through time and at the *influence of the unconscious and childhood experience* upon the ways in which we feel and behave. The third story, an experimental psychologist's account, drew attention to the role of the *body* and inherited characteristics in creating who we are. The second Reader article extended this biological perspective by presenting the sociobiologist's version of this story which tries to use the principles of evolution to gain insights about the nature of identity and to speculate about its origins. Three very different perspectives, then, focused respectively on conscious experience, on the unconscious, and on biology; each one opening us up to different aspects of identity and different ways of looking at it, and, in so doing, deepening our understanding.

The three perspectives contrast too in *method and approach*.

1   The phenomenological approach involves exploring conscious awareness and appeal to experience.

2   Psychoanalysis has developed concepts and techniques to investigate the unconscious and its origins in early development and inner conflict.

3   The biological perspective included two contrasting methodological approaches to investigating the bodily basis of identity: (a) experimental psychology, which attempts to measure personality and to use statistics, experiments and the methods of natural science to study it; and (b) sociobiology, which offers reasoned speculation based on placing the development of identity in the context of evolution and the origins of humankind.

─────────────────────── ACTIVITY 9 ───────────────────────

With which one (or more) of the three perspectives considered in this unit—(1) the phenomenological, (2) the psychoanalytic, (3) the biological (i.e. either Eysenck or sociobiology)—would you be most likely to associate each of the following statements?

1   'Love is a way of attempting to overcome the isolation we feel when we reflect on our experience of being.'

2   'Intense patriotism may be the outcome of early childhood identification with authority.'

3   'Reasons are usually rationalizations.'

4   'Consciousness is a mechanism for modelling and predicting the behaviour of others.'

5   'The capacity for reflecting on alternatives and predicting consequences enables us, partly at least, to change and transcend the influences upon us.'

6   'People who tend to be very sociable, probably are so because they need stimulation.'

5.2 COMPLEMENTARY OR CONTRADICTORY?

While presenting a series of perspectives in this way may have served to enrich your understanding of personal identity, it may also have caused you to wonder — where is the 'real self' in all this? Is personal identity best accounted for by some amalgamation or integration of these different accounts? Or are they so different that no real reconciliation between them is possible?

One way of regarding these different perspectives is to see them as casting light on different but interrelated aspects of identity. Human beings are biological animals, but animals with a highly developed capacity for symbolic awareness. To understand identity we need to look at these different aspects: our extraordinary capacity to be aware of what we think and feel, the long period of our childhood development, and the effects of biology (as well as, of course, the influence of society which will be taken up in the next unit). This is Erikson's position as expressed in his idea of 'triple book-keeping' (see Section 3.5): to understand identity we need to look at its biological basis, at a person's development and at the social context in which he or she lives, each in relation to the others. (We noted earlier how, in keeping with this position, he combined his psychoanalytic orientation with a phenomenological concern with the way in which people experience their lives.) Although the perspectives use different concepts and methods and this makes them difficult to integrate, they can be regarded as each having a different *range and focus of convenience*. What this means is that each focuses on, and is good at explaining, some aspects of identity, while other aspects which may be equally important may be outside its particular range. This position, then, regards the perspectives we have explored as complementary rather than contradictory. They may be difficult to integrate into one superordinate theory; but, taken in turn (for example, as we are doing in Units 19 and 20), they contribute different but complementary insights into the nature of identity.

But will this work? Is there not something contradictory about the perspectives? Do they not represent fundamentally different accounts? Certainly they often provide very different explanations for the same behaviour. Compare, for example, the reasons given in Section 3 (the psychoanalytic perspective) for the greater ability of women in comparison with men to express emotion. Chodorow argues that this arises because a boy is required to repress feelings in childhood as a result of turning away from the warmth and nurturance of the mother in order to establish identification with his father. The sociobiological account, in contrast, sees the same characteristics as having very different origins.

Can you recall from the Reader article the reasons a sociobiologist might give for greater female capacity for expressing feeling and relating to other people?

Sociobiologists assume that this capacity may well have been selected for because of the importance for females of relating to other adults in order to provide a protective environment to rear the comparatively few offspring (compared with males) they can have.

As another example, consider a likely psychoanalytic explanation of someone who finds it difficult to 'let go'. This would probably focus on fixation at the anal phase. Eysenck, in contrast, would see it as a manifestation of introversion and, at base, an attempt to avoid over-stimulation because of an already naturally high arousal level.

—————————————— ACTIVITY 10 ——————————————

Sexual jealousy would be explained very differently by the different perspectives. Try to account for sexual jealousy, (i) as a sociobiologist might explain it, and (ii) from a psychoanalytic point of view.

The sociobiologist would assume that sexual jealousy would have been selected for in males because, if it was successful in deterring a female from having contact with other males, it would have made it more likely that she would pass on to her offspring her partner's genes rather than those of another male. Because a woman is never in doubt that she is the parent of the child she bears, this would not apply to women and therefore this theory would assume that sexual jealousy would be more characteristic of males than females (a proposition for which, in fact, there is very little evidence, see Buss, 1989). The psychoanalyst, on the other hand, is more likely to ascribe sexual jealousy to unconscious fears arising from sibling jealousy in childhood or fear of loss of love in a childhood relationship with a parent figure.

These examples illustrate the very different kinds of explanation of the same behaviour which will be put forward by different perspectives. Not only may specific explanations given by the different theories or perspectives be in conflict, but, as we have seen, their methods are quite distinct and work from quite different assumptions. Thus, Eysenck prizes a positivist type of scientific approach which, like the natural sciences, regards measurement and experiment as essential. In contrast, psychoanalysis and the philosophical analysis of subjective experience emphasize the qualitative investigation of meanings which they regard as the only effective way of investigating the essential constituents of identity. Such methodological differences and their implications for the nature of social scientific understanding will be taken up in Unit 22, the Review unit for this Block.

The three perspectives we have explored differ not only in terms of the explanations they offer and the methods they use, but also with respect to the ways in which they conceptualize the nature of being a person. The phenomenological model, derived from subjective experience, views a person as capable of autonomy and self-direction. Psychoanalysis, in contrast, is somewhat more deterministic, seeing people as largely driven by forces beyond their awareness. At the same time, though, it allows that insights into these forces (particularly as a result of therapy) may make possible a degree of autonomous direction. The biological perspective is avowedly deterministic, assuming that personal identity results from factors like biological inheritance which are quite outside a person's control.

In line with these contrasting models of the person, the perspectives differ also in terms of their attitudes to the possibility of *personal change* and the means they would apply to bring this about. For the phenomenologist, the best method is likely to be heightening awareness, opening people up to possibilities and new ways of looking at things, and alerting them to their own power to initiate and bring about change. For the psychoanalyst, personal change is achieved through becoming more aware of the unconscious springs of behaviour and their origins in our developmental past. For the biologically oriented psychologist, such change may require the use of drugs or, possibly, the manipulation of the environmental stimuli which control our predispositions to respond in particular ways. For psychologists who emphasize the primacy of social influence (the fourth of our perspectives which we have so far mentioned only in passing but which will be the topic of the next unit), it is different again. For them, personal change is premised on changing the nature of the social context in which a person lives and modifying the images and values which this fosters.

There are, then, two opposing arguments — one that the different perspectives are complementary; the other that they represent fundamentally different and irreconcilable ways of accounting for identities. This is not a debate which is easily resolved but I would like to add a further consideration to your thinking about it. At several points in this unit I mooted the idea that a person's identity is not fixed — that it has multiple aspects and is open to change. We noted also Bandura's work on 'perceived self-efficacy' (see the end of Section 2.2), how this varies from individual to individual, and that it can be developed if so desired. These notions all suggest the importance of individual differences in identity, both between different people and between the kinds of identity that the same person can have at different stages of his or her life. It may be that the appropriateness and explanatory usefulness of any one perspective will vary depending on the particular individual in question and which life stage that individual has reached. One person may be guided by reflection and deliberate self-creation: in this case, the phenomenological approach is likely to yield useful understanding. In contrast, for another, perhaps someone who has experienced a traumatic childhood, the force of unconscious needs could be the dominant influence on identity: here, psychoanalysis would play the stronger part. For yet another person, identity may even be dominated by biological needs so that analysis at this level could provide the most fruitful insights. Although we have not yet specifically considered the social perspective on identity, it is worth noting that societies vary in their insistence on members conforming to social conventions and the degree to which they encourage individual style: this could be a factor which determines how relevant a social analysis of a person's identity might be. This position proposes then that all the perspectives have something of value to contribute, but that the explanatory usefulness of any particular perspective will inevitably depend on the kind of person whose identity it is you are trying to understand, and also, perhaps, on the situation of that person and on the nature of the society in which he or she lives.

This discussion is intended to open up the question of how we can deal with different perspectives on identity: a question that we will return to later in the block. First, though, we need to look more closely at the *social* nature of identity — at the role of images and ideologies and the influence of society in creating our sense of self. This is the topic of the next unit and to this we now turn.

A SUMMARY OF THE THREE PERSPECTIVES DISCUSSED IN THIS UNIT AND SOME OF THEIR MAIN POINTS OF DIFFERENCE.

Perspective	Main concepts	Methods	Person determined or autonomous?
Phenomenological	Subjective experience; sense of self: reflexive awareness, continuity, personal agency; existential issues: mortality, choice, search for meaning; multiple identity.	Introspection; reflection; 'thought experiments'.	Person capable of autonomy.
Psychoanalytic	The unconscious; psychosexual development: oral, anal, phallic stages; Oedipal conflict; fixation, regression; transference; psychodynamics: libido; id, ego, superego; defence mechanisms; ideal self.	Free association; dream interpretation; analysis of transference; introspection and observation.	Person largely determined but can become more autonomous with insight.
Biological (i) Eysenck	Extraversion–introversion; neuroticism (emotionality)–stability; autonomic nervous system; reticular formation.	Measurement of behaviour and responses to questionnaires and tests; statistical analysis (factor analysis); experiments; twin studies.	Person largely determined by personality type and conditioning. These in turn dependent on inherited biological characteristics.
(ii) Sociobiology	Genetic transmission; natural selection; sexual selection; reciprocal altruism.	Rational speculation based on principles of evolution; comparisons between social behaviours of different species.	Social behaviour determined by inherited pre-dispositions characteristic of species and the outcome of natural/sexual selection.

ANSWERS TO ACTIVITIES

ACTIVITY 4

1   Oral — particularly at the biting rather than sucking stage.

2   Anal — because of the concern with cleanliness (which is related to toilet training).

3   Oral.

4   Anal. This might result when a child has been praised a lot for 'producing'.

5   Anal — because of its association with holding on, retention.

6   Oral — pleasure in oral stimulation.

ACTIVITY 6

The answer is 17.

ACTIVITY 7

His/her N score is 2 and his/her E score is 4. They indicate that this person tends towards being a 'stable extravert'.

ACTIVITY 8

Responsive, easy-going.

ACTIVITY 9

1 Phenomenological (existential).

2 Psychoanalytic.

3 Sociobiological and psychoanalytic . Neither of them regards consciousness as a primary motivating force of human action. They would therefore see the reasons we give for our behaviour as often being equivalent to rationalizations.

4 Sociobiological (see Humphrey's ideas as discussed in the Reader article)

5 Phenomenological (existential).

6 Biological (Eysenck).

REFERENCES

Adorno, T. *et al.* (1950) *The Authoritarian Personality*, New York, Harper and Row.

Bandura, A. (1989) 'Perceived self-efficacy in the exercise of personal agency', *The Psychologist*, October 1989.

Bettelheim, B. (1976) *The Uses of Enchantment: The Meaning and Importance of Fairytales*, London, Thames and Hudson.

Bettelheim, B. (1985) *Freud and Man's Soul*, Harmondsworth, Penguin.

Bouchard, T. *et al.* (1981) 'The Minnesota study of twins reared apart', in Gellda, L. *et al.* (eds) *Intelligence, Personality and Development*, New York, Liss.

Broadhurst, P.L. (1958), 'Determinants of emotionality in the rat: strain differences', *Journal of Comparative Physiological Psychology*, vol.51 (1958), pp.55-9.

Buss, D.N. (1989) 'Sex differences in human mate preferences: evolutionary hypotheses tested in 37 cultures', *Behavioural and Brain Sciences*, no.12, 1989.

Child, I.L. (1968) 'Personality in culture', in Borgatta, E.F. and Lambert, W.W. (eds) *Handbook of Personality Theory and Research*, Chicago, Rand McNally.

Cottrell, M. (1979) 'Invisible religion and the middle class', unpublished conference paper, Linacre College, Oxford.

Darwin, C. (1859) *The Origin of Species*, London, John Murray.

Eardley, T. (1985) 'Violence and sexuality', in Metcalf, A. and Humphries, M. (eds) *The Sexuality of Men*, London, Pluto.

Erikson, E.H. (1950) *Childhood and Society*, New York, Norton (reprinted by Triad/Paladin, 1977).

Erikson, E.H. (1968) *Identity: Youth and Crisis*, London, Faber.

Erikson, E.H. (1975) *Life History and the Historical Moment*, New York, Norton.

Eysenck, H.J. (1967) *The Biological Basis of Personality*, Springfield, Thomas.

Eysenck, H.J. (1977) *Crime and Personality*, London, Routledge and Kegan Paul.

Eysenck, H.J. (1985) *The Decline and Fall of the Freudian Empire*, Harmondsworth, Viking.

Freud, S. (1905) *Three Essays on Sexuality*, vol. VII of Strachey, J. (ed.) *The Complete Psychological Works of Sigmund Freud*, 22 vols., London, Hogarth Press.

Fromm, E. (1960) *Fear of Freedom*, London, Routledge and Kegan Paul.

Glover, J. (1988) *I: The Philosophy and Psychology of Personal Identity*, Harmondsworth, Penguin.

Horney, K. (1950) *Neurosis and Human Growth*, New York, Norton.

Kamin, L. (1974) *The Science and Politics of IQ*, Potomac, Erlbaum.

Kline, P. (1981) *The Fact and Fantasy in Freudian Theory*, 2nd edn, London, Methuen.

Levinson, D.J. *et al.* (1978) *The Seasons of a Man's Life*, New York, Knopf.

Lifton, R.J. (1982) 'Medicalized killing in Auschwitz', *Psychiatry*, vol.45 (iv), 1982, pp.283-97.

Luckmann, B. (1976) 'The small life-worlds of modern man', in Brown, H. and Stevens, R. (eds) *Social Behaviour and Experience*, London, Hodder and Stoughton.

MacVicar, J. (1973) *The Sunday Times*, 4 November 1973.

Olweus, D. (1986) 'Circulating testosterone levels and aggression in adolescent males: a causal analysis', *Psychosomatic Medicine*, vol.50 (iii), 1986, pp.761–72.

Sacks, O. (1986) *A Leg to Stand On*, London, Picador.

Shields, J. (1962) *Monozygotic Twins*, London, Oxford University Press.

Stevens, R. (1983) *Freud and Psychoanalysis*, Milton Keynes, The Open University Press.

Stevens, R. (1985) 'Personal worlds', Block 4 of D307, *Social Psychology: Development, Experience and Behaviour in a Social World*, Milton Keynes, The Open University Press.

Thigpen, C.H. and Cleckley, H.M. (1957) *The Three Faces of Eve*, New York, McGraw-Hill.

Tolstoy, L. (1983) *Confession*, (trans. by Patterson, D.), New York, Norton.

ACKNOWLEDGEMENTS

Grateful acknowledgement is made to the following sources for permission to reproduce material in this unit:

Figure

Eysenck, H. J. *'Fact and Fiction in Psychology'*, (1965), © Eysenck, H. J., Penguin Books.

Cartoons

pp.12, 22, 23, 25, 31: Mel Calman; *p.17*: Courtesy of Punch.

Photographs

p.20: Mary Evans Picture Library/Sigmund Freud Archives; *p.29*: Harvard University News Office; *p.33*: Secker and Warburg; *p.36*: The Times; *p.42*: copied from Peter Watson *Twins*, Hutchinson, 1981 (source unknown).

UNIT 20   SOCIAL IDENTITY

Prepared for the Course Team by Margaret Wetherell

CONTENTS

1 SOCIETY AND IDENTITY: SOME CONNECTIONS

We hope it is becoming clear what is meant by identity — people's consciousness of who they are, the kind of person they are and how they relate to others. Unit 19 introduced you to three different ways of analysing these issues — from the phenomenological perspective of people's personal experience and then through the lens of the psychoanalytic and the biological perspectives. It touched too on a fourth perspective — the effects of social context on identity. The aim of Unit 20 is to develop this social perspective in much more detail.

The first five sections of Unit 20 attempt to describe how social forces affect identity. For example, we will look at the effects of different types of working environments, and compare ideas about identity found in different cultures — among the Balinese, the Javanese and the Inuit Indians, to name a few. Having described how identity and society interrelate, we then go on to look at some explanations of how this happens. Before we begin, however, I need to define the types of social influences this unit will try to cover.

READER

Now read the first two personal accounts in Chapter 16 of the Reader. Here, Phyllis Collins, a Yorkshire woman, talks about the effect on her life of being made redundant, and a middle-class West Indian man reflects on a typical moment in his day. Pieces of autobiography like these are useful sources in the study of identity because they tell us how one individual has understood themselves and their life. As you read, make a few notes on how the social context has affected the direction of each life story.

The social influence is, in many ways, very obvious. Phyllis Collins, for example, describes how her redundancy, due to the closure of a local factory, has affected her self-confidence. Her descriptions of her working life and the ways she reacts to it reminded me of the discussion in Unit 10 of 'real' jobs and the double role of women in the private domestic sphere as well as the public world of work. In her case, changes in the opportunities for women to work, in the status and pay of part-time jobs and the provision of nurseries could have had a substantial effect on her feelings about her life. The unnamed man in the other account describes how racist attitudes have affected his sense of identity. He also describes the opportunities for self-definition which are presented by his 'atypical', professional, middle-class status.

It is clear how these people, like all of us, struggle every day with social and economic facts which have a decisive effect on what we can be and do. Obviously people can also struggle to change and influence social facts and individuals clearly differ in the power and opportunity they have to make changes. The elements of the social seem to combine in ways which can produce both malign and empowering effects on identity.

One topic, therefore, a social perspective highlights is the influence on identity of broad socio-economic processes such as the division of labour, patterns of industry and class mobility, migration and colonization, as these are reflected through the particular social circumstances of any individual. We can ask questions like — what effects might redundancy have on mental health? How does discrimination affect feelings about oneself and strategies for getting by?

And what about those who discriminate — are their identities and sense of self affected by this power? What effect do social institutions, like the prison system for example, have on the psychology of both the guards and the guarded? Do people who were born in the 1960s or the 1980s and who grew up in times of economic boom, have a fundamentally different outlook from those who grew up in the 1930s? We can't answer all these questions in this unit, but Section 2 assesses some of these effects by looking at employment and unemployment, and at a suggestive study of the identities found in prisons.

Another topic the social perspective highlights is the influence of social categories. If Phyllis Collins were asked the question — Who are you?—she might give these responses — wife, mother, white, working class, former machinist, from Yorkshire, middle-aged, able-bodied. This list of social categories marks out the social groups she belongs to and 'positions' her in society. It allows us to define her 'place'. It says a lot about who Phyllis feels she is — her sense of identity.

Social categories define the *roles* people can play in society, and for each category there is a set of, sometimes contradictory, expectations about feelings, actions and motivation. For example, mothers are supposed to be caring and patient; the middle-aged are supposed to be mature, more sober than the young, and less interested in going to discos. One way social categories influence identity is through these sets of *representations* about the kind of person you should be if you belong to a particular category. Even if you disagree violently with the role you are expected to play, your identity will still be influenced by the very act of rebelling against convention and your struggle to change the prescriptions.

——————————————— ACTIVITY 1 ———————————————

Try describing yourself through a list of the social categories you belong to, or pick out the social categories in your response to the 'Who am I?' activity in the Block Introduction. What does this list say about your identity?

You may have concluded that a list of social categories gives some important information about your characteristics but doesn't tell the whole story — that there are other aspects like your personality and the phenomenological dimensions described in Unit 19. We will come back to this conclusion later.

Social categories provide one way of summarizing a person's identity and making predictions about their characteristics but they also raise some questions. Some categories, class for instance, are clearly social in origin. Others, like gender, age, sexuality and ethnicity have a biological as well as a social reference. How important is the social compared to the biological? Unit 19 looked at some of the arguments of socio-biologists about the effects of categories like gender on attitudes and relationships, in Section 3 we will take up these issues again but this time from a social perspective.

Finally, there is the question of culture. Culture was defined in Unit 3 as the customs, conventions, signs and symbols of a society which are passed on from individual to individual through learning. As members of a Western society we have particular ideas about what it means to be a person, about normal and abnormal behaviour, about morality and personal conduct. We have culturally defined ways of telling our life histories. The authors of the Reader pieces assume, for example, that they are free agents with some responsibility for their own lives, they don't attribute their actions to the spirits of the dead working through them. They assume they are unique individuals with a private, inner, mental life which they can choose to present publicly to others, and that life is a progression from birth to death. These basic ideas about identity seem quite natural to us, we take them for granted, but perhaps they are social in origin? Does every human social group think like this? Are these beliefs just specific to our culture at this moment in its history? We will examine this idea in greater depth in Section 4.

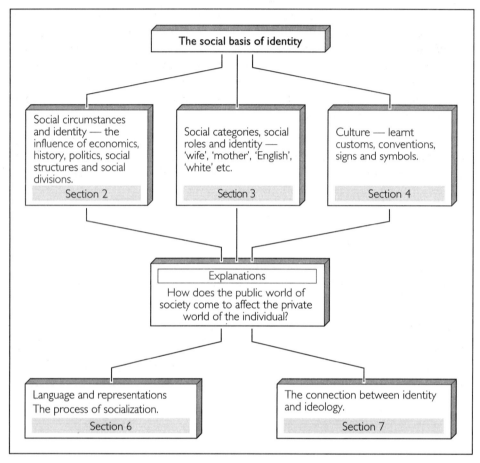

Figure 1   Summary and plan of Unit 20

2   SOCIAL CIRCUMSTANCES AND IDENTITY

2.1   EMPLOYMENT AND UNEMPLOYMENT

Experiences of employment and unemployment and indeed working conditions generally are likely to have major effects on a person's identity. But the effects may be contradictory.

> Frankly, I hate work. Of course, I could say with equal truth that I love work; that it is a supremely interesting activity; that it is often fascinating; that I wish I didn't have to do it; that I wish I had a job at which I could earn a decent wage. That makes six subjective statements about work and all of them are true to me.
>
> (Fraser, 1968, p.273)

The mixed feelings and inconsistencies in people's reactions complicate investigation. Jobs, joblessness and identity have been studied in two ways. *Qualitative studies* focus on particular work-places or the experiences of a particular group of the employed or unemployed through observation, interviews and other personal accounts like the autobiographies in the Reader. The advantage here lies in richness and detail. We discover what it feels like from the inside. There is the disadvantage however that we don't know whether the experience of some Ford car workers, say, is typical of all assembly-line workers. We can't make generalizations and estimates across large groups of people. *Quantitative studies* ask people to give responses on questionnaires and surveys which can be translated into numbers and compared across different workplaces; or they compare statistics, like rates of stress induced illness, across different groups. These studies make generalization possible but offer little insight into the meaning a particular person attributes to his or her social situation.

But what features of jobs and unemployment and what components of identity should we investigate? Peter Warr, the acknowledged British expert on the psychological consequences of work and unemployment, argues (1987) that in Western cultures there are five aspects associated with a positive attitude to oneself and a positive sense of identity:

1 Affective (i.e. emotional) well-being (an absence of anxiety, depression, and discontent).

2 Competence (a sense of being able to deal effectively with events).

3 Autonomy (a sense of control over the direction of life).

4 Aspirations (motivation to improve one's life).

5 Integrated functioning (a coordinated and harmonious identity).

These aspects concern people's personal experience and feelings about themselves. The question we are exploring then is: How do different working environments affect identity defined in this sense? Warr suggests nine features of working patterns which might be relevant:

1 Opportunity for control.

2 Opportunity for skill use.

3 Externally generated goals.

4 Variety.

5 Environmental clarity.

6 Availability of money.

7 Physical security.

8 Opportunity for interpersonal contact.

9 Valued social position.

—————————————— ACTIVITY 2 ——————————————

How would you rate your working situation (employed, unemployed, retired, child-rearing, domestic work etc.) on these environmental features? You could take each feature in turn and rate them on a scale from 1 to 5 where 1 stands for 'strongly characteristic of my working situation' while 5 stands for 'not at all characteristic'.

Warr proposes a 'vitamin' model of the relationship between features of the environment and well-being. Vitamins are clearly essential for physical health;

if a diet is deficient in them, health is impaired. Warr argues that control, contact, variety, environmental clarity etc. are the 'vitamins' for mental health. We need a certain level of vitamins to maintain a positive self-image. But the thing about taking vitamins is that eventually a plateau is reached, if you take a certain dosage there is no benefit from taking any more. Some vitamins taken in excess are even toxic. The same is true of some environmental 'vitamins'. A certain amount of variety is good, but add any more and you might decrease the job holder's feeling of being able to cope. It is this complex outcome which probably causes some of the mixed feelings people have about work. In a given day, the environment 'vitamins' your job or lack of a job offers might vary from optimum level to toxic level to deficiency.

If we apply this model first of all to compare paid employment with involuntary unemployment; it is clear that, in general, involuntary unemployment tends to have negative consequences for identity. The flavour emerges in qualitative studies.

> We were raised on work up here. I find myself even now thinking it's time to get up, and I put my feet out of bed, grab my trousers before I remember that I don't have to go. Then you get back in bed, and you're glad you're not late; till it dawns on you you'll never have to get up early again … You don't realize what it means to you (p. 109).

> You feel as if your whole life is crumbling. You feel devalued out of work; you feel your age, you feel you have less to offer. Instead of feeling you're getting richer in experience, you feel something is being taken away from you.

> (Seabrook, 1982, pp.122–3)

Quantitative studies, which test people as they move in and out of work, demonstrate a significant decline in well-being with unemployment which picks up again with re-employment. Research, which compares groups of unemployed with similar groups of employed people, demonstrates that the negative effects of unemployment concern all the aspects of identity described above. The unemployed are more likely to express anxiety, depression, and low self-esteem and are less likely to express happiness, life satisfaction and positive moods. Questionnaire data indicate less subjective feelings of competence, self-confidence, sense of control, and lower aspirations among the unemployed. Unemployment also spills over to other aspects of people's lives with detrimental effects on family relationships (Warr, 1987).

But these negative effects could simply be due to poverty. Money is crucial to well-being. Job satisfaction increases with increased levels of income while job-related psychosomatic symptoms decline. Low pay is associated with higher anxiety and stress symptoms (Warr, 1987). But psychologists argue that identity problems do not stem from financial hardship alone (Jahoda, 1982; Warr, 1987). Paid employment is an 'institutionalized social relationship' (Fryer and Ullah, 1987) offering environmental 'vitamins' which go beyond the wage contract (Henwood and Miles, 1987).

The jobless environment for many people tends to be low on opportunities for control, variety, structure, opportunities to use skills, and externally defined goals. Unemployment is also socially stigmatized and sometimes offers less chance for interpersonal contact and support from others. It is these aspects as well as poverty which affect identity.

So far I have considered the unemployed as a single group but in fact this group includes people of different sexes, ages, ethnicities, and social classes. Most research has focused on the adult male and it is the middle-aged man who is most likely to suffer the negative effects I have described. The findings for women are contradictory, with unemployment sometimes being associated with positive well-being. But the patterns for unmarried women and women who are the principal bread winners are similar to those for men. Obviously, different groups of women have different experiences because of the multiplicity of ways in which we work in the domestic and public worlds.

The points made so far refer only to the experience of involuntary unemployment, where the individual has no choice. Do these findings extend to other 'non-working' situations such as retirement and to women at home looking after young children? A lot seems to depend on people's attitude to their situation which can affect the environmental features Warr identifies. Poverty and the level of social support in both retirement and child rearing will always be significant factors, but if retirement, for example, is seen as a positive outcome and actively structured so that any environmental 'vitamins' lost are replaced with others then, obviously, the experience will be very different from cases where the person regards retirement as a form of banishment from the world of work. The point I am making is that people's perceptions can interact with features of the social environment — for a job to offer opportunities for control, those opportunities have to be perceived as such by the job holder.

The involuntary unemployed are also individuals with different feelings about their situation. An unemployed 55-year-old man whose previous job was highly stressful and who becomes active in voluntary work might well find that unemployment is good for his sense of identity. Although when asked, the majority of us say we would rather go on working even if we didn't need the money (Warr, 1987), jobs, too, can differ in their identity opportunities. We can't assume that not working always offers less 'vitamins' than working.

Assembly-line work is often taken as the classic example of employment which, like a bad diet, is low in 'vitamins' and particularly low in opportunities for control, use of skills, variety, and autonomy.

> I stand in one spot, about two or three feet in area, all night. The only time a person stops is when the line stops. We do about 32 jobs per car, per unit. Forty-eight units an hour, eight hours a day. Thirty-two times forty-eight times eight. Figure it out. That's how many times I push that button ... Repetition is such that if you were to think about the job itself, you'd slowly go out of your mind for yourself ... You dream, you think of things you've done.
>
> (Terkel, 1972, pp.159–60)

Quite small changes in work patterns can have significant effects on personal well-being. Warr describes a longitudinal study of workers in a confectionery factory where the transfer of responsibility from supervisors to workers, combined with increased control over the pace of production, the distribution of tasks, and the organization of breaks changed a job from low autonomy to higher autonomy with a general improvement in workers' attitudes to themselves both within and outside the work-place. Similarly studies of nurses and teachers show that as control over their job increases so does their mental well-being. Researchers followed one group of nurses as they moved from one. type of ward to another type and back again; the nurses showed significantly more anxiety, depression and psychosomatic symptoms in the more restricted and less controllable ward (Warr, 1987). So, it is important to compare not only employment with unemployment but different kinds of employment with each other.

SUMMARY — WORK AND IDENTITY

- The example of work strongly suggests that a person's social circumstances can have a significant effect on their identity.
- The effects concern aspects of personal experience such as feelings of autonomy, self-esteem, motivation and sense of well-being.
- These effects operate through features of the social environment which Warr calls 'vitamins'. Jobs and joblessness can provide deficient, sufficient or toxic levels of these environmental 'vitamins'.

2.2 PERSONALITY AND SOCIAL SITUATION

The research on employment and unemployment seems to provide clear evidence for the influence of social circumstances but it also raises questions about the contribution of individual differences and personality.

Perhaps people lose their jobs through particular personal characteristics, for example, which make them unemployable or they stay as assembly-line workers all their lives for the same reason. I also noted that individual differences in the way people perceive their situation can be important. Perhaps these differences between individuals explain the social circumstances people find themselves in and thus explain variations in well-being between groups.

As Warr points out, the 'individual difference explanation' for people's choices about work sounds plausible against a background of a booming economy and low unemployment. Then personal characteristics might account for whether people work or not, but the explanation becomes quite implausible in times of economic recession.

The relationship between personality and social situation can be studied in another way — by laboratory experiment.

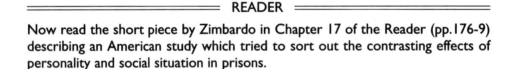

====================== READER ======================

Now read the short piece by Zimbardo in Chapter 17 of the Reader (pp.176-9) describing an American study which tried to sort out the contrasting effects of personality and social situation in prisons.

Most of the time it is easy for us to explain people's reactions by their personality, *X* feels miserable about being unemployed because he just isn't a fighter or an extravert; the influence of the social situation on people's feelings and attitudes is often much less obvious. Zimbardo asks us to think again.

The advantage of an experiment is that a 'pure' situation can be created. In a real prison, personality and social situation intertwine. It is not clear whether people with particular pre-existing personality characteristics are more likely to become prisoners, for instance. By selecting a group of young men with very similar backgrounds and with similar personalities, and imposing on them one of two different social situations — prisoner or guard — Zimbardo and his colleagues could see how each situation differentially affected the volunteers

and thus how a real-life social institution might come to structure people's sense of who they are and how they should behave.

Obviously a mock-up in the basement of a Psychology Department is going to depart from the realities of prison life in many ways. All the same, as the journal entries indicated, the experiment had dramatic effects on identity. The young men began to behave in prisoner or guard types of ways with profound consequences for their sense of identity and self-esteem. As Zimbardo notes in his article, many other social psychological experiments have reinforced this conclusion. The social situation has substantial power to determine attitudes, relationships and feelings about ourselves.

Before we get carried away, however, with Zimbardo's conclusion, we should note some limitations to his argument. There were still individual differences in Zimbardo's study, some of the guards found it easier to order prisoners about and some prisoners found their life more stressful than others. How do we explain those differences? Zimbardo discusses Milgram's finding that 60 per cent of people would apparently inflict pain on others when commanded by an authority. But how do we explain the actions of the remaining 40 per cent who didn't obey the order?

To explain these differences we could turn back to the perspectives discussed in the last unit. Psychoanalysts, for example, might look at people's upbringing and how that influences their resilience in stressful situations, the biological perspective would look at differences in temperament, extraverts might fare better in some situations than introverts, while the phenomenological perspective would look at how each person perceived their situation.

So, the conclusion is that social circumstances are extremely influential as the research on work and Zimbardo's study illustrate, but that's not the whole story. It depends, too, on what people bring to their social situation in the way of previous experience, personality characteristics and on the way they perceive what is happening to them.

> SUMMARY — PERSONALITY AND SOCIAL SITUATION
>
> - The social perspective on identity stresses the effects of roles and institutions on identity and action rather than personality and individual differences.
> - Zimbardo's study confirms the importance of social factors but leaves unexplained the remaining individual differences.
> - The psychoanalytic, phenomenological and biological perspectives offer different explanations of these individual differences but cannot explain the social effects. This indicates how the perspectives stress different aspects of identity but also how they could complement each other.

3 SOCIAL CATEGORIES AND IDENTITY

3.1 SOCIAL OR BIOLOGICAL?

The television programme associated with this unit, TV10, looks at one social category in detail — nationality — and how this identity, and the experiences associated with it (feelings of patriotism and belonging), are socially constructed. It is often assumed that each nation has a national character or personality: the English stiff upper lip, Scottish thriftiness, and German efficiency, for instance. These characteristics have been seen in the past as innate, a matter of the right kind of blood and 'race'.

> But I am haunted by the human chimpanzees I saw along that hundred miles of horrible country. I don't believe they are our fault. I believe there are not only many more of them than of old, but that they are happier, better, more comfortably fed and lodged under our rule than they ever were. But to see white chimpanzees is dreadful; if they were black, one would not feel it so much, but their skins, except where tanned by exposure, are as white as ours.
>
> (cited in Husband, 1982, p.12)

This observation written in 1860 assumes the classic premises of racism: a hierarchy of groups from uncivilized to civilized and the biological determination of group characteristics. The extract comes from a letter from the English author Charles Kingsley to his wife, in which he writes about his visit to Ireland and his impressions of the Irish. The same kind of assumptions have also been made in the past about social class; for example, that the working class were innately feckless. Women and men, too, have been seen in this light.

> The rather silly remark about women being privileged to change their minds is only a polite way of saying that women *do* change their minds. And they change them because they are swayed by fluctuating little moods — the children, as it were, of their deeper moods — which they make practically no attempt to regulate. It is true that men encourage them in this by tacitly acknowledging that it is merely what is to be expected, but I suppose they long ago discovered that it was wisest to accept the inevitable with good grace ... one must remember that

physiology plays a dominant part in directing women's outlook and that many of their unaccountable mental phases are due to forces over which they have no control.

(Curle, 1947, p.114)

The reasoning displayed here about the social categories of gender, race, nationality and class and their relationship to identity (i.e the way in which these points are approached) is often described as *essentialist*. It assumes that if you are born a woman or a man, black or white, Irish or English, the identity characteristics typically associated with your category, such as femininity and masculinity, or the different stereotypes about national characters, are part of your 'essence', a built in feature. Thus you will inevitably be moody if you are a woman, you just can't help it!

Although the prejudice displayed in these extracts is a serious matter, the sentiments expressed seem out of date and even laughable to the modern reader. Not only because we now have very different ideas about what women or men, the Irish or English, or the middle class should be like, but also because scientific and popular opinion about the categories of gender, race, nationality and class has gradually shifted further and further away from this notion of a built in, biologically determined, 'essence'.

Essentialism reached its zenith in nineteenth century science and has steadily declined since then, probably because of social changes and the development of competing ideologies of human nature. But also because research failed to back up some of the more extreme claims of nineteenth century essentialists: claims that women are less intelligent than men because their brains are smaller, for instance, or that black people are innately inferior. The effect of social expectations on identity characteristics has become more visible with time as social science has developed. This is not to say that essentialism will not recur or that it is not still an important element in ideologies of racism and sexism.

The historical variability in identity characteristics has also become more evident. As Michael Billig points out in TV10, in the past the English were not known for their stiff upper lip but as the fickle and emotional creatures of Europe, liable to burst into tears at the slightest provocation. Similarly historical studies demonstrate that women in Anglo-Saxon times were expected to be self-assertive and independent and modern writers on the Middle-Ages often note the 'surprisingly masculine' character of women in those times, surprising, that is, to today's historians (Oakley, 1972). At the time of the Crusades: 'The rule that such and such feelings or acts are permitted in one sex and forbidden to the other was not fairly settled. Men had the right to dissolve in tears, and women that of talking without prudery' (Oakley, 1972, p.59).

Characteristics which vary with each historical period can not be biologically built into the essence of women or men or into the English even though from the perspective of any particular period it is hard to imagine that things haven't always been that way.

The socio-biologists you encountered in Chapter 15 of the Reader, in connection with Unit 19, represent a modern attempt to revive and seriously question some of these issues. As you saw, they argue that some of the strategies women and men adopt and other aspects of relationships, like altruism, have a biological basis. But it is important to note that most socio-biological researchers would also dissociate their ideas from crude essentialism. They argue that biology will be modified by social factors. Some also note that any predictions they might make on the basis of biology will always be complicated by the immense variations among groups: the individual variation among groups of women and men, for example, often outweighs any aspects women or men as a whole might share in common. But, in general, one of the differences between a biological and a social analysis of identity is that biological explanations try to identify features that are part of the essence of people. Social analyses stress things like historically changing characteristics which are more flexible and not built in to individuals.

There are really two issues here for identity research. First, whether any characteristics associated with a category or group have social or biological origins or result from some combination of these and, second, a problem we haven't discussed before in relation to identity, the problem of distinguishing between representation and reality. I'll dwell a bit more on the social category of gender to explain what's involved in both these issues.

3.2   THE SOCIAL CATEGORY OF GENDER

For any given period in our society it is possible to identify various representations or stereotypes about femininity and masculinity. Studies of people's views in modern Western societies usually produce the following images. *Masculinity* is equated with aggressiveness, rationality, adventurousness, bravery, independence, and *femininity* with empathy, passiveness, irrationality, nurturance, kindness, and a caring orientation. That's a dominant representation and we could easily identify the dominant representations for other social categories like social class and ethnicity, but as social scientists we have to ask about the reality before we can begin to investigate the possible social and biological origins of gender characteristics. Are men actually more rational than women, for example? Are women really more emotional?

The debate continues about whether there are any real psychological differences between women and men and whether these differences might be social or biological in origin or consist of a complex mixture of environmental and physical factors. Note that I said *psychological* differences. There are many differences between women and men — according to insurance companies women are safer drivers, for example; the crime rate for women is lower, and there are all the differences in socio-economic position discussed in Block II. The question we are concerned with is — are there any differences in personality and abilities, in the psychological traits associated with gender categories, which might explain the different social position of women and men?

The present consensus among researchers is that, despite the representations and stereotypes which suggest strong differences, very few psychological differences between women and men can be reliably demonstrated. Despite a great deal of research, it is still unclear whether social or biological factors or some combination of them explain these differences (Nicholson, 1984). You looked at some of these arguments in relation to Unit 8 and there was an article by John Nicholson in the section of the Reader associated with Block II. Let's review some of the points again.

The psychological differences that have been established in Western societies come down to these: men seem to be more aggressive, better at visual spatial tasks like map reading, and better at mathematical reasoning. Girls have the edge in verbal skills over boys. These traits are tendencies rather than absolutes which means that girls of a certain age will tend *on average* to be better at verbal tests than boys of the same age but if you took any particular boy or any particular girl they need not be different, the boy might even be better, because the differences don't apply absolutely in all cases. Differences are also affected by training. Women are not condemned to be forever bad at visual spatial reasoning, a short training course can improve these skills dramatically, which suggests that social factors might be involved somewhere in the development of these skills.

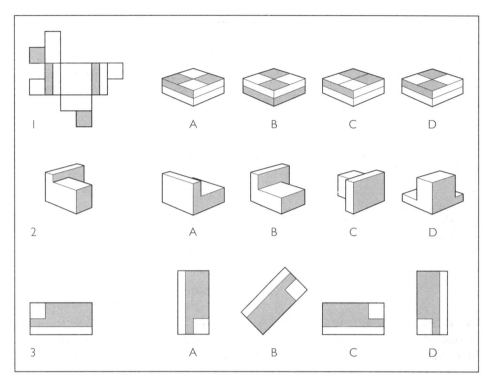

Figure 2   An example of psychological tests of 'spatial ability'; each shape on the left (numbered 1–3) must be matched with one of the shapes marked A, B, C or D.

Source: J. Sayers, (1980) 'Psychological sex differences', in The Brighton women and science group 'Alice through the Microscope', London: Virago.

Now that we know what the psychological differences come down to, we can ask whether these traits might explain other differences between women and men. There are very few women engineers, mathematicians and architects, for instance. Is this because of visual-spatial skills? Not at all. According to some calculations by Sayers (1980), the difference in visual-spatial abilities is such that if this was the *only* thing which determined the number of women in engineering we would expect to see 40 per cent women engineers and 60 per cent male engineers. Instead it is more like 5 per cent and 95 per cent. Social factors make the difference. Similarly, psychological tests indicate women have the edge in language usage, particularly spelling and grammar — if this psychological difference is the crucial factor in determining life chances then why are most journalists, famed writers, literary critics and social scientists men?

The results of research into the differences between women and men often surprise people, because there are so few established differences in personality and abilities and yet gender is so crucial to the organization of our society. Although it is important in social science to distinguish between the representation and the reality and to question the representation and popular stereotypes this doesn't mean that representations are unimportant for identity. After all if there really are only a few ways women and men actually differ, then representations must play a vital role in justifying a social structure based on gender.

Remember, too, the point made in connection with TV10 — because things like national character are a representation or construction of reality it doesn't make them any less powerful, persuasive, and psychologically real.

What people believe to be true is just as important to their sense of identity as the actual differences. If you grew up as a boy in the UK in the 1950s, you are probably familiar with the idea that boys shouldn't be sissies and real men never express their emotions. These representations and others like them are crucial to how men and women make sense of themselves and their lives, and how they see their opportunities. When it comes right down to it, men are just as capable of changing a nappy or comforting a child as women. Furthermore, in psychological tests, women have been found to be no more soft-hearted and emotional than men. Later sections of the unit will take up the relationship between representations and identity further and will look at how ideas, images, fantasies and expectations about identity can catch hold of us.

SUMMARY — THE SOCIAL CATEGORY OF GENDER

- One way of looking at how membership of social categories affects identity is to consider whether certain characteristics are inbuilt. If you are a woman rather than a man, or black rather than white, will your sense of identity automatically be determined by your biological make-up?

- Socio-biology is a modern version of what was once a very popular explanation for differences between women and men.

- But to sort out whether something is social or biological in origin we need first to discover the actual ways women and men differ psychologically. In the case of gender, there seem to be few real differences in personality and ability and many representations.

- The different contributions of social and biological factors to these psychological differences is still a matter for considerable debate with arguments on both sides.

3.3 EXPLORING THE SOCIAL

You saw in the Reader article associated with Unit 19 ('Evolutionary origins of identity' by Richard Stevens pp.150–61) the way socio-biologists explain differences related to gender using evolutionary arguments, but what does the social perspective draw upon in its analyses of categories and identity? I have hinted at some of the main elements already. Social explanations stress the role of upbringing and expectations, the influence of history, culture, and the economic and political organization of a society.

Let's look at two examples as a quick illustration: sexual orientation and identity and the effects of diagnosed disabilities such as learning difficulties on identity. In both cases there doesn't seem to be much scope for a social analysis. Disability and mental handicap are often assumed to be just a matter of biological impairment. While sexuality sometimes seems like one of our least social attributes. Male sexuality, in particular, tends to be seen as an inbuilt force, as a set of natural drives or instincts which require and demand expression (Weeks, 1986). But, as one researcher said, maybe the most important sexual organ in humans is located between the ears! (Vance, 1984). What would a social analysis focus on?

1 *History*. There is the history of the categories themselves, categories such as 'homosexual', 'heterosexual', and all the others by which we distinguish 'normal' and 'abnormal' sexual orientation. These categories seem merely descriptions of naturally occurring types of people, but a historical analysis questions this naturalness. We discover, for example, that these categories haven't existed for all time but emerged in particular historical periods, becoming particularly prominent in the nineteenth century. They are also clearly linked to changes in society occurring at that time. Similar investigations have demonstrated that some of the categories of disability once associated with mental impairment, such as the category of ESN (M) — which refers to mild or moderate educational subnormality — arose as a result of government policies and new systems of classification. Many people today prefer instead a category such as 'educationally disadvantaged' rather than 'educationally subnormal' (ESN) because of the implications that such a categorization contains about normality. We can analyse how new categories of people and thus new identities are created at different times in the history of society.

2 *Patterns of incidence*. We could then investigate patterns of incidence and investigate other characteristics of the people who seem to fit into the categories we are studying. The original Kinsey studies of sexuality in the 1950s, for instance, suggested that 37 per cent of the male population have homosexual experiences at some point in their lives but only 4 per cent go on to become exclusively homosexual. These findings were startling when they were first published, because they suggested that homosexuality is not, as was assumed, a fixed pre-determined disposition or an inevitable identity if you happen to be born that way, but is a more flexible identity.

Similarly studies of children labelled as ESN (M) demonstrated that if you are black, male or working class you were very much more likely to be diagnosed as having a learning difficulty or as handicapped (Tomlinson, 1982). But there is no biological reason to expect a greater incidence of learning difficulties in these groups, so these statistics point to some social process in the definition of category members. Tomlinson argues, on the basis of a detailed study of the process used to categorize children as ESN (M), that this diagnosis of disability has been used in schools to deal with children perceived as 'difficult' and 'disruptive'.

3 *Stereotypes, representations and social expectations*. How does society regard homosexuality and what are the effects of stereotypes on the identity of those so labelled? How does acquiring a disability like ESN (M) or being born with a disability affect the way people perceive you? Does the label interfere with a child's life chances compared to similar children who have not been categorized?

The reactions of other people to someone who has been stigmatized (for example, as a homosexual) can be crucial to that person's identity. The person must deal with social expectations reflected through parents, teachers, best friends and so on. Homosexual actions encourage others to react with particular labels and those actions come to be understood through common representations in our culture — for example, that male homosexuals are special kinds of people who can't have normal relations with women, that homosexuality is a negative condition. Consider this example from an interview study conducted by Plummer.

> I was told when I got myself into trouble, that I was a dirty, filthy
> queer. I did not even know what this was so I was told that this meant
> I would never be able to love a girl, that I could never have kids, that I
> had 'had' it, and would most likely end up my life in prisons for having

been caught interfering with small children ... I was half hysterical and I simply could not understand what they meant, as all that had happened had been weeks ago, I had forgotten it all by then, but somebody was made to blab by the Coppers and the Head had been brought in.

(Plummer, 1975, p.136)

As Plummer points out, social reactions reinforce the idea that to have homosexual experience is equivalent to being a certain kind of person. Similarly the disabled must deal with the reactions and assumptions of the able-bodied, with subsequent effects on their sense of identity.

―――――――――――――― READER ――――――――――――――

Now read the the third personal account in Chapter 16 of the Reader. This is one disabled woman's account of others' expectations about how she should feel and behave, and it indicates something of the stereotypes and representations associated with the identity 'disabled'. Analysis of these images would be a crucial aspect of any social scientific analysis of disability and identity.

4 *Comparison across cultures*. Finally, we can look across different cultures to cast more light on the particular social context operating around a category. We can also speculate about the connections between images of identity and particular forms of economic and social organization. In the case of the child labelled ESN (M) investigation might lead outwards to special education provision then to the education system as a whole and its function in society.

Plummer (1984) suggests the cultural element in sexual orientation is expressed in the 'who and how restrictions' — who you should have sexual relations with and how you should do it. Other cultures draw the boundaries between normality and abnormality rather differently.

For instance, homosexual acts, between male citizens and between male citizens and male slaves, were commonplace and regarded tolerantly in Ancient Rome and Greece (Veyne, 1985). According to the Roman citizen Artemidorus — relations that conform with normal behaviour are those with 'one's wife, with a mistress or with a male or female slave: but to let oneself be buggered by one's own slave is not right. It is an assault on one's person and leads to one being despised by one's slave' (Veyne, 1985, p.27). A Roman man might quite reasonably have both a wife and a catamite, a male slave for sexual pleasure. The pleasures of sleeping with women and with men were often publicly debated by the male poets.

The crucial moral distinction, as the comment from Artemidorus indicates, occurred between active and passive sexual acts. The male Roman citizen should take the active role and be the ravisher, most definitely not the one ravished; passive sexual roles, for men, were considered offensive, immoral and abnormal. Identity then was bound up, not with homosexuality or heterosexuality but with active or passive pretensions.

We will return to the connection between culture and identity in the next section but, as you can see from these two examples of sexual orientation and disability, the four stages in a social analysis of categories and identity involve many and varied research activities. Potentially the field is vast. After all there are many different ways of categorizing of people in our society and many possible identities associated with these. What about age (childhood, adolescence, middle age, old age), for instance? There is a clear biological process here but is that the complete story about the different senses of self we have at 3, 15, 30, and 80? TV11 takes up this question and provides another example of the role social and biological factors play in social categories and identity.

4   CULTURE AND IDENTITY

In Activity 1 in Section 1, I asked you to write out a list of the social categories which describe you and to consider whether this list comprehensively summed up your identity. If you are like me you probably concluded that there is more to your identity than this list, although social categories are crucial. What remains when you take away the social categories seems to boil down to the aspects which were discussed in Unit 19 — a sense of agency, of being a unique individual with a private inner life, distinctive personality traits, upbringing and so on.

The study of identity in different cultures, however, makes us think further about this personal experience of uniqueness and distinctiveness. Perhaps this view of ourselves is only possible in a particular social context? The most exciting thing about investigating different cultures is that it becomes possible, through comparison, to see the shape of what we tend to take for granted. Our ideas about identity become as unnatural and strange as the practices of others.

=============================== READER ===============================

To get you thinking about possible differences in basic assumptions about identity across cultures, now read the remainder of Chapter 17 of the Reader. In it, Maurice Eisenbruch cites the case history of a Vietnamese woman living in Britain. He describes how she and her family understand her illness compared to the theory expounded by the Western psychiatrist.

It seems reasonable to assume that mental disorders and, indeed, physical disorders will be the same all over the world. But is this the case, or do different cultures have different ideas and experiences of mental upsets? Keep this question in mind while reading Eisenbruch's article.

In this section on culture and identity, we will deal mainly with the work of anthropologists. Their research method is called ethnography and, like qualitative studies more generally, aims for disciplined observation. The goal of an anthropologist is to become totally immersed in a culture (through intensive periods of field work; living with the people being studied; and acquiring their language) with the object of systematically describing how the world looks from the other culture's point of view.

4.1   THE THOUGHTS OF DIFFERENT CULTURES ON HUMAN NATURE

It is not possible to live as a human being without having an idea of what it is to be human. People have always considered their nature. Their speculations have run along well-worn and reliable paths — those provided by culture and society.

(Heelas, 1981, p.3)

Each historical period, society and perhaps grouping within that society has its own common sense or 'good sense' about what life and human nature are about (Gramsci, 1971). If Gramsci is correct, then what is the 'good sense' of Western culture?

The account given below parochially refers to Englishmen but it contains aspects those of us who are neither English nor men might recognize too:

> An Englishman assumes, without undue reflection, that he is a unique individual, complete with a mind and an unconscious realm, and perhaps a soul or spirit, which are distinct from his physical body. Our common sense about identity focuses on the inner, private self: on emotions, states of consciousness, will, memories, the soul (if one is a Christian) and so forth. It also focuses on the self as agency. We regard ourselves as being capable of acting on the world, exercising our will power, and we feel that we have the ability to alter many of our psychological attributes (as when we 'make up our minds to be calm'). A number of expressions, in fact, focus on the powers of the self with respect to itself — e.g 'self-determination', 'self-possession', 'self-respect' and 'self-assurance'.

> (adapted from Heelas, 1981, p.4)

By expanding the key words in this statement a little bit, we get the following list — unique, integrated personality, self-governing, autonomous, in control, rational, responsible for one's actions, private inner self, separate, detached, acting on the world, and independent.

There is a powerful set of ideals here which reflect major assumptions about human nature. The good sense of Western society has been particularly strongly influenced by the liberal tradition of thought and its individualism. Remember the section on liberalism in the Traditions essay (Chapter 22 of the Reader)? Individualism is apparent in this stress on the uniqueness and the autonomy of the individual and the separateness of individuals from the social and natural world. We tend to see ourselves as the initiators of our own experience and as independent integrated centres of consciousness. We stress our control over the world and ourselves, emphasizing the power of our wills to make things happen.

The anthropologist Clifford Geertz has argued that these ideas about agency, uniqueness and individuality which seem very obvious to us might well seem very peculiar to other groups of people. He cites as an example two cultures — the Javanese and the Balinese — both distinguished by their highly ritualized and organized social life where the individual and society tend to be blurred together.

We tend to believe that personal expression is everything, the hallmark of the properly autonomous person. But the Javanese believe that personal expression is vulgar, impolite and uncivilized. Their ideal is as follows:

> Through meditation, the civilized man thins out his emotional life to a kind of constant hum; through etiquette, he both shields that life from external disruptions and regularizes his outer behaviour in such a way that it appears to others as a predictable, undisturbing elegant and rather vacant set of choreographed motions and settled forms of speech.

> (Geertz, 1984, p.128)

For us, the personal private life tends to be seen as the real world of the individual, in Java, it appears, the individual lives in the public facade but, most importantly, it is not conceptualized as a 'facade' because that implies there is a real self 'somewhere else', outside society, which doesn't apply in this case.

Geertz describes how the Balinese similarly attempt to wash out any hints of personal expression or personal style. The vital thing is not the individual but the social position the individual occupies and you behave appropriately for that position. The lack of attention paid to the individual and the strength of the focus on the self as always social and communal can be seen in this example from Geertz's research:

> All Balinese receive what might be called birth order names. There are four of these, 'firstborn', 'secondborn', 'thirdborn', 'fourthborn', after which they recycle, so that the fifthborn child is called again 'firstborn', the sixth, 'secondborn', and so on. Further these names are bestowed independently of the fates of the children. Dead children, even stillborn ones, count, so that in fact, in this still high-birthrate, high-mortality society, the names don't really tell you anything very reliable about the birth-order relations of concrete individuals. The birth order naming system does not identify individuals as individuals, nor is it intended to; what it does is to suggest that, for all procreating couples, births form a circular succession of 'firsts', 'seconds', 'thirds', and 'fourths', an endless four stage replication of an imperishable form. Physically men appear and disappear as the ephemerae they are, but socially the acting figures remain eternally the same as new 'firsts', 'seconds' and so on emerging from the timeless world of the gods to replace those who dying, dissolve once more into it.
>
> (ibid, 1984, pp.129–30)

Shweder and Bourne (1984) call cultures which do not make a clear distinction between the individual and society holistic or sociocentric cultures. Contrary to our own emphasis on the distinctive and special nature of individuals, these cultures regard individuals as simply parts of a whole. Human action is determined by one's social status, by family and kinship networks, and relations with others. These, rather than personal ideals, and individual desires dictate how you act and react.

The language of a people is a rich source for discovering their theory of identity. Our language, for instance, uses terms like 'I' and 'me' and 'you' and 'they' and 'it'. Harré (1983) notes that these terms correspond to our sense of a strong personal identity, distinct from others and of the self (the 'I') as a substance which acts on the world. He points out that the Eskimo or Inuit Indian language, in contrast, doesn't emphasize personal identity so strongly and talks about qualities or states of mind which incidentally happen to find expression in individuals. Thus to feel indignation is not 'I feel angry' but 'there is annoyance', 'I hear him' becomes 'his making of a sound with reference to me', and in answering the question 'Who is preparing dinner?'. We might say 'I am', the Inuit Indians would say 'the being here mine'.

Harré goes on to note that the Inuit have no term for our concept of 'creating' as in the sense of 'creating a work of art', a manner of speaking which stresses the role of the active self and the active individual who acts on the world. Instead the Inuit see the process of making a work of art as bringing forward or releasing the possibilities which are already present in the material itself.

Cultural differences extend to other important aspects of identity such as memory and desire. Heelas (1981) discusses the concept of the individual found among the Dinka of the Southern Sudan who, it is claimed, do not possess a concept of mind as an internal self which stores up memories. Thus when 'remembering' something the Dinka regard the place where the event happened as the agent which then acts upon the person 'remembering'. We, on the other hand, see ourselves as holding our memories in us and it is we who act as agents producing them from our minds. It is difficult to make sense of an alternative concept, and this idea of the place where the event happened holding the memory and then acting on the person at a later date.

The culture developed by the Chewong people of the Malaysian peninsula (Howell, 1981) is likely to appear similarly odd to Western eyes. The Chewong have developed rules (the 'punen' code) forbidding what they call 'speaking badly', which includes anticipating pleasurable events. The hunter, for example, who obtains some food, will not express any pleasure at the thought of the meal to come. To do so is thought to be dangerous and will result in death and disease. The Chewong believe that either you will be attacked by an animal such as a tiger or there will be a supernatural influence. If you are not bitten by an actual tiger or snake, you may still sicken and die, because the soul of the tiger can attack you too. The 'punen' code similarly forbids talking about any desire which is unfulfilled or making any emotional outburst when you injure yourself.

The *punen* and other rules make it unacceptable for the Chewong to not only express desires which as yet are unfulfilled but to discuss their emotions at all. They appear expressionless to the Western observer. Despite the British stiff upper lip, clearly we could be described as emotional compared to the Chewong. We spend a great deal of time anticipating pleasurable events, and are prepared to talk about our reactions in boring detail. These are activities which would seem extremely dangerous to the Chewong.

These systems for regulating desire which seem exotic to us are, of course, not simply arbitrary or random weirdness. Cultural systems for dealing with desires are closely tied to other aspects of the social system and structures of social control. To understand why the Chewong have developed 'punen' rules, Howell argues we need to understand systems of food distribution and food scarcity. The 'punen' rules actually ensure in a complex way, which I won't discuss here, that food is cooperatively shared. A culture's rules about emotional expression are closely linked to the organization of other aspects of social life.

It would be possible to develop example after example of cultural differences but I think there are enough here to make the point that ideas about agency, uniqueness and individuality are not shared by all cultures. Being a person, with an identity and a sense of self, thinking, feeling, and acting, just seem so natural that it is often difficult to appreciate that there is a theory of what it means to be human operating here at all. As Geertz (1984) points out, it is a bit like asking why do you call that object a hippopotamus? What else could you call a hippopotamus? Or getting the response, when asking about supernatural beliefs — of course the gods are powerful, why else would we fear them? Some answers to questions seem so obvious, they appear to be so natural, that they seem beyond reasoning and conceptualization, simply the way things are. From a Western perspective autonomy, self-control, uniqueness, separateness and mastery over the world seem like facts of nature — just the way people are by nature. It is hard to treat this view as an assumption, an idea, a theory, a representation which so firmly structures the way we understand ourselves that it seems as though we must have always thought in this way.

4.2   EVALUATING ETHNOGRAPHY

These cross-cultural examples may seem convincing but how should we evaluate anthropological work? Ethnography is a difficult and subtle business. How can the researcher be confident they have correctly interpreted the other's point of view? For example, take the Dinkas — do they *really* believe it is the *place* rather than the *person* who 'remembers' something that has happened or is this simply a metaphor for what they believe? Worse still, could they be making an elaborate joke at the expense of the anthropologist? In English, we sometimes use metaphors like: 'I was in two minds over that', or 'in my heart I knew it was wrong' but this does not mean that schizophrenia or a representation of the mind as being in the chest are dominant in our culture.

Another methodological problem is that societies can be diverse. How do you know your informant is truly representative of his or her culture? Within our own culture, for example, people believe in all kinds of things, astrology for instance. The American magazine the *National Enquirer* once ran a story headlined: SCIENTISTS DISCOVER THAT THE HUMAN SOUL IS 3mm THICK! What image of our culture and its theory of identity would an anthropologist gain from reading the *National Enquirer* or a British tabloid newspaper such as the *News of the World*? And who is to say that some groups are more properly representative of the the 'true' culture than others?

Perhaps, too, some of the practices of other cultures are not too far removed from practices in our own culture. The Javanese man, Geertz describes, might make a good civil servant and, as someone commented, the 'punen' rules of the Chewong resemble the rules of an English boys' boarding school! Similarly some British artists, the sculptor Henry Moore for example, have talked about their acts of creation in ways that are not dissimilar to that of the Inuit Indians.

Some researchers argue that the belief in agency, separateness and will-power which is accepted as typical of Western societies by many anthropologists may, in fact, only apply to the powerful in our society and that women have a different, more communal and less individualistic, theory of self (Lykes, 1985). Issues like these do not go away and are worth bearing in mind when considering the examples used in Section 4.1. In response to criticism, ethnographers like Geertz have tried to identify the *general* features of a culture repeated across a range of social contexts, and have also looked for differences among sub-groups.

SUMMARY — CULTURE AND IDENTITY

- Cultures vary in their notions about what it means to be human, specifically in the emphasis placed on individualism, in their ideas about memory, and in the display of emotions.
- Cultural variation provides another example of how identity is always influenced by social context.
- Good ethnography must be sensitive to who is saying what and to whom, looking at both the general context and the detail of differences.

5   A QUICK RECAP

You have now reached the end of three sections on the connection between society and identity. How far have we come?

In these sections, I have argued that the kind of society we live in has substantial effects on our sense of who we are and what we are like. To understand a person it is not enough to look only at their personal experience of themselves, at their developmental and psychoanalytic history, or at their biology (although these things are very important); we also need to ask about the person's social circumstances, about the social categories they are seen as belonging to and their culture's assumptions about identity. We have considered some evidence and noted the range of methods used from surveys to experiments, from analysis of autobiography to observation of other cultures.

I hope the distinctive aspects of a social perspective are becoming clear. One major contrast with the perspectives discussed in Unit 19 is the emphasis on factors which are external to the individual. The *public* domain has been stressed rather than *private* experience, traits, desires and motives. So, whereas Eysenck, for example, would look to characteristics within the individual to explain their response to violent crime or their sexual orientation, the social perspective turns to the person's society as the main cause of their reactions. In a nutshell, the social perspective argues that *private* experience is shaped by *public* events whereas the other perspectives argue that *private* events and experience shape the *public* presentation of oneself.

Another difference concerns the *local* and the *global* course theme. Whereas the perspectives in Unit 19, with the exception of the socio-biological strand of the biological perspective, are concerned with relatively local phenomena (individuals and their immediate lives), the social perspective tries to encompass global changes in social structure and social organization (such as international migration and economic prosperity and recession) and asks how these might affect our sense of identity.

One final contrast worth noting is the emphasis the perspectives give to continuity and change. Psychoanalysts, biologists and phenomenologists are interested in personal development and the possibilities for personal growth, but they also place a great deal of emphasis on the continuity of identity and the unchanging aspects of self-experience — patterns laid down in childhood, inherited traits, the existential truths of human experience. The social perspective pays more attention to flexibility and difference both for particular individuals and human beings as a whole. Social circumstances, of course, have continuity and thus so does identity *but* the suggestion is that if you move from one culture to another or take on a completely different role in life, your sense of identity could substantially change. Similarly it is suggested that human beings living in highly contrasting societies, or in highly contrasting historical periods, or even in markedly different social groups within a society can have extremely varied senses of identity. The social perspective claims that we are 'plastic', that we can bend and twist in many different directions and, like the chameleon, can take on the different identity colourings offered by our society.

It is important that we do not overlook some of the commonalities between perspectives. The biological, the social and the psychoanalytic perspectives tend to stress factors beyond individual control, whereas the phenomenological perspective emphasizes agency and choice. Social researchers like biological researchers use rigorous quantitative methods of investigation but social researchers also, like phenomenological and psychoanalytic investigators, study autobiographical accounts and people's reflections on their lives. Each perspective offers its own angle of vision and these angles coincide and cross over each other in different ways.

Let's turn now to the next section and move from review to explanation, how does the *public* (the social) mould and influence the *private* (the individual's experience and sense of identity)?

6   EXPLAINING SOCIETY AND IDENTITY: THE ROLE OF REPRESENTATIONS

So, just how do social forces 'take hold' of individuals? In part, it is inevitably a crude process. Win £300,000 on the pools or migrate from a society where you are part of the privileged majority group to a society where you become part of a stigmatized minority and the change in your material circumstances will quickly reshape your sense of identity. Social changes and social facts have their own logic and create their own pressures but how do they work psychologically? How are our minds and our hearts altered by changes in our social and cultural circumstances?

The problem can be seen as a developmental one. The development of a child as a member of society, from a purely physical being to a social being, can be used as a model for other kinds of changes where identity is reshaped. Children may have all kinds of understandings and experiences of the world. They can potentially be all kinds of people. They can think all kinds of things: that stones can talk, that the moon is a person. Yet this diversity becomes channelled into the acceptable schemes of the child's culture. Some experiences become almost 'culturally unusable' and may be repressed or forgotten in the process of becoming a proper member of society. This process of becoming a social being can be seen, then, as both a narrowing and a broadening of experience.

One of the most comprehensive accounts of how people develop as social beings can be found in the work of the American social philosopher and psychologist George Herbert Mead. Mead's theory, developed originally in the 1930s and later extended by his colleagues and students, focuses on the role representations play in identity. His contribution has been called *symbolic interactionism*. The reasons for this particular label will become clear shortly.

6.1   SYMBOLS, LANGUAGE AND SELF-CONSCIOUSNESS

Like many social scientists, Mead thought that social influences on identity work through the characteristics which distinguish us from animals and which make us distinctively human.

The world of animals, even sophisticated animals like chimpanzees, is very closely based on concrete objects and events — trees, tasty food, not so tasty food, predators etc. Animals can make associations between events, and note that one object stands as a sign or indicator for another object, but this is almost the limit of their capabilities. Your dog, for example, has probably learnt to associate some of your actions with dinner-time or with going for a walk, but can't go much further. Even the tricks displayed by the most clever and well-trained dog are simply extensions of these kinds of associations.

The distinctive thing about humans, which allows us to be social creatures and which separates us from other animals, is our ability to *symbolize*. We can make one object symbolize or represent another object. Language is the best example of a symbolic system and represents the most obvious difference between animal and human groups. An event happens and we can then talk about it to our neighbour over the fence. The words we use are symbols which stand for the sequence of actions being described.

The important thing about symbols is that they are arbitrary signs which rest on a social consensus or convention. The signs that our dog develops, such as overcoat and walking stick = going for a walk, are always based on concrete and relatively immediate connections between events. Human symbols do not need to be concrete and immediate in this way. Let's take an example. We use the word 'house' as a symbol for a physical object of a particular kind and shape, made of bricks and timber or whatever. This symbol 'house' has no necessary connection to the physical object, whatsoever, if we chose we could use another symbol, such as the French word 'maison' or make up our own word such as 'lokut' or 'bretch'.

Symbols are arbitrary then in the sense that humans are capable of making almost anything stand for something else. The constraint is this point about symbols depending on social consensus or social convention. We don't use 'bretch' for physical objects made of bricks and mortar, because no-one would have the faintest idea what we are talking about. The word 'house' works as a symbol because speakers of the English language agree that this particular word stands for that particular object. It would only be useful to talk about 'maisons' if we were part of the community or consensus of French speakers.

This capacity for language and symbolization enormously increases human potential. What does it allow us to do? It makes *intersubjectivity* possible, that is, our ability to communicate our internal world to each other. Symbols open up one mind to another mind. *Symbolization is the basis of representation.* You can understand what I'm thinking about when I watch sumo wrestling on television, if I turn to you and tell you, because we share the same symbols. We may argue about the significance and morality of wrestling but dispute is possible because we share a common set of terms from which the argument can be constructed and we can understand each other's different symbolizations or representations.

You may be asking, what has the capacity for symbolization got to do with identity? In Unit 19 it was argued, from the phenomenological perspective, that the sense of self depends on a highly developed capacity for symbolic thought, now we can build on that point and extend the argument a bit further using Mead's analysis.

Mead claims that the most fascinating symbolization is the possibility of *representing yourself to yourself.* An individual can use a symbol for themselves. We can create an image of ourselves in our minds, which stands for what we think we are, and manipulate that image. For example, you can imagine yourself in various situations and how you might act, what you might say and what you might look like. You can think about yourself and decide that a career in hairdressing or in the armed forces, for example, isn't 'really you'. People, like the assembly-line worker described in Section 2, often spend many hours mentally running through scenes in their lives, replaying, and sometimes rewriting, the figure they cut in vital episodes.

You also come to have a symbolic presence for other people in the sense that your body comes to stand for, *X*, a person of a particular type, with a certain name, certain likes and dislikes etc. Autobiographical accounts like those in Chapter 16 of the Reader depend on this ability to think about oneself and then represent that self to others.

This ability to reflect on yourself has been described as the capacity for *reflexivity*, or *self-objectification*: literally making yourself an object for yourself. There are clear overlaps here with the work described in Section 2 of Unit 19. Being 'self-conscious' allows you to regulate yourself and to monitor and change your behaviour.

One of the most interesting moments in child rearing is to see children gradually becoming self-aware in this way, turning into a person who has an image of herself or himself. We can tell this has happened when a child can look into a mirror and recognize the being in the mirror. It indicates that the child is beginning to carry around with them a mental image of what they are like. Using a play on the word 'mind', Hewitt refers to this as the moment when a person begins to 'mind their own conduct' (p.61), while Mead talks about 'being another to oneself' (Hewitt, p.69).

The capacity for symbolization and self-representation is closely allied to some other human abilities implicated in inter-subjectivity. For example, there is the capacity for empathy. We can put ourselves in the mind of another person and work out how they might be symbolizing themselves to themselves. We can anticipate what they might do next. Most importantly, we can do something Mead calls *role-taking*.

Role-taking means seeing ourselves from another person's perspective. You probably have, for instance, an idea of how your mother sees you, or what your best friend thinks you are like. You may be right or wrong in estimating your mother or best friend's representation but the crucial thing is that you can form an image of yourself based on the way you think other people are likely to see you. In other words, *you can symbolize yourself through the eyes of another person*.

Again the autobiographical accounts in the Reader illustrate this capacity. The professional West Indian man, for instance, imagines how the white visitors to his office see him. He represents to himself their likely view of him. The very act of autobiography similarly involves imagining an audience for whom you are constructing your history.

Mead notes that you can see yourself not just through the eyes of particular people but also in terms of how a *generalized other* might see you. The generalized other is people in general, a composite of people you know. Perhaps most self-consciousness is of this kind, imagining not just how a particular person will regard you but the impression people in general might gain.

─────────────── ACTIVITY 3 ───────────────

To consolidate what you have learned so far, try writing a very brief character reference for your self. First, note down in a *short* paragraph how you see yourself. What would you say were your main personality traits? How successful do you think you have been in your life? What are you most proud of and what are you most ashamed of? What do you think you will be best remembered for? That is, represent yourself to yourself.

Second, take the perspective of someone who is important to you, a parent for example, or a partner, your child, whoever, and imagine what their representation of you might be like, your personality, your successes and failures and so on and write another paragraph. Third, write a paragraph trying to see yourself from the point of view of people in general, the viewpoint of the *generalized other*, the kind of viewpoint a journalist who doesn't know you very well might take of your life.

Perhaps these three different perspectives have resulted in you writing the same paragraph each time, but perhaps there are significant differences in the three representations. Indeed, who is to say which is the most accurate representation? In making these judgements you have engaged in two fundamental activities: first, in *reflexivity* and *self-objectification*; and second, in *empathy* and *role-taking* from the point of view of *significant* others (your partner or child) and *generalized others* (the journalist), respectively.

6.2   SOCIALIZATION

Mead argues that the process of becoming a social being depends on our capacity for self-representation and emerges from the abilities of role-taking and reflexivity, abilities which the child acquires as they learn a language and develop in a social environment. Although the first stages of developing a sense of oneself as a certain kind of person occur in childhood, Mead thought the whole process would be a life-long affair. Whenever you change jobs, for instance, or become a parent, or become ill, or unemployed, or retire, a new process of self-education will take place as you acquire a new identity and a new set of self-representations. It is probably in childhood that the child gains the strongest and most durable sense of identity. The entire process is called *socialization*.

A new-born child is simply a physical being with the potential for becoming a social being: a being without culture, not yet shaped into human history. According to William James (1890), the baby's world is initially a 'buzzing, booming confusion'. Gradually the confusion of different sensations resolves itself as the child acquires symbols and language and learns to recognize objects as different from each other: different kinds of animals, for example, with different names and belonging to different categories — pet dogs, stray dogs, other people's pets, types of animals people never keep as pets and so on.

As the child becomes more competent at symbolizing their world in general, they also learn about themselves as separate selves with a particular identity. 'Only when the individual can symbolically designate objects in the environment can the self be designated as one of those objects' (Hewitt, 1984, p.67). The child gradually learns that they too are an object which is separate from other people. They learn how to refer to themselves by name and what kind of object this person, this self which acts on the world, is.

Mead placed special emphasis on the parents, the most *significant others* for the child, in this process of acquiring a complex symbolization or set of representations for the self.

> Individuals do not learn about themselves or experience themselves directly ... The person does not define himself as an object 'from the inside out'. Rather we see ourselves as others see us: In the simplest sense, we learn to use the name given to us by others; more subtly, all the terms of value, respect, hatred, liking, hope, social location and definition that people apply to themselves, they learn from members of their families and the other groups to which they belong ... The child does not learn to hate or respect himself by responding directly to his own conduct. Rather he learns both the terms of reference he should use and their specific application to him from others who are significant to him as he grows up.
>
> (Hewitt, 1984, p.55)

The child is surrounded by their parents' attitudes to this growing self. Parents' representations are a crucial source of evidence and information about the nature of this object — oneself. Parents give children names, they have views about good behaviour and bad behaviour, they attribute intentions and motives to the child, they act as if the child is a particular person, a girl rather than a boy, a valuable and worthwhile person rather than an object to be despised and ridiculed, and so on. Parents constantly interpret children's behaviour. Studies of mothers, for example, show how, long before children can possibly have acquired complex motives, the mother talks to the child *as though they already possessed these*—'that's a good girl, Susie, you wanted to kiss teddy and make him feel better because you trod on his foot'.

According to Mead, the social self is acquired by the child *internalizing* the parents' attitudes. To a large extent, the child takes over the parents' image about what kind of object this self called Susie or Bill is. In doing so, the child becomes *socialized*. They find out how their particular culture, which may differ from any other culture, believes the two sexes should behave, the significance given to gender and how one should display emotions and so on. A social self emerges from this ability to represent oneself to oneself, from *role-taking*, and from the fact that for the growing child, the parents' attitudes to the child or the parents' representation of the child are the basic materials from which the first kind of self can be constructed.

This process is difficult to understand and difficult to write about. To try and clarify it further let us think for a bit about a metaphor developed by the sociologist Charles Cooley (1902). Cooley stated that our selves are always looking-glass selves. We look to society for an image of ourselves and the image society reflects back becomes our self. The child looks to the parents and the parents act as a mirror in which the child can see herself. She sees her shape in her parents' eyes. This process ensures that culture and the conceptions of identity held by a society, and we have seen that different cultures have very different ideas about identity, are transmitted to the next generation. The child's caretakers act as the representatives of society. They represent their society's or their sub-groups' expectations and notions about normal behaviour to the child.

Clearly as children grow, the environment created by parents or other caretakers becomes less embracing. These particular 'significant others' lose their importance. The self once put into position is capable of creating new representations and new self-'reflections', rejecting some possible selves in favour of other selves, creating new meanings, new symbols. Parents, as significant others, have tremendous power but they are also destined, in Mead's account, to lose that power.

Low self-esteem and self-hate in adult life may indicate the power of the parents' earlier conviction of the inadequacy of the child. This adult may have learnt from their parental mirror that they are an unworthy self of little value. Yet the ability to be aware of oneself as an object and to change that object also gives the child autonomy. Control moves from the adult to the child. Using Cooley's metaphor, it permits the child to move out of the range of the parents' mirror and even to reverse the looking glass so the parent now, for example, discovers themselves reflected in the eyes of their adolescent child.

6.3   IDENTITY AND REPRESENTATIONS

So far in this section of the unit, I have argued that representations are vital in the process of constructing an identity or a sense of who we are, and also that representations are the bridge between the individual and the social and between the public and the private. Mead's argument is that in talking about our identity we rarely create new representations, most of the time we are working with the representations which already exist in our society. Representations which Mead sees being transferred to the child by parents. This transfer from parent to child or from society to its members is what is meant by socialization which continues at every stage of life.

We saw in Sections 3 and 4 that the social representations of identity which are already in existence, and which are transferred from society to the individual, span a number of levels. There are very broad representations in Western culture about what it means to be human, to be a private individual, to have a personality, to be sane rather than insane and there are the more specific representations associated with different social categories. These might be contradictory or in the process of change. Traditionally, as I noted, masculinity has been represented as about assertiveness, dominance, logical and rational thinking, independence and mental toughness. But this representation is being challenged and new representations are emerging.

We have also seen that representations can be distinguished from reality. It is important to remember that dominant images of gender and ethnicity are sometimes simply that — images, stereotypes, fantasies. But they are powerful images all the same.

They are powerful because, as we have seen, the social representations available in our society are the materials from which we must construct our personal sense of identity. We each have to tell the story of our life. We have to fit ourselves as characters into stories we understand and other people will understand. This is maybe why soap operas are so amazingly popular. They provide very simple story-lines with clearcut character types, simple dilemmas, and stereotyped social relations. They make the business of self-representation look easy and exciting! Indeed, you could tell the story of your life as a dramatic soap opera. This kind of narrative might have been a fourth form of description you could have given for Activity 3.

The point is that although there is a lot of choice around about how we can tell our story, we are not free to make up any kind of story. The *way* you tell the story of your life and the representations a child internalizes as they acquire an identity reflect not only the experiences open to you due to your particular social circumstances, but also reflect a collectively shared vocabulary and accepted sets of images for talking about human nature, motives, and desires. Every person has their own unique story but in conveying this autobiography we have to rely on recognizable narratives for talking about oneself.

Take a look at this piece of self-description from a female university student:

> Describe myself? Em — I'm one of those people who's like really over the top — but underneath is really sort of shy and retiring, and who puts on like different shows for everybody, who is quite extravert but underneath is sort of doubting and I analyse things a lot and get very depressed; I over-analyse things. Is that it?

The speaker here represents herself by making a distinction between appearance and reality. She says that on the surface (appearance) she comes across to others as a jolly and extravert sort of person but really, underneath, she is more shy and retiring. This statement seems sensible to us, you hear people make this sort of distinction the whole time. It makes sense because we share with the speaker a set of cultural meanings about what people can be like, which structure and organize the way we understand and talk about the story of ourselves.

In other cultures and at other historical periods this idea of two selves, appearance and reality, might not have seemed in the least bit sensible. It could have been seen as a sign of insincerity or duplicity and thus immorality, or simply as crazy, a symptom of mental illness or possession by evil spirits.

The next section will extend the discussion of representations and identity to include the concept of ideology. A great deal of socialization and a great number of the self representations transferred from parent to child are, of course, not concerned with ideology. For example, parents teach their children how to be polite in public, how to treat their friends and, indeed, what a friend is. But some of the identity representations offered to us seem to be more intimately related to the structure of our society and to power relations within it. In these cases the concept of ideology, as we will see, can be useful for thinking about identity.

SUMMARY — THE DEVELOPMENT OF SOCIAL BEINGS

- The social 'gets inside' the individual through the human capacity for symbolization and self-representation.

- Mead argues that children become socialized because parents act as a mirror for their children. Children see from their parents the kind of person they can be and actively take on that self.

- Parents present already existing representations to the child and thus the representations of our culture and society are transmitted from generation to generation.

- Our identity and autobiography are based on our experiences. These experiences depend on our distinctive social circumstances but if our story is to make sense to others it can only be expressed through culturally recognizable narratives.

---

7   IDENTITY AND IDEOLOGY

7.1   FROM REPRESENTATION TO IDEOLOGY

Think back to Section 6.1 where I presented Mead's views on symbolization and representation. You may have noticed at the time some parallels with the concept of ideology introduced in Unit 17 of Block IV.

Several different features of ideology were noted in Unit 17. If you remember, the unit author argued that to merit the description 'ideological' ideas and beliefs had to be shared by significant numbers of people. To be influential ideologies must be collectively held. They are more or less systematic chains of linked ideas and symbols which develop over time and which pre-exist any particular individual person.

Mead similarly stressed in his work on symbolization the importance of cultural understandings that have become shared social frameworks. There is a strong overlap here. Mead also argued that cultural representations pass from generation to generation and pre-exist the new-born child, providing a ready-made social space into which that child is born.

The concept of ideology, however, has the potential to go a bit further than Mead's analysis. It can add some additional features and for this reason it is useful to extend our analysis from the study of representations and identity to the study of ideology and identity. What are these features?

The clue comes in the claim in Unit 17 that ideologies, as opposed to ideas, beliefs and representations more generally, are intimately connected to the operation of power within a society. Ideologies are those sets of ideas, assumptions and images which help us make sense of society and which in some way *legitimate* particular relations of power.

This emphasis which links the collective sharing of ideas with power ties in with some of the social functions often attributed to ideology. It connects with the claim that ideology can act as a 'social cement', maintaining social order and distorting social reality in the interests of powerful groups (functions 3 and 4 in the list in Section 1.3 of Unit 17). This definition also highlights some of the ways ideologies are thought to work by smoothing over social contradictions.

With this brief revision of ideology under our belt, I want to move on and see what ideology could contribute to the topics we have been exploring in this unit. The next two sub-sections use the tools of ideological analysis introduced in Unit 17 and look at some concrete examples of ideologies surrounding gender, ones which sustain specific feminine and masculine identities.

7.2   PERFECT BODIES AND FACES

'The most important business in the post-industrial world is the creation and manipulation of identity' (*Arena* on the fashion designer Giorgio Armani).

Take a look at the following ideological statement which is analysed by Rosalind Coward in her book, *Female Desire*:

> Have you ever envied models and actresses their slim and supple bodies and glowing good looks? Have you ever thought I could never have a body like that, because ... and reached for another chocolate biscuit in the same breath? Do you recognise any of these excuses? — Big Bones — No will-power — Husband likes me cute and cuddly. Well no more excuses! You can have a beautiful body if you really want one. After all, it's your body in the first place — and it is your responsibility to take care of it. All you need is a little know-how and some will-power.
>
> ('Look Great, Feel Better,' article in *Annabel*, December 1980, cited in Coward, 1984, p.24.)

Although this is only a short piece, you may recognize it immediately as part of the general subject matter found in a certain type of magazine addressed to women. These magazines concern the body beautiful, clothes, attaining the ideal home, relationships and families. They are closely related to the development of consumer markets for cosmetics, fashion, interior decoration and food.

The interesting thing about subject matter like this is that it is not simply responsive to what women want, nor is it providing a service, it is *producing* and *creating* women's desires, to help sell certain products. It sets up ideals, which women are encouraged to aim for and promises pleasures if those ideals are attained. A particular feminine identity and subjective feeling is being constructed here. We tend to think of psychological states such as pleasure, interest and desire as simple natural reactions to situations. But, Coward argues, we should recognize that pleasure and interest are also created through ideology.

In Unit 17 (Section 1.5) it was suggested that there were five main ways ideologies work:

1   By presenting ideas as 'only natural' and as the only rational way to act.

2   Through concealing contradictions.

3   By presenting norms and human motivations as eternal, unchanging and universal.

4   Through chaining together packages of symbols and using evocative language.

6   By making a personal appeal to the individual.

It is relatively easy to see all these techniques operating in the magazine's exhortation to women. The desire to be thin and the pleasure to be gained from having a 'perfect' body are presented throughout as straightforward unquestionable common sense: a natural, universal, and eternal desire. As Coward points out, when we read this piece it is difficult not to agree — yes, of course, we want better bodies — to reject this conclusion, given the way the piece is framed, would be like choosing to be stupid when you could be intelligent.

I am not so sure if the magazine meets the second characteristic of ideology — concealing any contradictions. Perhaps there is one if we consider the often quoted statistic that more than 50 per cent of British women wear size 14 or over. 'Beautiful bodies', in the parlance of these magazines, are usually not the bodies most mature women actually have, they are the thin and under-developed bodies of prepubescent women. But encouraging size 14 women who are normal in terms of the population in general to try for a 'beautiful body' is good for the sale of products advertised in the magazine.

Another way ideologies work is through personal appeal and it is worth dwelling on this a bit because of the connection with identity. Ideological statements construct *subject positions*. They often seem to speak directly to the person and construct the person as being a certain kind of listener.

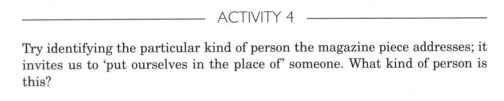

——————————— ACTIVITY 4 ———————————

Try identifying the particular kind of person the magazine piece addresses; it invites us to 'put ourselves in the place of' someone. What kind of person is this?

It helps to rewrite the statement in the first person. It constructs the reader as the kind of woman who might say to herself:

> I want a beautiful body; I want a body like that of a fashion model or an actress. I am eager to enter into a struggle to attain this ideal body. It will be hard work but I will feel good about myself. This desire is normal, every woman wants this and I can do it too if I can control myself.

As was noted in Unit 17, ideologies are powerful because they recruit us to some cause, they both invite and command at the same time. Ideology, therefore, gives us a stance from which to view the world; it positions us through giving us a self-definition and creates a logic to acquiesce in. Hence the term 'subject position' — subject equals self or identity here.

Another term introduced in Unit 17 to describe this process was *interpellation*, which comes from Althusser (1971). Althusser said that we know ideology is working when it creates a reaction like — 'oh, you mean me', or 'yes, that's me alright, I think just like that'. He suggests we should be suspicious of these moments of recognition because what is happening is that an ideology has

successfully 'hailed' us. It is a bit like someone hailing you on the street, you turn around and recognize that it is you who is the object of the greeting and accept that the hailer knows you and has successfully greeted the right person.

The statement from the magazine is not an isolated piece of ideology moreover. Women readers have been hailed or invited and commanded in this way many, many times before. There is a familiarity effect from all those previous hailings so no wonder there is the — 'yes, that is just like me' — response.

Whether we should be worried by this process of self-recognition and suspicious of the hailing depends on your point of view. For instance, why should we see this magazine piece as a piece of 'ideology' in the first place?

Rosalind Coward argues that in her opinion the article fits into the category of ideology because she sees it as oppressive for women and thus connected to power relations and the division of labour in our society along gender lines. The piece suggests that the will-power, discipline, effort, autonomy and self-control of women should not be focused outwards into the world but inwards onto the shaping of her own body. Coward connects the incidence of anorexia and other eating disorders among women with this kind of interpellation. This particular beautiful body is always an impossible ideal. The other side of pleasure in relation to the subject position constructed here is, therefore, guilt and failure.

But here we are back to one of the conundrums involved in defining ideology noted in Unit 17. If you disagree with Coward's view, then you could accuse her of simply labelling the things she finds personally offensive 'ideology' and presenting her own reaction not as ideology but as a 'simple representation'. A better criterion, therefore, might be whether this magazine piece can be seen as legitimating power, as in the definition of ideology from Unit 17 I quoted above: presumably in this case the power to sell products.

———————————————— ACTIVITY 5 ————————————————

Two advertisements follow this Activity, one appearing below the other and printed on pages 86–7. Have a go at analysing these as pieces of ideology. What kinds of identities are being presented to readers here? How are readers recruited into seeing themselves as certain kinds of subjects? You might like to compare your results with other students' conclusions at your local study centre. The first one is interesting because it covers the same sort of ground as Coward's example, but comes from the period of the Second World War, while the second is a modern advertisement directed at men.

No

surrender...

We have a chance to show our
mettle in this war. We wanted
equal rights with men and
we have been taken at our word.
We are glad and proud to
work for victory beside them.
And work is not our only task.
We must triumph over the daily

round, keep within ourselves
the spirit of lightheartedness.
We must see that personal
troubles are not mirrored in
our faces. We must aim for
masculine efficiency without
hardness. Above all, we must
guard against surrender to
personal carelessness. Never must
we consider careful grooming
a quisling gesture. Now that
we have little leisure and few
beauty-aids, it is specially
creditable to look our best.
Let us face the future with
high-held heads. And let us
honour the subtle bond between
good looks and good morale.

Put your best

face forward . . .

FEW ENOUGH MEN MAKE A MARINE. WHAT DOES IT TAKE TO MAKE AN OFFICER?

The Royal Marines. The Royal Navy's amphibious spearhead. The Commandos.

You don't get to be one simply by filling out the application form.

Can you imagine yourself commanding a whole troop? 30 Marines, including men with years of active service behind them in places you've only read about.

And you just one year out of school or university. If you're honest with yourself, it probably sounds beyond you.

But don't worry. If you ever make a Royal Marines Officer, you'll make it on merit.

And by the time you do, there won't be a lot that'll intimidate you.

Training that'll make you or...

If you've heard the stories about the rigours of Commando training, chances are they're all true. There are no short cuts to the level of physical fitness we require.

The 30-mile endurance test. The Tarzan course. The timed cross-country runs in full kit. Mud, tunnels, hills and ditches.

And that's just the first step.

Because the object of all this rough stuff is to get you used to physical stress.

So used to it, it ceases to matter.

As a Royal Marines Officer, you're paid to think. Whatever the conditions, however shattered you feel, we expect your brain to go on working. Because it's on that piece of equipment, more than any other, that the lives of you and your men will so often depend.

If you check the history of Royal Marines operations, you'll find very few came risk-free. To minimise those risks as far as possible, the planning needs to be meticulous, the thinking alert, the mind sharp.

A cross between
Daley Thompson and Einstein?

As a Young Officer under training, your intellect will be stretched as hard as your body will be pushed.

Military History, International Relations, Guerilla Warfare. You'll be expected to know as much about subjects like these as you will about the SA80 rifle and crossing rope bridges.

That said, we're not looking for a hybrid of the two gentlemen named above.

Determination. Guts. A good brain.

If you've got those qualities, the right academic qualifications, and you're between 18-25, you could be serving in places as diverse as Nato's Arctic Flank or a frigate in the Indian Ocean within two years.

Write to: Major P. N. Ward RM, Dept 389A, Old Admiralty Building, Spring Gdns, London SW1A 2BE. The Armed Forces are Equal Opportunity Employers under the terms of the Race Relations Act 1976.

ROYAL MARINES OFFICER.

7.3 COMICS FOR GIRLS

The aim of this sub-section is to consolidate the points already made about ideology and identity. On pages 89–91 you will find part of a comic strip story reproduced. This strip is from *Bunty,* which is a popular comic read by pre-teenage girls, mostly working-class. The market the comic is aimed at gives us some context in which we can interpret it as a piece of ideology. Valerie Walkerdine, a developmental psychologist, has analysed comics like *Bunty* and *Tracy* with a view to making a general connection between identity and ideology.

 ACTIVITY 6

Before I discuss Walkerdine's points you might like to read the strip reproduced on pp. 89–91 and note down any themes in the narrative and the identities constructed. Who are presented as the good characters here and who as the bad ones? What constitutes goodness or evil?

In her analysis, Walkerdine claims that the stories in comics like *Bunty* repeat the same themes over and over again — 'they are nearly all about girls who are victims: of cruelty and circumstance … In the majority of stories, the children do not live with their biological parents or siblings, but are removed by various tragic circumstances to surrogate families who are cruel to them' (Walkerdine, 1984, pp.167–8). The remaining stories, Walkerdine says, cover such themes as the girl who is clever and beautiful but who is the object of envy at school and thus unpopular, and the girl whose mother teaches in a rough comprehensive school with the girl helping her mother manage the school by various good deeds. Another typical story concerns a horse who is jealous of the heroine's horse but the heroine's horse unselfishly helps the jealous horse in spite of all.

In all the stories cruel and bad circumstances are resolved by fantastic solutions and twists of the plot. Mainly these involve the heroine in selfless acts and her private endurance of awful situations carries the day. This is in strong contrast to boys' comics where the heroes engage in action to change the situation and rout the villians. For the heroines of *Bunty* and *Tracy* triumph comes through quiet good deeds and patient acceptance of others' wrongdoing.

Walkerdine suggests that we should look at these stories as ideologies which produce a particular *subject position*, through fantasy, for the young female reader. That is, as ideologies, these stories address the reader and ask the reader to 'take the part' of the heroine. There are five features about this subject position which emerge from Walkerdine's analysis:

1 Heroines are victims but this victim status and the cruel circumstances are exciting because they indicate an adventure is in progress.

2 Heroines win through selfless helplessness, they are rewarded by taking a passive rather than active response to violence and to the bad motives of others. This righteousness brings pain and suffering but produces a good outcome.

3 Thinking and acting for oneself and emotions of anger, desire for change or longings are presented as bad. These unacceptable emotions are acted out by other characters, the bad characters, not the heroine. Interestingly these are also usually female characters.

4 If the heroine is sufficiently 'good' and suppresses selfishness, suffering long enough in silence, then the reward is often the return of the

Come Home, Kathleen

The next day, Emma and her mother arrived—

MOTHER! THEY'RE HERE!

LOOK, MOTHER   THEY HAVE A REAL CAR!

DOESN'T EVERYONE? OH, DON'T TOUCH ME WITH THOSE GRUBBY HANDS!

—AND THIS IS KATHLEEN, MY ELDEST CHILD!

NO SHOES! AND A DIRTY OLD DRESS! YOU MIGHT HAVE PUT ON YOUR BEST CLOTHES.

THIS IS MY BEST DRESS.

THE HORS-D'OEUVRES WEREN'T BAD. WHAT'S FOR NEXT COURSE?

NEXT COURSE? THERE IS NO MORE!

THIS VISIT HAS OPENED MY EYES, MARY. I HAD NO IDEA YOU WERE SO POOR. BUT THIS MAKES IT EASIER FOR ME TO TELL YOU THE REASON WHY I'M HERE.

AUNTY THERESA HAS NEVER TAKEN AN INTEREST IN US BEFORE.

MY POOR EMMA IS LONELY. SHE HAS NO BROTHERS OR SISTERS, AND AS YOU HAVE TOO MANY MOUTHS TO FEED, I'D LIKE TO ADOPT ONE OF YOUR CHILDREN.

OH, BUT I COULDN'T BEAR TO PART WITH ANY OF THEM!

THAT'S A SELFISH ATTITUDE WHEN YOU CAN'T FEED OR CLOTHE THEM PROPERLY. LOOK AT MY EMMA—SHE WANTS FOR NOTHING, AND THE CHILD THAT I TAKE WILL BE TREATED IN THE SAME WAY.

YOU'RE RIGHT. IT IS WRONG FOR ME TO DENY A BETTER LIFE FOR MY CHILD. B–BUT WHICH ONE WILL IT BE?

TO MAKE IT EASIER FOR YOU, I SHALL CHOOSE. YOU MUST HELP ME, EMMA.

I DON'T LIKE BABIES—

2

—AND BOYS ARE HATEFUL!

WHICH ONE WILL THEY CHOOSE? I CAN'T BEAR TO LOSE ANY OF THEM!

11.3.89 BTY

3

11.3.89 BTY

idealized family, a traditional nuclear happy family, who live in a good home with many possessions.

5   Finally, the story presents good girls and bad girls as mutually exclusive personalities, one cannot be both good and bad but either one or the other.

The stories are, of course, fictitious and will be recognized by the girls who read them as not being true to life. But, Walkerdine argues, fiction like this can still have an effect on the reader's identity through working on her desires and fantasies. The stories don't deal with the real circumstances of their readers' lives and in that way might be thought to be ineffective. But what they do achieve is to suggest general ways girls can resolve difficult situations and what being a 'good girl' means. They propose escapes, ways out, fantasy solutions, the means through which things could romantically be otherwise by becoming a particular kind of person. These stories suggest that miserable and difficult circumstances can be resolved through girls becoming martyred victims who will win in the end because of their 'goodness', passivity and selflessness.

Walkerdine goes on to argue that this ideology and the subject position it creates helps prepare girls for heterosexual relationships. The ground is set for a theme which emerges strongly in adolescent girls' magazines such as *Jackie*, and in Mills and Boon's novels. This theme shows men as princes who will save the heroine if only she is good enough. Girls discover that being a woman involves being sensitive to others' needs and passive. If you are sufficiently selfless then you will be rescued, not by your own actions, but by a man who will take on the assertive and active role for you.

People get enormous pleasure from reading fairy stories, comics, novels, and watching films or television. The main point of Walkerdine's ideological analysis is to ask why the experience is pleasurable. With whom are women and men being asked to identify, and how does the sense of satisfaction gained emerge from that identification? What are the social implications of putting oneself in this position for this pleasure?

It is important to note here that people are surrounded by many different ideologies. The author of Unit 17 referred to an 'ideological field' of contrasting possibilities. Thus a girl might read her brother's comics as well as *Bunty*. She might also read the comics produced by a collective of girls in Birmingham who wish to develop radically alternative images of girls. She also goes to school and is constructed in different ways by the ideologies through which the school operates and so on and so on. In other words, people are constantly presented with many contradictory choices and can therefore resist appeals of one particular kind in favour of others.

SUMMARY — WHAT DOES IDEOLOGY ADD TO THE STUDY OF IDENTITY?

- The life-long process of socialization involves internalizing many different and contradictory representations of oneself.

- The concept of ideology suggests we think about the social functions of some of these representations and how they might relate to the structure and organization of society.

- This type of analysis poses questions about the connection between the representation of women and men found in some forms of popular culture and power relations between the sexes.

- Ideological messages work by constructing identities or subject positions which readers or viewers apply to themselves.

8 CONCLUSION

The aim of this unit has been to review the social influences on identity. We have looked at several types of evidence: work connecting social circumstances with well-being, cross-cultural studies, studies attempting to tease out the relative influences of social and biological processes and research indicating how ideologies might shape the individual's sense of identity with consequences for the social system in general.

The two D103 course themes that have been particularly relevant here are the *public* and the *private* and *representations* and *reality*. The material reviewed suggests that a simple distinction between the private individual and public social life can no longer be maintained. Individuals are private in the sense that ultimately you are free to think anything you like within the confines of your own head and you are usually free to communicate those thoughts or keep them to yourself, as you please. However, it is also clear, that the raw materials of those thoughts, the content of what an individual can think, depends very strongly on social processes. Perhaps even this sense of being a separate private individual depends on your culture, on the public domain!

We have analysed the elements of identity as representations which can operate as ideologies. That is, a person's sense of themselves can be seen as a story or set of narratives acquired through the process of socialization. These narratives can be many and varied and perhaps may be quite contradictory; there are many ways you can tell the story of your life. But there are constraints. If you are either Chewong, Dinka, or British you will tell the story of your life in very different ways. If you are a woman rather than a man, gay or lesbian rather than heterosexual, described as disabled, you will struggle with some narratives more than others. Representations of oneself are cross-cut by culture, gender, ethnicity, nationality, age, social class and so on, and are shaped by the practices and processes of society. And when representations, or these stories of identity, are viewed as ideologies we can begin to see some connections between identity and forms of power in society.

You are now almost at the end of Units 19 and 20 on identity and in Table 1 (see p.94) you will find the completed version of the grid begun in Unit 19 which puts the social perspective alongside the three other perspectives. As a result of holding in mind and comparing four different angles on identity we can see the truth in the statement that understanding people involves many layers of knowledge from biology and individual differences, reflections on personal experience, psychoanalysis, as well as all the different facets of social being. As was noted in Unit 19, the trouble is that those layers might not fit neatly together. Are the perspectives developed in Units 19 and 20 competing or complementary? Can we put all the bits together into one grand integration or will you have to choose which layers are most significant in this integration? This question was raised in the Conclusion to Unit 19. Let's have another look at the issues involved.

You could see the different perspectives on identity we have presented in Units 19 and 20 as being like political parties. Are these parties opposed to each other or could they be put together in a workable coalition? Who would you vote for? Would you like to see a coalition and who would hold the balance of power in your coalition?

In Unit 19 it was pointed out that theories differ in their *focus and range of convenience*. All scientific theories have a focus, that is, there is a set of topics, questions and phenomena with which they deal best. You could think of the theory as being like a spotlight illuminating one area very brightly but as you

Table 1   Summary grid of identity perspectives in Units 19 and 20

Perspective	Main concepts	Methods	Person determined or autonomous
Phenomenological	Subjective experience, sense of self, reflexive awareness, continuity, personal agency, mortality, choice, multiple identity.	Introspection, reflection, 'thought experiments'.	Person capable of autonomy.
Psychoanalytic	Unconscious, psychosexual development, oral, anal, phallic, Oedipal conflict, fixation, regression, transference, psychodynamics, libido, id, ego, superego, defence mechanisms, ideal self.	Free assoc., dream interp., analysis of transference, introspection and observation.	Person largely determined but can become more autonomous with insight.
Biological (i) Eysenck	Extraversion–introversion, neuroticism (emotionality)—stability, autonomic nervous system, reticular formation.	Measurement of behaviour and responses to questionnaires and tests, statistical analysis (factor analysis), experiments, twin studies.	Person largely determined by personality type and conditioning. In turn, dependent on inherited biological characteristics.
(ii) Sociobiology	Genetic transmission, natural selection, sexual selection, reciprocal altruism.	Rational speculation based on principles of evolution, comparisons between social behaviours of different species.	Social behaviour determined by inherited pre-dispositions characteristic of species and the outcome of natural/sexual selection.
Social	Socialization, representations, ideology, subject positions, role-taking, culture, the looking glass self, social categories, internalization.	Eclectic approach: surveys, questionnaires, experiments, ethnographic observation, analysis of the content of representations.	The options for a sense of identity are largely determined by what is available in society but people can and do choose among socially structured possibilities and in this way have some autonomy.

move away from the main beam of light, it becomes more difficult to see. For example, biological theories can have a lot to say about the role of hormones in motivating different kinds of behaviour, but Freud makes no mention of hormones, and researchers working from within a phenomenological perspective are also silent on this subject. Similarly, social theorists are interested in the effect of large-scale changes in the economy on identity; biologists, in contrast, don't feel that topic is part of their focus.

Theories also have a range of convenience; they differ roughly in how broad their beam of light is and the number of topics they can explain conveniently. The social and the psychoanalytic perspectives have a broad range, for instance, there are many phenomena they try to illuminate. The range of Eysenck's biological theory is rather narrower, restricted to the topic of personality and individual differences. Although you will remember (from Unit 19) that Eysenck also wanted to apply his theory to explain social phenomena such as criminality and political attitudes. Here, the range of Eysenck's theory overlaps with a social account and as a result there are two conflicting explanations of the same phenomenon. There are lots of cases in these two units where theoretical ranges of convenience overlap. The biological and the social perspectives in the hands of some advocates can both become very extensive theories with very grand ambitions, struggling to explain the same phenomena.

While notions of focus and range of convenience are helpful to us in thinking about theoretical perspectives they don't solve the problem. What do you think? Would you like to see an integration, a grand combined theory of identity — a little bit of Marx, a little bit of Freud, a little bit of phenomenology, put together as an explanation of human action? Or do you think that there are really only one or two main causes of human action, that, for instance, when it comes down to it, biology is primary and the rest just a secondary reflection of this basic cause? Perhaps you will be persuaded by the suggestion made in Unit 19 that different perspectives are appropriate for different individuals at different stages of their lives.

AUDIO-CASSETTE

The debate about the competing or complementary nature of the perspectives is continued in Part 2 of Audio-cassette 5 which you could listen to at this point.

We are not asking you to solve the problems of working with multiple perspectives in your TMAs and exam answers, social scientists haven't reached a satisfactory conclusion themselves, so we can hardly expect you to sort out the disputes. As the Audio-cassette notes, the choice between perspectives will partly be decided by the relation of each to the evidence in the manner described in Unit 18, but not completely because it is also a problem of values and the broader views you have about human nature.

It is worth remembering that these questions are often best decided on practical grounds. What do you want to do with this material? The perspective you take is often determined by the kind of questions you want to ask. For example, if you were a clinical psychologist working with a patient who has a problem with anxiety, what might be useful would be for you to have some knowledge of how personality problems develop in relation to family difficulties. You might also want to bear in mind the 'social being' of the patient — that in this case, for instance, the patient is a single parent with financial problems. Similarly, if you were a school teacher who wanted to understand the reasons for the rebellious behaviour of a group of boys in your class, you might begin by looking at things like identity and ideology, social class, and the educational system but you might also want to keep in mind questions of individual differences and ask yourself why these *particular* boys were rebellious while others in roughly the same social situation remained cooperative.

This is where we leave the topic of identity. Unit 21 moves on to social interaction but there are many continuities and you haven't quite left behind all the debates. Social interaction research also has its biological and social perspectives, for instance, and it is an another arena where we can explore the different influences of the private and the public.

READER

By now you should have read all of Chapter 22 on Traditions of Social Thought, except perhaps Section 3 on their 'presence in the study of society'. Because part of your Summer School work will be on the *traditions*, it is important that you complete your reading of Chapter 22 *before* you go to Summer School. It would also be useful preparation (if you have time) to look back over the sections you read earlier and remind yourself of the main points which are in the section Summaries.

REFERENCES

Althusser, L. (1971) *Lenin and Philosophy and Other Essays*, London, New Left Books.

Cooley, C. (1902) *Human Nature and the Social Order*, New York, Schocken Books.

Coward, R. (1984) *Female Desire*, London, Paladin.

Curle, R. (1947) *Women: an Analytical Study*, London, Watts & Co.

Fraser, R. (1968) *Work: Twenty Personal Accounts*, Harmondsworth, Penguin.

Fryer, D. and Ullah, P. (eds.) (1987) *Unemployed People: Social and Psychological Perspectives*, Milton Keynes, Open University Press.

Geertz, C. (1984) 'From the native's point of view: On the nature of anthropological understanding', in Shweder, R. and LeVine, R.A. (eds.) *Culture Theory: Essays on Mind, Self, Emotion*, Cambridge, Cambridge University Press.

Gramsci, A. (1981) *Selections from the Prison Notebooks*, London, Lawrence and Wishart.

Harré, R. (1983) *Personal Being: A Theory for Individual Psychology*, Oxford, Blackwell.

Heelas, P. (1981) 'Introduction: indigenous psychologies', in Heelas, P. and Lock, A. (eds.) *Indigenous Psychologies*, London, Academic Press.

Henwood, F. and Miles, I. (1987) 'The experience of unemployment and the sexual division of labour', in Fryer, D. and Ullah, P. (eds.) *Unemployed People: Social and Psychological Perspectives*, Milton Keynes, Open University Press.

Hewitt, H, (1984) *Self and Society: A Symbolic Interactionist Social Psychology*, (3rd edn.), London, Allyn and Bacon.

Howell, S. (1981) 'Rules not word', in Heelas, P. and Lock, A. (eds.) *Indigenous Psychologies*, London, Academic Press.

Husband, C. (1982) *'Race' in Britain*, London, Hutchinsons.

James, W. (1890) *Principles of Psychology, Vol. 1,* New York, Wiley.

Jahoda, M. (1982) *Employment and Unemployment: a Socio-Psychological Analysis*, Cambridge, Cambridge University Press.

Kinsey, A., Pomeroy, W.B., and Martin, C.E. (1948) *Sexual Behaviour in the Human Male*, Philadelphia, W.B. Saunders.

Lykes, M.B. (1985) 'Gender and individualistic vs collectivist bases for notions about the self', *Journal of Personality*, vol.53, pp.356–83.

Mead, G.H. (1934) *Mind, Self and Society*, Chicago, University of Chicago Press.

Nicholson, J. (1984) *Men and Women: how Different Are They?*, Oxford, Oxford University Press.

Oakley, A. (1972) *Sex, Gender and Society*, London, Temple Smith.

Plummer, K. (1975) *Sexual Stigma: an Interactionist Account*, London, Routledge.

Plummer, K. (1984) 'Sexual Diversity: A Sociological Perspective', in Howells, K. (ed.) *Sexual Diversity*, Oxford, Blackwell.

Sayers, J. (1980) 'Psychological sex differences', in The Brighton Women and Science Group, *Alice Through the Microscope*, London: Virago.

Seabrook, J. (1982) *Unemployment*, London, Quartet Books.

Shweder, R. and Bourne, E.J. (1984) 'Does the concept of the person vary cross-culturally?' in Shweder, R. and LeVine, R.A. (eds.) *Culture Theory: Essays on Mind, Self, Emotion*, Cambridge, Cambridge University Press.

Terkel, S. (1972) *Working People Talk About What They Feel About What They Do*, New York, Panthenon Books.

Tomlinson, S. (1982) *A Sociology of Special Education*, London, Routledge.

Vance, C. (ed.) (1984) *Pleasure and Danger: Exploring Female Sexuality*, London, Routledge.

Veyne, (1985) 'Homosexuality in Ancient Rome', in Aries, P. and Bejin, A. (eds.) *Western Sexuality, Practices and Precepts in Past and Present Times*, Oxford, Blackwell.

Walkerdine, V. (1984) 'Someday my prince will come', in McRobbie, A. and Nava, M. (eds.) *Gender and Generation*, London, Macmillian.

Warr, P. (1987) *Work, Unemployment and Mental Health*, Oxford, Clarendon Press.

Weeks, J. (1986) *Sexuality*, London and Chichester, Tavistock and Ellis Horwood Ltd.

ACKNOWLEDGEMENTS

Grateful acknowledgement is made to the following sources for permission to reproduce material in this unit:

Figures

Figure 2: J. Sayers (1980) 'Psychological sex differences', in The Brighton Women and Science Group, *Alice through the microscope*, Virago Press, © Brighton Women and Science Group.

Illustrations

p.61: Danny Lyon/Magnum; *p.84*: Reproduced by kind permission of Peters, Fraser and Dunlop/Posy Simmonds; *p.85*: Yardley advertisement, courtesy of The Advertising Archives; *pp.86–87*: Royal Marines advertisement which appeared in the *Radio Times*, 19 March 1990, reproduced with permission from the Royal Marines and Young and Rubicam Ltd.; *pp.89–91*: 'Come Home, Kathleen', Bunty, 11 March 1989, © D. C. Thomson & Co. Ltd.

UNIT 21   SOCIAL INTERACTION

Prepared for the Course Team by Margaret Wetherell

CONTENTS

1   SOCIAL INTERACTION INTRODUCED

Units 19 and 20 focused on identity and the way identities are 'manufactured' or put together from different kinds of materials. We tried to discover the elements which constitute the person and it became clear how personal experience, development, biology and social identity can be interwoven in the construction of a life story, but also how the perspectives derived from these different levels can contradict each other. Let's now extend this analysis a bit further and turn from the study of identity to the study of interaction. We need to take account of the fact that most of daily life takes place in relationships, in conversations with others, and involves collective social action and reaction. Autobiography and biography are ultimately about one person's life, but unless the person is a hermit like Robinson Crusoe the complete story also involves his or her pattern of interaction with others. And even Robinson Crusoe, as Unit 6 pointed out, had his memories of past interactions to guide him.

The first section of this unit defines the term 'social interaction' and discusses some of the problems and issues the investigation of interaction raises. The middle sections of the unit then turn to different types of explanation. Two of the explanatory perspectives from previous units — the biological and the social — are taken up in detail, although you will also find references to phenomenological and psychoanalytic perspectives. Because interaction is largely about the *public* presentation of oneself, our analysis will emphasize its social basis. We shall look at two facets of a social analysis: the influences deriving from the broad organization of society, and the influence of local rules operating in specific social situations. The last section of the unit tries to reach some conclusion on the relationship between the individual and society and describes some practical applications of interaction research.

1.1   WHAT IS SOCIAL INTERACTION?

You will find below a collection of excerpts from sources such as etiquette manuals, novels, agony columns, and research reports. The study of social interaction takes behaviour of the type described as its subject matter. You can see what sorts of activities the term covers: relationships both serious and trivial, conversation, mutual influence, the actions involved in presenting one-self to others, the impressions we create, the rituals of civilized and uncivilized behaviour, and all the problems of generally getting on with others in the modern world.

SOME EXAMPLES OF SOCIAL INTERACTION

Order even in disorder

Four Sheffield fans sit eating crisps on a pile of concrete slabs opposite the tea stall. A number of Oxford Rowdies gradually move over and silently surround them. Taunts and subtle threats are made by the Oxford boys and one of their number moves in closer to lead the antagonism. A Sheffield boy, who has so far been looking steadfastly at the ground in front of him, glances up for an instant at the leading Oxford fan. He is immediately accused of 'staring' and is challenged to stand up and fight. The challenge is ignored. Other Oxford boys now move in closer and become more vocal. The leading Oxford fan continues his taunting and starts to flick the reluctant Sheffield boy's collar and hair. At this point the Sheffield boy leaps up, his face red with anger. Adopting a stance with feet apart and arms outstretched,

he faces his opponent. The two stand silently facing each other while
the onlookers step back a pace. After what seems to be a very long
period of inactivity, an intermediary in the form of an older Oxford fan
arrives on the scene — in fact, one of the Town Boys. He moves the
younger Oxford fan to one side and escorts the Sheffield boy out of the
conflict area. The police having been onlookers themselves up to this
point, now grab the Oxford antagonist and push him roughly in the
opposite direction. There is an almost audible sigh of relief and
everyone returns to watch the second half of the match which has now
been in progress for about ten minutes.

(Marsh *et al*., 1978, pp.88–9)

Husband driving her insane

Dear Abby: My husband is trying to make me, and other people, think I
am insane. He takes things out of my drawers, hides them, and then
after I have searched the house for days, he puts them back in their
original places and tries to tell me they were there all the time. He sets
all the clocks ahead, and then sets them back until I am so confused I
don't know what time it is! He calls me vile names and accuses me of
terrible things like going with other men.

(Goffman, 1974, p.37)

Families

Two people exchanging the same behaviours may be said to relate in a
symmetrical fashion. For example, exchanging either compliments or
insults would each be regarded as symmetrical. The participants
compete to be in the 'one-up' position so each attempts to define the
relationship on his or her terms.

A husband said that he and his wife had argued every single day since
they got married except Christmas Day 1971. The wife responded by
claiming that it was on Christmas Day 1972 that they had not argued.
'No', the husband insisted, 'it was 1971'. This couple displayed a
remarkable talent for maintaining a symmetrical relationship.

(Burnham, 1986, p.13)

The Pimp Roll

Just then there was one of those drops in sound, one of those holes in
the roar you get when a door opens between subway cars. Into the car
came three boys, black, fifteen or sixteen years old, wearing big
sneakers with enormous laces, untied but looped precisely in parallel
lines, and black thermal jackets ... He saw boys like this every day in
court ... They walked with a pumping gait known as the Pimp Roll ...
He saw the Pimp Roll in the courtroom everyday too ... On warm days
in the Bronx there were so many boys out strutting around with the
Pimp Roll, whole streets seemed to be bobbing up and down ... They
drew closer, with the invariable cool blank look ...

(Wolfe, 1988, pp.45–6)

Such stupid self-destructive macho egos thought Kramer. They never
failed to show up with the black jackets and the sneakers and the Pimp
Roll. They never failed to look every inch the young felon before judges,
juries, probation officers, court psychiatrists, before every single soul
who had any say in whether or not they went to prison or for how long.
Lockwood pimp-rolled to a bench in the rear of the spectators' section

and sat down next to two more boys in black thermal jackets. These were no doubt his buddies, his comrades. The defendant's comrades always arrived in court in their shiny black thermal jackets and go-to-hell sneakers. That was very bright, too. That immediately established the fact that the defendant was not a poor defenceless victim of life in the ghetto but part of a pack of remorseless young felons of the sort who liked to knock down old ladies with Lucite canes on the Grand Concourse and steal their handbags. The whole pack entered the courtroom full of juice, bulging with steel muscles and hard-jawed defiance, ready to defend their honor ...

(*ibid.*, 1988, pp.127–8)

A wife or a person?

The classic story is that I met somebody — Matthew introduced me to a director he was working with and he didn't take me in, he said how do you do and made a little small talk, and obviously didn't take much interest. Then Matthew had to go away and we were rather unfortunately left together. And he obviously with an enormous effort sort of turned to me and said you're a physiotherapist aren't you? And I said no, no I work in television. And he said who are you — what's your professional name? And I said Sophy Bates, and he knew of me — it's a very small world — and his whole attitude changed, his whole face changed. And suddenly I was a person and somebody it might be interesting to talk to. That was awful and I don't like him for it but it was an absolute indication of how I was not of any interest if I was Matthew's wife ... It was very alarming ... I've always said that I want to go on working when I have children: it's very important to me.

(Oakley, 1981, p.62)

Manners through the ages

Thirteenth century

313   You should not drink from the dish, but with a spoon as is proper.

315   Those who stand up and snort disgustingly over the dishes like swine belong with the other farmyard beasts.

319   To snort like a salmon, gobble like a badger, and complain while eating — these three things are quite improper.

1558

You should not offer your handkerchief to anyone unless it has been freshly washed ...

Nor is it seemly, after wiping your nose, to spread out your handkerchief and peer into it as if pearls and rubies might have fallen out of your head.

1714

Frequent spitting is disagreeable. When it is necessary you should conceal it as much as possible, and avoid soiling either persons or their clothes, no matter who they are, nor even the embers by the fire. And wherever you spit you should put your foot on the saliva.

At the houses of the great, one spits into one's handkerchief ...

Do not spit so far that you have to look for the saliva to put your foot on it.

1731

If you pass a person who is relieving himself you should act as if you had not seen him, and so it is impolite to greet him.

(Elias, 1978)

This material might seem like rather poor stuff for a social scientific analysis: either because the routines are so banal and familiar that there is nothing to be said about them, or, in contrast, because human relationships are so subtle, variable and complex that only a poet or novelist could hope to say anything meaningful. However, despite these rather contradictory restrictions, social scientists continue to be interested in social interaction and have made great efforts in their investigations of the topic. So let's first ask why this is the case, and how the study of social interaction connects with some of the other concerns of social scientists.

1.2   THE MICRO AND THE MACRO

As the Block Introduction noted, the study of identity and interaction is sometimes described as the study of the 'micro-social', and distinguished from the 'macro-social' or the world of economics, politics, social structures and large-scale social processes. The need for a distinction and this categorization implies that there may be little connection between the micro-social and the macro-social — that they could be two different worlds.

But this can't be so. To have social relations on the grand scale it is necessary to have social relationships on the small-scale. One world informs the other. Shopping in a supermarket and conversations with the assistants, for example, are real for us in a way that laws of supply and demand and the market-place may not be, yet we know from Block III that during those conversations in supermarkets we are servicing the economy, and acting in a market, as well as passing the time of day. Similarly, we can study the interactions which take place in classrooms between teachers and pupils. Our main interest may be in the pattern of influence teachers exert on their students, but conversations between teachers and students repeated many times all over the country result in the institution of education and contribute to the formation of social classes with different skills and levels of qualifications.

There are several complex issues here about how the micro-social and the macro-social connect together and we shall come back to these later. For the moment, the point to note is that one of the reasons why social scientists are interested in studying patterns of interaction is because they form the everyday reality of a society. The routines of social interaction can be seen as the glue of social life. You can look at everyday social interaction as the arena in which the processes you discovered in earlier blocks of the course occur on a day-to-day basis.

1.3   THE INDIVIDUAL AND THE SOCIAL

A closely related reason for being interested in social interaction is that it raises in a particularly acute way the question of the relationship between individual human agents and social forms. Any kind of interaction automatically involves the individual in a social act, in the move from 'I' to 'we', from the *private* to the *public*. Social interaction involves joint or collective action; it involves people in coordinating their actions together, which results in the emergence of new bits of social life. An interaction involves human agents but it also involves the social. Think about a tutorial. The atmosphere of a tutorial depends greatly on the particular human agents who attend, but, regardless of who is there, it is a social situation with a pre-existing structure and rules for behaviour.

An issue which has exercised the minds of many social scientists is the question of primacy in the relationship between the individual and the social. Which is the crucial determinant of social interaction — the individual agents taking part and their psychological natures or the social structures and practices? How do these two relate together? The dilemma becomes clearer if we take another example.

Consider the crowd at a football match or some other sporting event — social interaction in one of its most spontaneous and unorganized forms. The interesting thing about crowds is that they often act in unison, chanting and singing. Perhaps you remember the Mexican Wave which became popular during the 1986 World Cup? At such times we often say 'The crowd had a mind of its own', or 'The crowd moved as one'. The same phrases are also often applied to mobs in riots and to the revolutionary crowds of history. A crowd can itself seem like a gigantic human agent. Watching a crowd, we have a sense of something superordinate, above and beyond individuals, which must, none the less, emerge from the individual.

It is this problem of explaining the emergence of the social and the influence of the social on the individual which interests researchers. There are a number of possibilities here. We could conclude that human agents are always primary; they always create and determine the form of any social interaction. We could conclude that the members of a family solely determine the form of their family relationships, for example. This is like the *methodological individualism* described in Block II, Unit 6. Alternatively, we could say human agency is an illusion. On this view, people's behaviour in interactions can be totally predicted in advance from existing social forms. Social roles and social structures will predetermine any family relationships. This solution resembles the *collectivism* of Durkheim which you also read about in Unit 6. We could equally conclude that both of these alternatives ring true and that the individual and the social influence each other in complex ways. This debate between the individual and the social will be becoming familiar to you. It was discussed, for instance, in Block II. In this unit you will see some of the arguments played out again.

1.4   THE INTERACTION ORDER

Order, regularity and pattern are the stock-in-trade of any scientist. The business of theorizing and explaining depends on the identification of some patterning worth all this conceptual activity.

But, where is the order and pattern in social interaction? Is there any pattern? Or are relationships and conversations too unpredictable and random to study?

————— ACTIVITY 1 —————

The North American sociologist, Harold Garfinkel, used to ask his students to carry out tasks which disrupted the fabric of social life and then to discuss the results. An example would be trying to engage in barter for goods in a high street shop: asking the assistant in the Californian equivalent of Boots if she or he will take 50 cents instead of 75 cents, or whatever, for a tube of toothpaste.

Other examples could be acting for a day in one's own home as though one was a highly esteemed visitor, or, perhaps, treating a distant acquaintance as though one had known them intimately for the past twenty years. Now I'm not suggesting *you* necessarily do these things, but mentally rehearse what might happen. What does the discomfort at the thought of the action indicate?

It indicates that although social interaction may seem unstructured, it is usually highly predictable and regular. The kind of violations recommended by Garfinkel reveal the social practices which rule our lives. These social practices are so commonplace it is often difficult to say what the rules are, but carry on violating them and you might find yourself regarded as mentally deranged or, at best, as extremely eccentric.

Take a look, for instance, at these two cases where interaction was disrupted by asking people to clarify common-sense remarks (Garfinkel, 1984, pp.42–4). The student experimenter in the study is (E), and (S) is the unknowing participant:

Case one:

(S)   Hi, Ray. How is your girlfriend feeling?

(E)   What do you mean, 'How is she feeling'? Do you mean physical or mental?

(S)   I mean how is she feeling? What is the matter with you? (He looked peeved.)

(E)   Nothing. Just explain a little clearer what do you mean?

(S)   Skip it. How are your Med School applications coming?

(E)   What do you mean, 'How are they'?

(S)   You know what I mean.

(E)   I really don't.

(S)   What's the matter with you? Are you sick?

Case two:

The victim waved his hand cheerily.

(S)   How are you?

(E)   How am I in regard to what? My health, my finances, my school-work, my peace of mind, my … ?

(S)   (Red in the face and suddenly out of control.) Look! I was just trying to be polite. Frankly, I don't give a damn how you are.

Social interaction depends on the operation of a mutually agreed *working consensus* among the participants (Goffman, 1959). This working consensus includes things like what kind of social situation it is, who the proper participants are, how they should behave *vis-à-vis* each other, and the appropriate rituals of conversation.

Order in interaction applies even in the most minimal social situations, even when walking down the street as one pedestrian among many. Although there is usually no direct communication with other pedestrians, we none the less orientate to their presence and engage in a minimal interchange, in the ritual of 'civil inattention'. This minimal ritual involves not looking directly at others; noticing their presence but not commenting on it in any way; not dramatically ignoring others, but behaving in such a way that you acknowledge their passing but do not indicate hostility, threat, or fear (Goffman, 1971).

As Garfinkel (1984) points out, this interactional order presents a technical problem to social scientists. A further reason, therefore, for our interest in social interaction is that it presents an unsolved puzzle. What are the sources of this order? How is it maintained? How should interaction patterns be described and explained? Of course, for members of society, including social scientists, the interaction order is also a *moral* order in that it is about the right and appropriate way to behave towards others. It is about matters of trust and tact.

1.5   SOCIAL SCIENCE AND COMMON SENSE

The story is told of the guest who approached the hostess at a party:

> 'I find the whole situation absurd, no one seems to realize the silliness, the grotesque artificiality of their behaviour.' 'Ah,' said the hostess, 'you must join the sociologists in the far corner. The rest of us realized all that long ago but decided to ignore it and enjoy the party.'
>
> (Cohen and Taylor, 1978, p.45)

One important goal of science is to reveal hidden things — the 'secrets of nature'. Natural scientists often begin with obvious facts — the sun rises and sets — and provide surprising explanations: our apparently stationary earth spins on its axis. A lot of social science also has this revelatory potential. For example, think back to Block III. The ordinary person shopping and working may have little idea about the operation of markets and the balance of payments, but we saw there how the study of economics can help to illuminate daily life.

With social interaction it is more difficult to provide surprising analyses. As we have seen, order in social interaction seems to depend on social practices which at some level everybody knows already: otherwise, we couldn't take part in the micro-reality, have conversations, develop relationships, and attempt to influence other people. The social scientist's job is still to make the invisible visible but in this case the invisible is something we half know in advance! None the less, it is important to continue to explain patterns and develop systematic knowledge. Interaction researchers are often accused of just revealing the obvious. That is inevitable. Indeed, in some sense, interaction research would probably be on the wrong track if it told you something you found completely startling.

Because of this aspect a complex relation operates between social science and common sense in investigations of social interaction. Elsewhere in the course, common sense has sometimes been seen as a source of bias, and therefore as an untrustworthy basis for developing an analysis. Think, for example, of the discussion on ideology in Unit 17. The study of social interaction also needs to preserve a detached and critical attitude to what everybody knows already, but it can make use of common sense as a resource, as a source of knowledge. Sometimes it can be useful to treat ordinary members of society as *participants* and informants in the research process and adopt methods which aim to elucidate people's existing knowledge about how to behave.

But perhaps social interaction is crucially determined by biology or macro-social organization beyond the range of everyday knowledge? In trying to explain the order in social interaction we shall consider these influences first, before looking at approaches which focus solely on the micro-social practices and the 'working consensus' identified in Section 1.4.

SUMMARY: WHY STUDY SOCIAL INTERACTION?

- The study of interaction is the bridge between the familiar events of daily life (relationships, conversations) and broader macro-social processes (economics, politics, social structure).

- This investigation might help us understand the relationship between the individual and the social: how people create social forms and the ways in which their actions might be shaped by those social forms.

- The order and pattern apparent in social interaction demand social scientific investigation and some explanation.

- Interaction research helps us to investigate common sense and what we take for granted in everyday life.

---

2 SOCIAL INTERACTION, BIOLOGY AND SOCIETY

2.1 THE CONTRIBUTION OF THE BODY

Obviously the human body is central to social interaction. What could a disembodied interaction (without movement, voice or facial expression) possibly be like? In this sense interaction, like identity, is shaped by the physical. But do genes, hormones and the other apparatus of our biology have an effect on what we actually do with these arms, legs, faces and voices?

Identifying the role of biology is beset with methodological problems. The ethologist Robert Hinde argues, however, that there is good evidence for some biological constraints on patterns of social interaction:

> These constraints and predispositions may arise from the very nature of our bodies, from the properties of our sensory/perceptual apparatus, from the motor patterns at our disposal, or from properties of the nervous system which become apparent in specific learning situations.
>
> (Hinde, 1987, p.63)

A predisposition is a *tendency* to act in one way rather than another. Hinde argues for the following tendencies, seeing them as the pre-programming human nature might bring to social interaction:

- withdrawing from painful stimuli and avoiding situations which bring pain;

- establishing and constituting relationships conducive to survival and reproduction;

- efforts to make sense of the world, to construct a notion of reality.

Hinde also argues that humans everywhere show a preferential or positive response to the facial features (high bulging foreheads, small noses and large cheeks) of babies, which explains some of the appeal of teddy bears and certain animals and cartoon characters. Young children appear to automatically follow these rules: 'If it is new investigate its properties'; 'Class together things seen at the same time'; 'Watch what your parent does and imitate' (Hinde, 1987, p.65). These tendencies are stable, seem universal in human society, and have clear adaptive potential in human evolutionary history. For these reasons, Hinde concludes that they are built-in features which structure human action.

Hinde's argument draws on the work of the sociobiological researchers you studied in the Reader chapter associated with Unit 19. You can see that, like the sociobiologists, Hinde stresses inherited tendencies and the evolution of our species. Remember how sociobiologists explained certain aspects of relationships between women and men? But note, too, that Hinde's claim is a muted one. He argues that any pre-programming provides only a framework and a set of possible directions for social interaction; it does not determine the form or content of any particular conversation or relationship. Biology alone, he says, can tell us little unless this knowledge is combined with social scientific analyses.

To further clarify both the contribution and the limits of biological study, let's look in a bit more detail at some actions which are crucial to human relationships — smiling, laughing and crying.

——————————————————— ACTIVITY 2 ———————————————————

Pause and think about how you might establish that smiling, laughing, or crying were biologically determined or that they were cultural traits. What sort of evidence would be convincing? Would it be any help, for example, to show that people in two very similar cultures smile and laugh in the same way? If not, why not?

Smiling, laughing and crying are universal communicative signals found in all cultures. They also occur in infants who are both profoundly deaf and blind at birth, who have not seen or heard others smiling, laughing or crying and, in this sense, are outside cultural influences (Hinde, 1987). So in answer to the question about methodology, one research strategy would be to look for situations where cultural influences are negligible (as in the case of profoundly deaf and blind infants). Another strategy would be to look comparatively across human groups. Cultures vary markedly, but if the trait you are investigating stays constant you can be more confident it is due to something shared across groups, such as common human biology, although this rule is not infallible, as we shall see later. It may therefore not help very much to look at two similar cultures, say America and Britain, but it would be more useful to know that British people and the tribes of the Kalahari Desert, for example, express grief and pleasure in the same way.

An alternative way of establishing biological influence is to look to animal studies. Other primates also display mouth and face movements which resemble smiles and laughs (Van Hooff, 1972). Chimpanzees display two movements — baring their teeth and a relaxed, open-mouth display. Bared teeth is associated with submissive and friendly behaviour, while the relaxed, open-mouth display is associated with play. Van Hooff argues that the bared-teeth display is related to our smile, while the relaxed, open-mouth display is related to our laugh. He traces out a possible evolutionary sequence for the development of our smile and laugh, arguing that our human ancestors passed through a stage similiar to that currently displayed by the chimpanzee (see Figure 1).

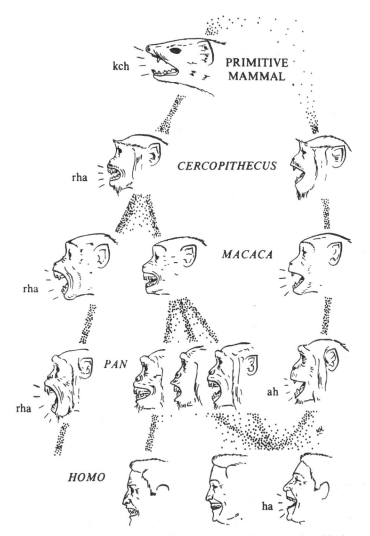

Figure 1   The phylogenetic development of laughter and smiling as suggested by homologues in existing members of the phyletic scale leading to *Homo*. On the left is the speciation of the *silent bared-teeth* display and the *bared-teeth scream* display. The *sbt*-display, initially a submissive, later also a friendly response, seems to converge with the *relaxed open-mouth* display (on the right), a signal of play.
Source: Van Hooff, 1972, p.237

Other expressions which are important in interaction also seem to have biological roots. For instance, Hinde notes the case of the 'eyebrow flash'. In many cultures, including our own, people nod and rapidly raise their eyebrows as a communicative signal. But, as Hinde notes, the *meaning* of this signal is quite

Figure 2   The eyebrow flash
Source: Drawing by Priscilla Barrett from a photograph in Eibl-Eibesfeldt, 1972; in Hinde, 1987, p.94

variable. In Greece, the raised eyebrow indicates disapproval and signals 'no'. In Polynesian societies, the raised eyebrow substitutes for the word 'yes', while in Japan the eyebrow flash is considered indecent and suppressed.

Other emotional expressions also seem to have a considerable degree of generality. People in different cultures are good at recognizing emotional expressions such as fear, anger, shame, or disgust when shown photographs of people from very different cultural backgrounds (Ekman *et al.*, 1972). Physical proximity seems to signal intimacy in all cultures (Gahagan, 1984).

But when we move from the physical movements involved in smiles, laughs and cries to the meaning of an eyebrow flash or the significance given to an angry expression, we are moving beyond the limits of the biological and into the realm of the social and the cultural where local culture begins to become more important than universally shared biological tendencies. Take the smile, for instance. All cultures smile but smiles are interpreted in many different ways. For the Japanese, smiling is a social duty; it is polite to maintain an appearance of happiness even in extreme circumstances where we would think it inappropriate, such as the death of a husband or wife (La Barre, 1947).

Cultures are sometimes divided into the 'cold' and the 'hot', according to the patterning of their non-verbal gestures (Gahagan, 1984). 'Hot' cultures (such as Arabic, South American and Mediterranean cultures) use more gestures, more eye-contact, stand in closer physical proximity, and touch more. Gahagan notes that people from a 'hot' culture like Greece maintain that a conversation with people from a 'cold' Northern European culture is like eating left-over boiled rice with no salt!

The importance of the cultural dimension, and the local rather than the universal, comes into sharper focus if we consider how differences might affect inter-ethnic relations in the UK.

2.2   INTER-ETHNIC MISCOMMUNICATION

SUPERVISOR: Can you speak English?

APPLICANT: No. *(ironically)*

SUPERVISOR: *(addressing observer)* Oh, you see, he can't speak English.

APPLICANT: If I can't speak English, what am I speaking to you now?

This exchange between an Asian job applicant and a white supervisor was recorded in a textile mill (Etherton, 1975, cited in Jupp *et al.*, 1982). The applicant had been speaking in fluent English for some time before this interaction, which occurred as the supervisor began to fill in the relevant record form. Jupp *et al.* argue that the supervisor's image of Asian workers and his previous experience simply led him to fail to register the evidence of his own ears.

The UK is a multi-ethnic and multilingual society. Problems in inter-ethnic interactions, however, are more subtle than lack of knowledge of each other's languages. Gumperz (1982) and his colleagues argue that learning a language is not just about acquiring a vocabulary and learning the grammatical rules; it involves being *socialized* into the speaking practices of a culture and into the way social interaction is typically organized. Shifting from one culture to another, even from Scotland to England or from America to the UK, reveals how much of our behaviour and our notion of what is normal is learnt during childhood.

Gumperz has demonstrated many contrasts in what is taken for granted about interaction among different ethnic groups. We shall look at just three examples. The first concerns intonation patterns:

> In a staff cafeteria at a major British airport, newly hired Indian and Pakistani women were perceived as surly and uncooperative by their supervisor as well as by the cargo handlers whom they served. Observation revealed that while relatively few words were exchanged, the intonation and the manner in which these words were pronounced were interpreted negatively. For example, when a cargo handler who had chosen meat was asked whether he wanted gravy, a British assistant would say 'Gravy?' using rising intonation. The Indian assistants, on the other hand, would say the word using falling intonation: 'Gravy'. We taped relevant sequences, including interchanges like these, and asked employees to paraphrase what was meant in each case. At first the Indian workers saw no difference. However, the English teacher and the cafeteria supervisor could point out that 'Gravy', said with a falling intonation, is likely to be interpreted as 'This is the gravy,' i.e. not interpreted as an offer but rather as a statement, which in the context seems redundant and consequently rude. When the Indian women heard this, they began to understand the reactions they had been getting all along which had until then seemed incomprehensible. They then spontaneously recalled intonation patterns which had seemed strange to them when spoken by native English speakers. At the same time, supervisors learnt that the Indian women's falling intonation was their normal way of asking questions in that situation, and that no rudeness or indifference was intended.
>
> (Gumperz, 1982, p.173)

Because these aspects of interactions are taken for granted, strangeness is often interpreted, not as a communicational problem, but as due to the problematic personality of the other, or is understood in terms of racist stereotypes. Some interactional conventions are very specific to certain social situations and this can disadvantage not only ethnic minorities but also certain social classes. For instance, consider the standard procedures in job interviews, taken for granted by middle-class, usually white, British people, and demonstrated in the following typical utterance: 'One last question, Mr Sandhu, why are you applying for this particular type of job in a college — a librarian's job in a college?' (Jupp et al., 1982, p.252).

Interviewers ask such questions to give candidates an opportunity to talk about the special qualities and interests which make them eminently suited to a job — a chance to sell themselves. In this particular case, the interviewer indicated this by stressing the word 'college'. However, not being familiar with this code, the applicant quite reasonably interpreted the question to mean, 'Explain why you are looking for work?' He therefore went on to describe how long he had been out of work, his financially desperate straits, and the number of job applications he had sent out. It is likely that the interviewer would perceive this applicant unfavourably, not seeing such a response as a legitimate or competent answer to the question.

The impressions we gain of others are usually a mixture of non-verbal and verbal elements. Misperception can build quickly from the slightest social contact, and a vicious circle can develop. As a third example of inter-ethnic miscommunication, look at the two following extracts from a review by Jupp *et al.* of a study conducted by Gubbay. In the first extract, Mrs J, a white, middle-

aged supervisor in the packing department of a large food-processing company, is giving her impression of Mrs K, an Asian worker under her supervision. The second extract is Mrs K's description of Mrs J:

> Well Mrs K you see, she came on the afternoon shift. I've never interviewed her, whatsoever, so I knew nothing about her, I'm just told on Friday afternoon, 'You'll have Mrs K Monday morning, she's on the afternoon shift. She's alright.' Oh well of course I done a few days with Mrs K I thought to myself 'Ooh I don't know, I think they told me a fast one here,' you know. I used to go up and tell her things, she used to laugh at me ... never look at me, if I was to say something, she'd laugh, head down and laugh. So 'Oh dear, she couldn't care less, couldn't care less about me,' you know. And this went on for a long while. 'I mustn't get wild, I mustn't get wild, I must play it cool, I've got to play it cool.' I thought, 'Oh dear, they've really pulled the wool over my eyes, they've put her on my shift, you know, but she's like this.'

> We never mix up English ladies and Asian ladies. We didn't bother to each other ... we are going in the factory, we are working, we're getting our money and come back. Our supervisor, she don't want to talk to us. She prefer English lady to us — we thought she don't like us ... we are not like friend with her. We respect her like in our country we respect our boss and have to listen to them ... if they talk to us we are happy, if they don't bother we don't bother ... if we want anything from Mrs J we didn't say, because we are frightened that if we say she will refuse... we thought Mrs J, she upset very quick — we feel it — we never look on her face.

> (Jupp *et al.*, 1982, pp.240–1)

The sort of misperception demonstrated in the above examples stresses the importance of the cultural dimension. It supports the point made earlier that the study of biology can only tell us about the very broad possibilities for interaction and very little about the meaning and significance of any particular interaction.

The above examples also suggest that the *global* social context is relevant to the study of interactions in the *local* UK scene. The multi-ethnic nature of the UK is the result of patterns of colonization and migrant labour. It is within this global framework that the inter-ethnic interactions examined above take place. For a complete picture, these interactions need to be placed in their broader social context. For instance, it is necessary to look at the patterns of socio-economic disadvantage, described in Unit 8, which determine the respective roles in the workforce of white and British Asian people, the differential power relations between white and black workers, and thus the bases on which these interactions are constructed.

In thinking about this broader social context we are thus also returning to the relationship discussed in Section 1.2 between the macro-social world of economics, politics, social structures and divisions and the micro-social world of identity and interaction. So, what does the macro-social context contribute?

2.3 THE MACRO-SOCIAL CONTEXT

The UK is an industrial, perhaps even a post-industrial, democratic state with a capitalist economic system. Your reading of the previous blocks of this course has given you a detailed picture of the nature of our type of society. You have seen how the division of labour and class relations are changing and noted different political systems which clarify our UK model. This macro-social context provides the backcloth for everyday life, but what distinctive flavour does it give to daily interaction?

Giddens (1989) contrasts western industrial societies and the traditional society of the !Kung people of the Kalahari desert. He notes how the !Kung lived intimately in small groups of thirty to forty people, within which all activities of food foraging and ceremonial rituals were shared. Division of labour was minimal and confined to the different food-gathering roles of women and men. The !Kung were bound together by a common way of life, and a single value system. As a result, all interaction was with familiar others. For example, until recently the !Kung did not have a word for 'stranger'. Privacy was limited, with families living in open dwellings, and most activities were open to public view.

The UK, in comparison, can be described as differentiated, bureaucratic, technological, urbanized and rationalized. One interaction pattern which starkly demonstrates our difference from the !Kung is the relations we have with 'familiar strangers'. How can a stranger be familiar? Studies of commuters in large cities show that many recognize others on the railway platforms or on the buses: people they see repeatedly, but never speak to or acknowledge (Milgram, 1971). Similarly, the shop assistants in your supermarket might be familiar strangers to you. These 'diluted forms' of interaction are characteristic of our type of social environment.

The programming and timed organization of modern lives and work relationships are equally characteristic (Berger *et al.*, 1974). As a result of the industrial revolution, the *private* has been separated from the *public* world of work for us in a way which has not occurred for the !Kung. This public–private division has had substantial consequences for interaction and everyday life: for relations between women and men; for the organization of domestic and leisure activity; for urban and rural living; and for styles of architecture and house design which affect the types of relationships we can have with others.

The UK is a technological society and technology too has had a considerable effect on relations with others and the way everyday life is organized in the workplace. Typically, in technological modes of production, we become part of a

Familiar strangers?

hierarchy of people with different levels of expertise. Unlike the !Kung we experience others not just as concrete, unique individuals but as functionaries who serve particular roles in a bureaucracy, for example, and who could be replaced with other people who would serve the same functions in the hierarchy.

Modern societies rely on reproducible and mechanistic work patterns. Factory workers may experience their work as one component in a sequence of production, often knowing just their component and being quite unfamiliar with the sequence as a whole or how their actions contribute to that sequence. For the !Kung, social life is seamless, with all sharing the same value system. By comparison, our society is full of disjunctures as we move from one community or social situation with its particular roles and values to another with a radically different orientation.

Modern, particularly urban, life is often criticized as unnatural. But, as Block V has demonstrated, perhaps being unnatural (that is, socially rather than biologically driven) is the most natural thing about human beings! Unlike most animal species we are quintessentially social creatures and thus have the capacity to move beyond and redefine our particular 'state of nature'. All the same, it is important to compare and evaluate different forms of social life from the standpoint of human happiness and well-being, and those in the social reformist tradition have been particularly concerned with the technological and bureaucratic effects of modern life.

It is clear that both biological and macro-social analyses of the economic, political and structural organization of society are crucial to the study of social interaction. In their different ways they indicate some broad constraints guiding the who, where, what, why, and how of interaction. Biology informs about some of the origins of non-verbal expressions, emotional reactions and some general tendencies which might constrain interaction. The macro-social describes how the modern environment sets the scene for interaction and demonstrates how the forms of everyday life have altered in response to social changes.

Despite major differences in the constraints which they emphasize, biological and macro-social perspectives have things in common. Both perspectives tend to minimize the role of human agents and individual choice. Agency implies the capacity to control, initiate, and flexibly adjust one's actions. Biological and macro-social analyses emphasize the automatic and inevitable nature of certain patterns which are beyond the control of particular human agents. You don't choose your biology or the structure of your society.

Similarly, both approaches downplay the importance of the micro. The micro-social world of everyday life, the world of identity and interaction, is *reduced* to something else: to a biological substrate, or to history and social structure. But what do I mean when I say that something has been reduced?

Think back to the studies conducted by Garfinkel's students, described in Section 1.4. These revealed a form of order, constructed by human agents responding to their knowledge of how they should act. Interactions and conversations seem to be guided by people's expectancies and shared understandings. These expectancies are shaped by biological imperatives, such as 'Avoid pain', and by macro-social constraints: 'Clock into work at nine and go home at five', or 'Cope with an environment which presents you continually with strangers'. But biology and the macro-social don't help us discover the details of our 'working consensus' and the way it is applied from moment to moment.

In saying, therefore, that the study of interaction cannot be reduced to or collapsed into the study of biology or social structure and history, I'm saying that there seems to be more involved in human relationships than biological tendencies and macro-social organization — that these provide only a limited or one-dimensional analysis.

The next two sections look at research which takes micro-social reality as its central focus and develops a more complex view of the connection between the individual and the social. This research takes the social perspective a bit further and tries to identify what other social factors, apart from broad macro-social processes, might be involved and what else might be influential.

SUMMARY: BIOLOGY AND THE MACRO-SOCIAL

- Interaction seems to be biologically pre-programmed only in very general ways, leaving considerable room for contrasting meanings and significances to be attached to expressions and movements.

- Local cultural influences on interaction are subtle and far-reaching. Failures in communication are often wrongly attributed to the participants, thus neglecting cultural expectations about interaction.

- The macro-social context has a decisive effect on the actual patterns of daily life and the scope for interaction but, like biological research, it is uninformative about the mechanics of any particular interaction.

3 THE MICRO-SOCIAL APPROACH: PART ONE

3.1 TAKING MICRO-REALITY SERIOUSLY

The research described in this section and in Section 4 assumes that social interaction should be treated as an intellectual domain in its own right, just like the domains of political science, economics or biology. Interaction is thought to have its own specific forms of order and its own brand of social practices which require unique theories and concepts. One of the leading researchers in this area, Erving Goffman, sums up his interest in the *particular* character of interaction in a typically engaging manner:

> I make no claim whatsoever to be talking about the core matters of sociology — social organization and social structure ... I am not addressing the structure of social life but the structure of experience individuals have at any moment of their social lives. I personally hold society to be first in every way and any individual's current involvements to be second; this report deals only with matters that are second ... The analysis developed does not catch at the differences between the advantaged and disadvantaged classes ... I can only suggest that he who would combat false consciousness and awaken people to their true interests has much to do, because the sleep is very deep. And I do not intend here to provide a lullaby but merely to sneak in and watch the way people snore.
>
> (Goffman, 1974, pp.13–14)

As you'll discover shortly, in this approach individuals are viewed as both *constructing* social interaction (relationships and conversations) and as dependent on pre-existing social resources. In the very act of breaking silence and uttering words to others we become active agents bringing an interaction into existence, but in order to break the silence we must rely on social forms that were there before us, such as language, manners, and gestures, which we merely borrow for the occasion (Fontana, 1980, p.62).

Social interaction makes the *private* (thoughts, motives, intentions) *public*. But researchers such as Goffman see the private inner world of the individual as partly made up of stocks of public knowledge about how to act in different situations. An important part of an analysis of interaction from a social perspective is the description of these private/public stocks of knowledge, which are seen as the resources people bring to social situations.

The properties of the micro-world make this task difficult. Social interaction is open-ended; speakers can change course in mid-conversation and can flexibly vary their actions. Social interaction is predictable but also unpredictable. As we have seen, when society changes over the long term so do patterns of interaction. There is therefore a danger that any research findings may have limited validity and may only apply to a particular historical moment.

Despite these limitations, a considerable amount of work has been conducted on social interaction. This unit can only pick out a small part of this work and will concentrate on the approach taken by two prominent researchers whose names you have already encountered: Harold Garfinkel and his colleagues (in Section 3), and Erving Goffman (in Section 4).

3.2   THE ART OF CONVERSATION

Conversation is one of the most basic building blocks of social interaction. If conversation is an art, it is one we take for granted. It is a good place, therefore, to begin our description of some of the detail of the micro-social world. We shall look at a branch of study called *conversation analysis* inspired by Harold Garfinkel. Garfinkel's general perspective is called 'ethnomethodology': literally, the study ('ology') of people's ('ethno') procedures for making sense of social life ('method').

Garfinkel and his co-workers in conversation analysis (Harvey Sacks, Emanuel Schegloff, and Gail Jefferson in the USA and Max Atkinson, Paul Drew, and John Heritage in the UK) were fascinated by the minutiae of how people build social interactions and how they slot the pieces together in all the various combinations possible. To understand their work and its practical implications which will be discussed later we need to follow conversation analysts into their detailed study. The point, however, is to give you a general impression of this investigative strategy and its broad findings, *not* that you should remember and reproduce in your writing all the technical terms and specifics.

Although a great deal is known about the rules of syntax or grammar and phonology which make speaking possible, work is just beginning on actual speech performance. This work has received a powerful impetus from attempts to build computers or 'intelligent knowledge-based systems' which can act and react in relation to their human users. If a computer is to talk to us intelligibly, it not only needs to know its grammar but also something about the routines humans go through in setting up and developing a conversation.

The first stage in a conversation-analytic study is to gather together a large collection of naturally occurring conversations from many different sites. In fact, conversation analysts' methods resemble coincidentally the activities attributed to one well-known British playwright who is said to be equally fascinated by conversation and who is inclined to walk around with a tape-recorder, recording snippets of conversation on buses, in pubs, etc., building up a huge tape library of the flotsam and jetsam of human interaction. In their collection of specimens, conversation analysts perhaps more closely resemble botanists, and like good naturalists they attempt to find as many variations of interactional events as possible to allow systematic comparison and the establishment of a pattern (Heritage, 1988). Every tape-recording is painstakingly transcribed into a written record with every detail of the intonations, emphases, pauses, and overlaps between speakers reproduced. (The written records, as you will see from the examples on the following pages, include unfamiliar symbols which signal the various linguistic features. You will find a guide to these symbols in an appendix at the end of this unit, to which you can refer when you are reading the extracts.)

Working from an increasingly large corpus collected over the years, conversation analysts have identified many different regularities, examining, for instance, the patterning of turn-taking in conversations, methods for closing down conversations, topic changing, methods for the repair of conversations which go wrong, or the structuring of accounts and explanations. I will consider one regularity in detail here — *adjacency pairs* and the *preference structure*.

Adjacency pairs are a particular structural feature of talk. Typical examples of adjacency pairs are questions and answers, greetings and return greetings, offers and acceptances, assessments and second assessments. For instance:

(1)   A: Uh you been down here before // havenche?
      B: Yeah.

(Sacks et al., 1974)

(2)   J: T's — it's a beautiful day out isn't it?
      L: Yeah it's jus' gorgeous …

(Pomerantz, 1984)

(3)   L: You're not bored (huh)?
      S: Bored? No. We're fascinated.

(Pomerantz, 1984)

(*Note*: The examples of adjacency pairs in Section 3.2 have been numbered in sequence for ease of reference.)

These pairs have a first part produced by one speaker and a second part produced by another. Adjacency pairs are 'typed'. This term doesn't refer to the way they look on the page but means that a particular first — a question, say — requires a second from a restricted range of utterances — most likely an answer (Schegloff and Sacks, 1973). In other words, you could say that there are types of paired utterances.

This is not earthshattering news, of course. Adjacency pairs are exactly the sort of truism which sometimes gives social scientists a bad name. Remember how I pointed out in Section 1.5 that social scientists sometimes need to tell you the obvious? But, taken further, these pairs give insight into some rather more complex features of conversation.

The first thing to note is that the notion of adjacency should not be interpreted strictly. The second part of the pair is not always exactly adjacent to the first. For instance, insertion sequences are commonly found. Thus, in the next extract, certain things have to be sorted out before the question is answered:

(4)   K: What's on next?
      J: On this channel or Four?
      K: Four.
      J: Ah, it's that thing on the Sandinistas.

(Potter and Wetherell, 1987)

Before J answers K's question she checks on its specific meaning; a second question/answer adjacency pair is inserted into the first. Sequences of this kind obviously have the potential to get quite complicated, when a number of different things have to be attended to before the second part is offered.

So adjacency doesn't mean the second part will immediately follow the first; instead, conversation analysts suggest the relation is one of 'conditional relevance' (Schegloff, 1968); that is, given that the first part of an adjacency pair has been uttered, the second part is immediately relevant and expected — although its actual production may depend on sorting out a variety of other things. The first and second parts are not bound together by a strict rule; the uttering of the first sets up 'normative expectations' to which speakers must attend. A normative expectation operates like the shared expectancies revealed by Garfinkel's studies with his students, described in Section 1.4; people are aware at some level of what is the appropriate way to behave and they use this knowledge as a kind of social resource for understanding the significance of other people's actions, without always strictly conforming in a mechanical or automatic way.

How do we know there is a normative expectation or a conditional relevance? Look at the following extract:

(5) A: Is there something bothering you or not?
         (1.0 second pause)
     A: Yes or no?
         (1.5 second pause)
     A: Eh?
     B: No

(Atkinson and Drew, 1979)

The conditional relevance relation means that if you ask a question it is normative (usual behaviour) for the other person to answer. Not answering *inevitably* becomes a socially significant act because of this conditional relevance. In effect, it becomes a form of communication. In this extract, A asks a question and a long pause follows (1.0 second: a second is a very long time in conversation). Because the question is not answered, it is repeated until an answer is forthcoming. A is orientating to B's failure to offer the second part.

Conversation analysts have tried to systematize further this principle of the conditional relevance of adjacency pairs and the notion of normative expectations. They have noted that there is a 'preference structure' operating in conversations. For the first part of every adjacency pair there is a 'preferred' second part and what they call, using a rather awkward term, a set of 'dispreferred' responses (see Table 1).

Table 1   Preference formats

Action	Preferred format response	Dispreferred format response
Request	Acceptance	Refusal
Offer/invitation	Acceptance	Refusal
Assessment	Agreement	Disagreement
Self-deprecation	Disagreement	Agreement
Accusation/blaming	Denial	Admission
Question	Answer	Failure to answer

Source: Adapted from Heritage, 1984, p.269

Thus, for a request, the preferred second part is an acceptance and the dispreferred second is refusal. When an accusation is made the preferred second part is a denial and the dispreferred second is an admission. But what do conversation analysts mean by preferred and dispreferred? Do they mean that a denial is the response the accuser prefers to hear, or that an acceptance is the second part a speaker making a request prefers to hear?

This is not what they mean. Preferred and dispreferred are not descriptions of speakers' wishes or hopes; a speaker might actually prefer to reject a particular invitation rather than accept it. They are preferred and dispreferred in terms of general normative or social expectations. Turning down invitations is always the more socially awkward option; it is the dispreferred second normatively speaking. Instead of preferred and dispreferred then, we could say that an acceptance is the normatively usual second part, and refusal the normatively unusual second part.

But how do conversation analysts establish that some second parts are more socially expected or preferred than others? Look at the following set of extracts. In each case the first part of an adjacency pair (an assessment: Extract 6; a self-deprecation: Extract 7; a request: Extract 8) is followed by the preferred second part (agreement: Extract 6; disagreement: Extract 7; acceptance: Extract 8).

(6)   A: (It) was too depre//ssing
      B: O::::h it is te::rribble

(Pomerantz, 1978)

(7)   L: ... I'm so dumb I don't even know it. hhh!
              heh
      W: Y-no, *y-you're not du:mb* ...

(Pomerantz, 1984)

(8)   Child: Could you .hh could you put on the light for my .hh room
        Father: Yep

(Levinson, 1983)

Now look at the next set of extracts where the first part of the adjacency pair (a request: Extract 9; an invitation: Extract 10; a question: Extract 11) is followed by a dispreferred second (a refusal: Extracts 9 and 10; and a failure to give information: Extract 11).

(9)   C: Um I wondered if there's any chance of seeing you tomorrow
              sometime (0.5) morning or before the seminar
              (1.0)
      R: Ah um (.) I doubt it
      C: Uhm huh
      R: The reason is I'm seeing Elizabeth.

(Levinson, 1983)

(10) Mark: We w're wondering if you wanted to come over Saturday, f'r
              dinner
              (0.4)
      Jane: Well (.) .hh it'd be great but we promised Carol already

(Potter and Wetherell, 1987)

(11) Dave: What's in Justice for=All
              (0.3)
      Paul: Its (.) ah (.) its about
              (1.0)
              Well you've got na:h I'm not going to tell you
              (1.0)
              'cos you wo:n't belie:ve the reason I like the film.

(Potter and Wetherell, 1987)

When first parts are followed by preferred second parts, the response is produced with the minimum of delay. Often the second part comes with a slight overlap, with the second speaker anticipating and slightly speaking over the first speaker. This is indicated by // in the transcript and you can see it in Extracts 1 and 6. Preferred responses also tend to be brief, with no hedging or qualification. Dispreferred second parts, in contrast, come with delays (of 1.0, 0.4, and 0.3 of a second in the extracts above), and with *accounts*; that is, with justifications and explanations.

──────────────── ACTIVITY 3 ────────────────

Bearing in mind that you don't need to remember all the details, you might still like to try this question to make sure you have followed the general drift of the argument. On the basis of the analysis given above, predict what kind of response might be given when: (i) an assessment is followed by a disagreement, (ii) an accusation by a denial, and (iii) a request by an agreement?

(Answers at the end of the unit.)

───

These patterns of adjacency pairs, conditional relevance and preferred and dispreferred responses are extremely regular. I have gone into them in detail not just to indicate some research methods used in studying interaction but so that you can see for yourself that, although conversation may often seem haphazard and chaotic, this appearance is deceptive. Conversations are organized around a limited number of principles and these principles can be seen as some of the procedures, tools or methods we carry around and use when, like construction workers, we assemble or build a piece of social interaction.

How universal or culturally specific are the principles which organize conversations? This is still an open question. Systematic research on cultural differences in turn-taking or adjacency pairs is still in its infancy. Work in Germany, the UK and in America finds the same sorts of patterns which suggests that the same principles apply in these quite similar cultures. You probably noticed that some of the examples above were from American English speakers and some from UK English speakers. The patterns also seem to hold across different social classes within western societies.

However, although the basic organization of conversation could possibly be the same all over the world, it is clear that the content, style and interpretation of turns *within* conversations differ across cultures. Remember the earlier examples of inter-cultural miscommunication in the UK, discussed in Section 2.2? Here people were taking conversational turns in the usual way but the interpretation of what each person meant differed. In the case of the job interview, for example, Mr Sandhu answered the question he was asked (he provided the preferred second part for the first part), but interviewer and interviewee had different interpretations of what the question was.

If it was found that the organization of conversations, unlike the interpretation of content and style, was universal across cultures, would this mean that adjacency pairs, for instance, are biologically programmed into us? Earlier, in Section 2.1, I argued that if something was shared across cultures then there was probably some biological basis, but that this rule was not infallible. Cultural universality need not mean biological inheritance. In the case of adjacency pairs, the reasons for universality could be practical or pragmatic rather than genetic. To have any kind of social interaction, to get any kind of society off the ground, there has to be an expectation that conversation will be organized in turns and that some conversational initiatives normatively require certain types of responses. Time will tell whether these are in fact universal patterns, and will also show the relative importance of biology and practical considerations.

You follow conversational principles every day, but could you lay them out clearly enough to enable you to teach them to a computer? Conversation analysts argue that since much of this everyday knowledge is tacit and unconsciously applied, it is vital to study conversational patterns systematically and to develop a set of concepts which capture regularities, such as conditional relevance and adjacency pairs. However, this claim that it is worth studying conversation in great detail seems rather abstract. What do you think? Does this type of research seem a valuable outlet for social scientists' energies? Before you reach a conclusion, read Section 3.3 which looks at some more immediate applications of conversation analysis.

3.3   CONVERSATION, POWER, CHARISMA AND RHETORIC

The study of conversation may not only help us communicate with computers but may also provide a means of sorting out how dominance is organized in interaction. Unit 15 looked at power and social relations in UK politics, but how is the power to get something done and to set the agenda manifested in day-to-day relationships between members of society? Conversation analysis may help to explain the effectiveness of different politicians. Charisma and the power to persuade and influence seem mysterious and enigmatic, but in part, it seems, they are to do with how one organizes one's rhetoric.

Researchers into gender issues have for the last twenty or so years been interested in differences between the speech styles of women and men with regard to the display of dominance. Many differences have emerged: from the fact that men tend on average to take longer turns than women, despite the stereotype of women as the gossips and chatterers, to differences in the use of certain adjectives, adverbs, pronunciation forms, and intonation patterns (Smith, 1985). Like the differences between ethnic groups noted earlier, these patterns have been attributed to socialization and to the different occupational worlds that women and men inhabit.

───────── ACTIVITY 4 ─────────

What does the phrase 'on average' in the paragraph above mean to you? Does it mean that every man will display this pattern all the time? That most men show it some of the time? That 51 per cent of men will display it all the time?

(Answer at the end of this unit.)

───────────────────────────

One very interesting common finding is that men and women tend to assume different conversational rights (Thorne *et al.*, 1983). Not only do men tend to talk for much longer, taking up a great deal more of the conversational space, they also, on average, interrupt women to a much greater extent than women interrupt men. Take a look at the following sequence from a classic study by two conversation analysts:

Woman	How's your paper coming?=
Man:	Alright I guess (.) I haven't done much in the past two weeks
	(1.8)
Woman:	Yeah:::know how that [can
Man:	Hey] ya' got an
	extra cigarette?
	(.)

Woman: Oh uh sure (hands him the pack)
          like **my** [pa —
Man: How] 'bout a match?
          (1.2)
Woman: Ere ya go uh like **my** [pa —
Man: Thanks]
          (1.8)
Woman: Sure (.) I was gonna tell you [my —
Man: Hey] I'd really like
          ta' talk but I gotta run (.) see ya
          (3.2)
Woman: Yeah
(West and Zimmerman, 1977)

Zimmerman and West surreptitiously recorded a large number of conversations between women and men on a university campus. They left their tape-recorder running in coffee bars, outdoor seating areas and so on, always asking people afterwards for permission to include the conversation in their analysis. They recorded twenty conversations between members of the same sex and eleven conversations between women and men. In the same-sex conversations they found seven instances of interruptions and twenty-two overlaps in speaking, while in the mixed-sex conversations there were forty-eight interruptions and eleven overlaps. In those conversations men were responsible for forty-six of those forty-eight interruptions and for all the overlaps. The extract above is a typical example from their data.

Feminist researchers working in this field argue that conversation, talking, and the opportunity to express one's views and be listened to are resources like money and economic goods (Spender, 1980; Thorne *et al.*, 1983). Men have a monopoly on this resource in the same way that they monopolize other resources. These researchers note that the conversational patterns of women and men talking together strongly resemble those occurring naturally between high status and low status workers in organizations, and between parents and children. Features of men's conversational styles indicate the greater status and power they are accorded, as a result of the gender division of labour described in Units 8 and 10.

Are men and women aware of these different conversational patterns? Are they consciously behaving in this way? Not necessarily. As the work on adjacency pairs suggests, certain conversational procedures are so habitual, so normatively usual, that they are, for all intents and purposes, unconscious. In this sense the conversation analyst can make something that is often invisible visible.

The second example of conversation and power which we shall consider concerns politicians and their audiences. The interaction pattern here is somewhat different because one party in this interaction, the audience listening to a politician's speech, is more silent than usual.

What makes a politician effective and charismatic? Traditionally, psychologists have looked to the personality of important figures, such as Martin Luther King, J.F. Kennedy, Lenin, or Adolf Hitler, to explain their impact. Ideology is even more crucial in winning hearts and minds. But is political influence also due to interactional style? Is charisma just a set of rhetorical skills which could be taught to potentially anybody? Recent conversation analytic work

(Atkinson, 1984; Heritage and Greatbatch, 1986) has demonstrated that speaking style plays a vital role in attributions of charisma.

Atkinson argues that the effectiveness of political oratory arises from skills used in everyday conversation. He studied audience reactions to different speakers (their applause, boos and heckles), using video-recordings of political party conferences to identify successful techniques.

In ordinary conversation people are very good at predicting in advance when the person speaking is about to stop, so they can start their own turn without delay. The change-over of speakers is incredibly smooth and fast, with often only micro-second delays between speakers. In ordinary conversation, of course, there are a variety of cues we can use to make these predictions. What about political speeches? These could be seen as long conversational turns; the audience has the same problem of predicting when to respond, in this case by clapping. If the audience fails to predict effectively then there will be a delay between the speaker's point and the applause, making the latter seem half-hearted or reluctant. When Atkinson timed the delay he found that the applause was typically instantaneous or even in slight overlap with the speaker's words.

Applause in political gatherings usually occurs at the end of a speech and after the speaker has attacked or criticized other parties and boasted about the achievements of his or her own party, but what kind of cues do audiences orientate to and what makes something worth applauding? Not all boastings, attacks, etc. are rewarded with applause. Atkinson argued that there are two particularly effective rhetorical strategies — *three-part lists* and *contrast structures*. Here are two examples of three-part lists, one from the former Conservative Prime Minister, Margaret Thatcher, and the other from the Labour MP, Eric Heffer:

Thatcher:		This week has demonstrated (0.4) that we are a <u>party</u> <u>uni</u>ted in
	(1)	<u>pur</u>pose (0.4)
	(2)	strategy (0.2)
	(3)	and re <u>solve</u>.
Audience:		Hear hear ---------(8.0)-------------------
Audience:		x-xxXXXXXXXXXXXXXXXXXXXXXXXXXXXXXxxx-x

(Atkinson, 1984)

Heffer:		The National Executive decided (0.8) that we <u>agreed</u> in <u>PRINCIPLE</u> (0.8) that we <u>MUST AGAIN TRY</u> AND <u>GET</u> SOME <u>CONSTITUTIONAL AMENDMENTS</u> (0.5)
	(1)	BE <u>FORE</u> YOU (0.2)
	(2)	<u>AT</u> CONFERENCE (0.2)
	(3)	THIS <u>WEEK</u> SO THAT YOU CAN <u>STILL</u> MAKE
Audience:		xxxXXXXXXXXXXXXXXXXXXXXXX
Heffer:		YOUR <u>MINDS</u> UP
Audience:		XXXXXXXXXXXXXXXXXX

(Atkinson, 1984)

The three-part lists in these extracts are indicated by the numbers (1), (2) and (3), and you can see how the combination of speech stress and emphasis (indicated by the underlining and capitalization), and the pauses (given in brackets) makes the sequence audible as a list and allows the audience to predict a completion point at which they can applaud. Rising intonation in the first part of the list with falling intonation in the third part and standard hand gestures, which are not reproduced here, particularly help the audience project an end at which clapping would be appropriate.

The next extract from a speech by David Steel, the former leader of the Liberal Party, displays a contrast structure:

Steel: THE TRUTH IS BEGINNING TO DAWN ON OUR
                PEOPLE THAT THERE ARE TWO CONSERVATIVE
                PARTIES IN THIS ELECTION
     (A)   (0.6)
            ONE IS OFFERING THE CONTINUATION OF THE
            POLICIES WE'VE HAD FOR THE LAST FIVE YEARS
     (B)   (0.2)
            AND THE OTHER IS OFFERING A RETURN TO THE
            POLICIES OF FORTY YEARS AGO

Audience: Heh heh heh
Audience: xXXXXXXXXXXXXXXXXXXX

(Atkinson, 1984, p.74)

The two parts of the contrast are marked (A) and (B). Again the stress patterns and the pauses indicate to the audience when a completion point will be reached and thus when to clap. In this case a rising intonation around 'five years' indicates to the audience that there is more to come, the 'and' which follows indicates this is the last part, while a falling intonation around 'forty years' suggests completion. Atkinson notes that the second part of a contrast generally mirrors the first part in grammatical structure, phrasing and idiom.

Norman Tebbit, former Conservative Party Chairman

Successful orators often combine three-part lists and contrast structures. Here, for example, is former Conservative Party Chairman Norman Tebbit:

Tebbit:	And I have a duty (.) a duty that falls upon all responsible politicians
	(.)
	to lead others to f:<u>fi</u>- to <u>face</u> reality.
	(0.4)
(1)	Not a duty to feed the people a diet of compromising <u>pap</u>
	(0.2)
(2)	<u>pie</u> in the sky:
(3)	and <u>false</u> <u>hopes</u>.
Audience:	Applause (10.7 seconds)

(Heritage and Greatbatch, 1986, pp.129–30)

In this case the three-part list comes as the second part of the contrast structure. Again, pauses and intonation prepare the audience for a suitable completion point at which they can clap. Skilful management of this 'conversational' routine with the audience (and we have only looked at two possible rhetorical devices) is crucial to the maintenance of a politician's identity as a persuasive and effective speaker who can generate the support of his or her party. Next time you want to get a massive amount of applause, work up some three-part lists and some contrast structures! Indeed, to demonstrate the validity of his analysis, Atkinson did just that. Someone who had never spoken in public before was trained by him in the use of these devices and then gave a delegate's speech at a political party conference. The result?—a standing ovation for the delegate.

SUMMARY: CONVERSATION ANALYSIS

- Ethnomethodology and conversation analysis aim to study the procedures involved in an interaction through painstakingly analysing everyday conversations to identify the rules of production.

- These procedures, which are like 'traffic' rules (Goffman, 1981) regulating the flow of interaction, are so routinized and habitual that we may only perceive them in a fragmentary and semiconscious way.

- Analysis of these procedures can help us understand the way the power structures embedded in social relations are managed on a daily basis in face-to-face relationships.

---

4   THE MICRO-SOCIAL APPROACH: PART TWO

4.1   THE PRESENTATION OF SELF IN EVERYDAY LIFE

Social interaction is not just about holding sensible conversations, it is also about presenting oneself to others, about giving and receiving impressions. The study of power and rhetorical style begins to raise broader questions about the general goals of social interaction and the positioning of ourselves and others, and here the study of interaction begins to meet up again with the concerns of identity. But how do we know what kind of impression is appropriate and how do we manipulate our verbal and non-verbal communications to create different effects?

At this point we can turn to the work of Erving Goffman. Goffman worked at a different level from the ethnomethodologists. Their tactic was the methodical study of particular examples of interaction, but Goffman preferred a more speculative approach. One of his main contributions to the study of interaction was to develop analogies which might cast light on the kind of questions raised above. The aim of an analogy is to gain an understanding of something complex by indicating its resemblance to something easier to grasp. Remember the model of the market as a set of balances and scales from Unit 11? An analogy says: take this messy piece of social life and think of it like this — view it through these spectacles. The analogy allows some order to be imposed on the mess and offers a set of concepts for structuring observations.

The theatre and drama have provided some of the most productive analogies for social interaction. The dramatist talks about roles, plots, scripts, props, on-stage and off-stage, 'cameo' parts, prompts, costumes, rehearsals, and there is the audience, the critic, the director and the producer. All of these could potentially be applied as analogies in the study of social interaction.

The concept of 'role' has proved a particularly useful way of thinking about some of the regularities in the ways we present ourselves to others. Actors on a stage act out a role they have been assigned by a director. An actor can't speak any old lines or perform any old character. The actor playing Macbeth has to act out the part of a Scottish nobleman tormented by the murders he has committed. Those who adopt the theatre analogy suggest there are similar constraints on people in ordinary life.

A complex society like the UK can be analysed as a set of social positions. A social position might be an occupation, such as waitress, doctor, prime minister; a position related to cultural and leisure pursuits, such as opera patron, football referee, lace-maker, pop star; or a position in a kinship network, such as mother, uncle, daughter, etc. These social positions carry with them sets of expectations about behaviour. Mothers, in the eyes of their children if not in their own eyes, should be kind, caring and good at washing dishes; football referees should be firm and fair in applying the rules. The combination of social position and a set of expectations constitutes a *social role*.

As players of such social roles, we are constrained rather like stage actors. Knowledge of our parts guides our conduct and influences our behaviour. We have a limited repertoire of roles and lines to speak which reflect our social positions. A doctor in his or her surgery might decide, for a day, to stop behaving like a doctor and behave like a tourist visiting an interesting museum. Fair enough. But patients expect doctors to have some knowledge and to be ready to display it; conversations in surgeries proceed on the basis of these pre-existing social expectations. Social roles like actors' roles are impersonal; whoever takes on the role will be expected to act in much the same way with only a few little individual touches. The show goes on regardless of who takes part. Some people play their roles well, others have trouble fitting the bill. As on the stage, there is often an extended period of training or rehearsal (socialization) before the performance proper begins.

Now, note that Goffman and others who use this analogy are not necessarily suggesting that social positions and associated roles *determine* our actions. It is more as though people in life off the stage are following some memory of a play they have read and are constantly ad-libbing the dialogue. We could add, therefore, another term from the theatre—'improvisation'. Goffman is arguing that scripts in real life just provide an outline and that the detail needs always to be improvised from situation to situation.

Goffman (1959) has tried to show how people *actively bring* social roles, and thus social forms, to life. He says that inevitably we 'realize' our characters in society and depend on socially-shared roles and rules to make ourselves intelligible and he is interested in the performances involved. Bringing a role to life involves, consciously or unconsciously, intentionally or unintentionally, displaying oneself as a particular kind of person or social actor. Goffman noted that actors have stage-craft and learn acting techniques, and he wanted to try to describe some of the techniques ordinary people might use in their performances on the stage of everyday life. How does the bank manager convince others that he or she is to be trusted and has authority? How does the nurse display an image of competence and compassion? How does the teenager 'act out' adolescent rebellion? Through what non-verbal signs does Kramer in the 'Pimp Roll' extract in Section 1.1 develop his impression of the defendants in the courtroom? People's actions are continually expressive of whom they think they are, or should be, and there are routines for managing this expression.

Appearance, clothes and non-verbal manner are clearly crucial in the presentation of 'personal fronts', as Goffman calls them. A public display presents two kinds of information to the observer: information directly *given* and information *given off*. When we talk to other people, there is the information they supply directly, the content of what they say, and there is the information we deduce from other signs. We generally try to look behind the public into the private. Do they look anxious, do they look like they know what they are talking about? We tend to assume, rightly or wrongly, that signs given off are involuntary and thus more revealing of a person's real character: 'He that has eyes to see and ears to hear may convince himself that no mortal can keep a secret. If his lips are silent, he chatters with his fingertips; betrayal oozes out at every pore' (Freud, 1905).

In psychoanalysis, which you encountered in Unit 19, these unintentional signals become important subject matter. Freud made a particular study, using self-observations and the observations of others, of what he called the 'psychopathology of everyday life', arguing that slips of the tongue, mistakes, forgetting names, and fumbled actions have unconscious origins in desires or conflicts which are repressed:

> Some years ago I was acting in a subordinate position at a certain institution, the front door of which was kept locked, so that it was necessary to ring for admission. On several occasions I found myself making serious attempts to open the door with my house key. Each one of the permanent visiting staff, to which I aspired to be a member, was provided with a key, to avoid the trouble of having to wait at the door. My mistakes thus expressed my desire to be on a similar footing and to be quite 'at home' there.

> At a certain point in the analysis of another woman patient I had to tell her that I suspected her of having been ashamed of her family ... and of having reproached her father with something we did not yet know about. She remembered nothing of the kind and moreover declared that it was unlikely. However, she continued the conversation with some remarks about her family: 'One thing must be granted them: they are certainly unusual people, they all possess Geiz [greed] — I meant to say "Geist [cleverness]".' And this in fact was the reproach which she had repressed from her memory. It is a frequent occurrence for the idea one wants to withhold to be precisely the one which forces its way through in the form of a slip of the tongue.

(Freud, 1966, pp.164 and 64)

4.2 TRACKS, FRAMES AND RITUALS

In later analyses, Goffman went on to develop other analogies for describing the performative aspects of social interaction — moving from theatre to film-making (1974) and pulling out the notion of ritual from purely ceremonial contexts in order to apply it to everyday contexts (1967). He argued we could see interaction as running along *attentional tracks*, like the sound tracks in a movie. One stream of messages is treated as the main-line track, which we pay attention to and which forms the main story line of an encounter. But there is also the disattend track, which includes things like a person's appearance, yawns and scratches, smiles, frowns, and body movements, which are politely unattended. 'Disattend' doesn't mean that we don't notice these things, or that we fail to draw conclusions from them about the kinds of people we are dealing with, what they think about us, whether they are interested in the conversation, and so on. Rather, it means that ordinarily these aspects do not become part of the main story line of the encounter.

In addition, Goffman argued that it is insightful to see everyday life as a series of *frames*. A teacher, for example, might move through several frames in the course of the day, from the frame of family breakfast, to the frame of school assembly, to the frame of active teaching, to the frame of disciplining pupils, to the frame of the staffroom at lunch-time, and so on. We often think of conversation as involving the meeting of minds, as an unstructured give and take. Goffman instead emphasizes how the frame defines the meaning of the bits of talk, the significance given to them, and imposes a likely sequence of events. For instance, the comment 'three spades' means something quite different within the frame of gardening from its meaning within the frame of playing cards (Collins, 1988, p.51). Similarly, complaining about a friend has quite a different significance in casual gossip and in a court-room.

This notion of framing has obvious architectural implications. Frames tend to have 'brackets' around them in the sense that each frame is associated with a distinctive physical space, and as we journey from space to space we move from frame to frame. A well-designed building creates spaces which are appropriate for different frames. Goffman points out that, like actors, we need back-stage and front-stage regions. In a typical house, for example, the living room is more 'on show' than bedrooms and bathrooms. In the back-stage regions, people, like actors, prepare themselves for the outside world, working on the less impressive bits of themselves, putting on a front-stage self: the make-up, the clothes, and so on (Collins, 1988).

Goffman understood these aspects as indicating the *ritual* nature of much of social life. Ceremonial rituals, like the opening of Parliament or a christening service, are carefully 'scripted'. There is a predictable sequence and appropriate words for different moments. In contrast, daily life is much freer. But is it?

ACTIVITY 5

Try describing a day in your life (today or yesterday) in terms of the frames you have moved through, thinking about the physical and social architecture of each one. Are there any ritual sequences? Standard patterns of greeting, gossiping, moaning, celebrating? Do you find that, through the habits of years of interaction, conversations with others fall into predictable sequences — maybe satisfactory, maybe unsatisfactory?

4.3   THE IMPLICATIONS FOR IDENTITY

The two topics of Block V, identities and interaction, cannot easily be separated from each other. As Goffman's work demonstrates, interaction creates identities just as it is clear that the particular identities of the participants in a conversation will affect the shape of that conversation.

Goffman has been criticized for presenting a view of individuals as 'tricky, harassed little devils', always engaged in cynically manipulating the impression they give (Gouldner, cited in Fontana, 1980). But this is unfair to Goffman. His analysis of performances and techniques for self-presentation applies both to occasions when we consciously put on an act, and to normal, natural and unselfconscious action. As Giddens (1988) notes, the moral dimension of interaction and issues of mutual trust and tact are a major preoccupation in Goffman's work. This is particularly evident in his argument about embarrassment and fear of 'loss of face'. Goffman points out how participants in an interaction tend to work jointly to maintain the 'faces' or identities presented to each other. If there is loss of face, or a threat to identity, interaction goes into remedial mode to recover the situation:

> People accommodate to each other's constructions of their social selves. They tend to accept the way they define what they are. The politeness of everyday interaction is largely oriented towards protecting these self-definitions. The ritual code calls for people to avoid threatening topics in conversation, and to avoid questioning claims that people have made about themselves; to show tact in overlooking errors in what one's conversational partner has said. What Goffman calls 'face work' in conversation includes not insulting others ... avoiding lulls or 'embarrassing pauses' which would reveal a lack of interest in the other's line.

> ...Each person defers to the other's demeanour self, and in return receives deference which helps them to uphold their own demeanour. One's personal self is partly based on other's reactions via deference to one's demeanour. Every individual relies on others to complete one's picture of one's self.

> (Collins, 1988, p.49)

Actors on the stage are always conspiring together to some degree. They are collaborating to produce a performance, and if one actor forgets lines or muffs an entrance, others will try cover for this person so that the show can go on. Goffman is making the same point about social interaction: it is a cooperative endeavour where participants try to shore up and sustain each other's performances.

The identity construction aspect of interaction can reach very deep indeed. Goffman (1961) makes the point that in some circumstances the impression of human agency itself rests on interaction. Agency has many facets. On the one hand, we can feel a sense of agency when we formulate a goal and successfully carry out our aim. This need not have anything to do with interaction; our goal could be simply to do with the physical environment: mending a broken car, for example. But some feelings of agency, purpose and control do depend on interaction. Our feelings of agency do depend on the reactions of others.

Goffman argues that we often have to behave in certain ways before people will treat us as rational, self-motivated agents capable of controlling our own destinies. His studies in mental hospitals alerted him to the point that certain kinds of performances lead others to treat patients as though they are indeed passive dopes without agency. He noted how certain of the initiations and interaction rituals, which he called 'mortification rituals', associated with institutions such as the army, prisons and hospitals, have the effect of re-positioning their recipients as non-agents.

The point that the interaction order is also a moral order becomes especially evident when we remember that if social life is a stage, it is one where we negotiate crucial identities of personal effectiveness or ineffectiveness, accomplishment, popularity, autonomy, and our sense of ourselves as reasonable and reputable individuals. This aspect emerges most clearly in work which has tried to apply Goffman's framework, and similar insights, to relationships between doctors and patients, and between the young and the elderly.

For instance, Strong (1988) notes, in his studies of consultations between Scottish NHS doctors and mothers, how the interaction rituals between doctor and patient idealize the participants. Doctor and patient contrive to maintain each other's integrity and moral character, delicately skirting around discrediting information. Thus, every doctor tends to be treated as competent and every mother as good, loving, honest, and intelligent.

Strong gives the following example of a consultation between a doctor and a mother concerning a grossly fat baby who is twice the expected weight. He comments that this mother and the family were notorious among health and social service staff, and that there were grave doubts about the mother's competence as she had ignored all previous advice:

Doctor	And you feed him on Farex?
Mother	In the morning and evening.
Doctor	And porridge?
Mother	Aye.
Doctor	Does he get anything else for elevenses?
Mother	Just biscuits …
Doctor	How much does he get at lunchtime?
Mother	Oh just mince and tatties …
Doctor	And what does he get for his tea?
Mother	Oh a boiled egg or a scrambled egg.
Doctor	And this is as well as milk?
Mother	Aye …
Doctor	If I were you, I'd miss out the Farex and the porridge at breakfast and the biscuit as well. It is best to do this now because if children get fat now then they tend to be fatter later on in life. He's supposed to be twice his birth weight now and he's a good bit more than that, isn't he? This is very important. He's putting on a bit too much weight.

(Strong, 1988, p.241)

The doctor suggests that the mother's conduct is wrong here, but does this carefully, through a neutral series of questions which set the mother up throughout as a good person who simply needs advice about the best way to proceed. The self-presentation of the doctor as a polite and friendly supporter and the mother as a cooperative patient who wishes for the best is preserved during the criticism.

The same ritualistic patterning can be seen in conversations between the elderly and young people, but in this case with pernicious effects on identity. Ageism (or negative stereotypes of the elderly) is clearly evident in our society. One common stereotype, as the extract below from an interview with two young women indicates, is that elderly people are difficult to talk to — that they moan a lot, are absorbed in their own problems, and rave on and on:

> RHW: Well I've got a granny of 85, who is continually saying she's lonely, she's not lonely at all because there is a visitor just about every hour of the day into the house. But she says she's lonely and that nobody comes to visit her. In some respects you have to take it with a little pinch of salt what people say.

> DG: Yes, they play for sympathy, they're very much like, some elderly people, are very much like young children, they want to be the centre of attention for as long as possible.

> (Henwood *et al.*, 1989, p.58; transcription symbols have been omitted)

Recently, some very interesting studies have tried to pin-point precisely the conversational rituals which occur between the elderly and younger people. This research concludes that stereotypical expectations about the elderly lead to both parties constructing an interaction or developing a working consensus which reinforces a negative 'face' for the old person, to the detriment of the elderly person's sense of control, autonomy, and sense of participation in social life.

In a research paper entitled 'My life in your hands', Coupland *et al.* (1988) report a study of twenty interactions between elderly women and young women. Commonly, elderly women spent a large amount of the conversation talking about their troubles (ill-health, bereavement, loneliness, family problems, financial worries). This fits the stereotype. However, close study of the pattern of conversation demonstrated that most of this talk about troubles was initiated by the younger women. They often assumed the right to question their elderly partners — rights which are not commonly assumed when talking to people — which frequently left the elderly women with little option but to disclose perhaps painful information about themselves (Henwood *et al.*, 1989, p.4).

TV 11 takes up the topic of ageing and transitions in life in more detail, but for the moment we can note that this pattern fits into a class of events that social psychologists call *self-fulfilling prophecies*. Often we go into an interaction with a strong expectation or image of the other person (a prophecy). Our definition of the situation may give the other person little choice but to act in the way we expect, and so our prophecy is fulfilled. But it is self-fulfilled; we made it come true. We subtly shape each other's identities and self-presentations and this shaping may have a strong psychological impact. If someone acts continually as though you are incompetent, maybe you become incompetent.

Studies of teachers and pupils suggest that if teachers believe a child is bright, regardless of whether they are specially intelligent or not, the academic performance of the child improves markedly. The child becomes bright as a result of the teacher's expectations. It is for this reason that some teachers and educational psychologists argue that all assessments of children should be confidential and should be treated with care. In studying interaction, therefore, it is crucial to know who holds the power to define the situation and slant the working consensus.

It seems that what is important is how different types of interaction lead to different representations of our identity. And as we saw in Unit 20, the public representation — how others choose to define us — can become the private reality. Think back, for example, to Mead's arguments about the growing child and the way children internalize their parents' images. Goffman's work and the examples above demonstrate that this process doesn't stop with childhood.

4.4 REFLECTIONS

Erving Goffman was one of the first social scientists to study social interaction as a micro-reality in its own right. He was committed to the view that order in social interaction cannot be reduced to the workings of social structure or biology. Goffman's work, however, is still within the social perspective and thus extends the concerns of Unit 20. Individuals bring about interaction but on the basis of their knowledge of social expectations. Furthermore, their very identity and their understanding of themselves as individuals are structured by that social interaction. As we saw, there is a strong affinity between the notion of a self-fulfilling prophecy and Mead's account of the child becoming socialized.

Goffman's work also has a strongly phenomenological flavour, if you think back to the description of that perspective in Unit 19. Goffman sees individuals as capable of reflecting on their experience and self-consciously working over the resources brought to social interaction. Indeed, it is this which makes social interaction open-ended and difficult to study.

Once again, thinking through the unit as a whole, we can see how different perspectives focus on different issues. The biological perspective looks for cultural universals in interaction, the psychoanalytic perspective tries to 'get behind' our words and deeds to find unconscious motives, while the phenomenological perspective focuses on the 'here and now' experience of interaction and stresses human agency. In this unit, the social perspective on identity and interaction has gone in two directions. Macro-social investigations, like the biological perspective, have stressed broad forces beyond human agency, while the micro-social analyses of Goffman and the conversation analysts, in their emphasis on the specific social situation and the individual person, have more in common with the phenomenological perspective. Perhaps you can see other similarities and differences. We shall return to comparison of the perspectives in Unit 22.

SUMMARY: GOFFMAN'S ANALOGIES

- Goffman's investigations of micro-reality depend on developing analogies and models of social interaction. Analogies from the theatre, film-making and the ceremonial have been particularly prominent.

- Goffman argues that the sources of order in interaction are publicly available and socially shared stocks of knowledge about appropriate behaviour which people draw on in making their actions regular, predictable and intelligible to others.

- The individual and the social and the public and the private are intertwined. Individuals both construct and are constructed by social interaction. Interaction can define identity as well as reflect pre-existing identities.

5   CONCLUSION

5.1   PRACTICAL RELEVANCE?

Social science research can be evaluated in a number of ways. Is a theory logically consistent? Does it fit the evidence? Does it make a contribution to social problems? This last criterion is particularly relevant to the study of social interaction. People often experience difficulties in their relationships with others or want to present themselves in more effective and positive ways to improve self-esteem, self-confidence, and to develop a sense of control over their lives. How could the work described in this unit help?

READER

At this point, read Chapter 18 by Judy Gahagan in the Course Reader. The author describes an important aspect of clinical psychology known as social skills training. You will see how the identification of skill elements draws heavily on the work of Goffman and on conversation analysis.

ACTIVITY 6

As a check on your reading and note-taking, you might like to attempt to answer these questions once you've read the piece, and compare notes with other students at your study centre:

- Action therapies differ from insight therapies in that ...
- Action therapies have the advantage that ...
- What values does Gahagan say should guide therapy?
- What assumptions does the notion of interaction as a set of skills make about the components of interaction?
- Give three examples of ways people could be deficient in social skills, and the remedies.
- Finally, what do you think of the argument that people can be trained to present themselves in certain ways — an appealing idea, frightening, sensible, overly calculating, or what?

Gahagan describes the basics of social skills training, but it is clear how the ideas can be applied in many different arenas. There is family therapy, for example — the type of therapy which works with a family as a group. The focus here is often on severe conflicts of interest and pathological patterns developed over many years, but therapists find it useful to look for interaction rituals and disabling self-fulfilling prophecies which might underlie mutual misperception. Similarly, those who work in personnel and public relations apply the ideas of social skills training to improve channels of communication, morale, and the efficiency and productivity of management and workers. Courses on assertiveness training are another area where the general assumptions of self-management and interaction as a skilled performance are applied to change patterns of behaviour.

In schools, social skills training can make a contribution to problems of bullying and to racist attacks in the playground. Bullying is a serious social problem. One estimate suggests that as many as 10 per cent of children in UK schools are at any given moment involved in bullying, either as the victim or the bully (Besag, 1989).

Besag reviews profiles of typical bullies and victims and suggests a number of fronts on which bullying could be tackled. Here, for example, are four descriptions of typical characteristics of victims from four separate studies (Besag, 1989, p.19). Your reading of the Gahagan article will probably immediately suggest to you some ways in which work on social interaction might help:

1 Shy, withdrawn, anxious, passive, non-gregarious, showing little interest in others, poor communication skills.

2 Socially insensitive, obsessive behaviour, ineffectual social skills, poor ability or wish to conform, submissive.

3 Feelings of inferiority, below average self-esteem, rate themselves low in intellectual ability and attractiveness, and describe themselves as detached, critical, moody.

4 Feel unable to cope alone or to elicit support from peer group, feel helpless and ineffective.

Certain characteristics recur in these descriptions, indicating a general weakness in social skills. Work with the victims of bullying has tried not only to change attitudes in the classroom and the physical environment of schools to decrease the opportunities for bullying, but also to improve the communicational skills of victims and short-circuit the aggressive routines of bullies. The development of cooperative work routines within the classroom also seems effective in changing the patterns of relationships between pupils which lead to bullying.

These applications of social interaction research are in keeping with the social reformist tradition. They indicate both the strengths and weaknesses of social reformism: strengths, in that practical solutions are sought to limited practical problems; weaknesses, in that little emphasis is placed on the macro-social context in which problems arise.

For example, take the problem of racist attacks in school playgrounds. Social interaction research suggests ways in which teachers might work with individual pupils and in the classroom to change racist attitudes, thus creating a less prejudicial social atmosphere and alternative patterns of social interaction. That would be a major achievement. But the teacher and the social interaction researcher can do little about the power relations and patterns of inequality and disadvantage which structure relations between ethnic minorities and the white majority in the first place. Some would argue that applications such as social skills training can ameliorate bad situations but can't address the root causes of those situations. In defence, the social reformer might argue that it is better to do something in the short-term, and that critics underestimate the extent to which local social interactions in classrooms and playgrounds determine global macro-relations between ethnic groups.

5.2 A COMPLEX INTERACTION?

The individual and the social and the macro and the micro have recurred throughout this unit. Several positions have been reviewed within the social perspective, from the macro-social which often pays little attention to human agents, to Goffman's emphasis on the intertwining of the individual and the social. Before leaving this topic I'd like to describe in a bit more detail the position which says there is a complex interrelationship between the individual and the social and the micro and the macro. Take a look at Figure 3.

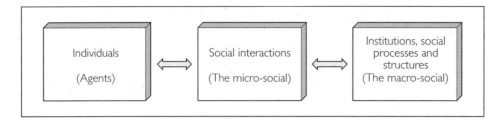

Figure 3   Three levels of analysis: individuals, social interactions and institutions

Individuals, social interaction and the macro-social context have emerged as different levels of analysis, each with its own properties. (Biology provides another level, but one which is not the main focus for the social scientist.) Individuals have the property of agency: of being able, sometimes, to choose to do otherwise and to create relationships and new social forms. Interaction is a micro form of social life with, as we have seen, its own order, norms and rules. The macro-social context has its own properties: structures, institutions, and social processes. These levels are in complex interrelation. The character of each level is changed by its interaction with other levels and yet each has its own decisive impact, as you can see from the two-way direction of the arrows in Figure 3.

I will talk further about the interrelation of levels in a moment, but first an analogy to get you thinking. Forget about Figure 3 temporarily and draw a small square on a piece of paper. Now draw four separate straight lines in a row, ensuring that each of these lines is equal in length to the side of the square. The analogy I am about to develop concerns parts and wholes.

You can see that the square on your page forms a whole. It is an entity in itself, made up of parts — four lines of equal length. What should be clear is that the whole, the square, can't exist without the parts, the four lines, and yet a square is something different from its constitutent parts. Combining the four lines has brought a new thing into being, but that new whole also redefines the nature of the parts. A line which is part of a square is quite different from a line standing by itself. Parts make up wholes, but the wholes define the nature of the parts.

Going back to Figure 3, we can see that agents, social interaction and the macro-social context operate like the lines and the square. Bring agents together and a social interaction is created; develop many many interactions over time and an institution emerges. Combinations of parts create new wholes at each stage; and the characteristics of those parts, such as the characteristics of the individuals in an interaction, are crucial in determining the nature of the whole. Yet social interaction, as we saw with the example of old and young women talking together, also defines the identity of its particular parts, the participating individuals. Finally, as we saw with the contrast between our society and that of the !Kung, the institutions, processes and structures of a society define the character of its parts (that is, the many social interactions which constitute institutions like schools or factories), just as the nature of these interactions defines the atmosphere of the institutions in a society.

The really challenging task for social science is to study the bridges between all these levels of analysis. We have also ignored another important contributor, the physical space and material environment in which interaction occurs. Every interaction has not just a history but a geography. It takes place in a particular geographical area with particular regional characteristics. D103 has said little about this dimension so far, but sometimes it is crucial to know whether an event takes place in the North or the South of the UK, and whether that divide is a real one in terms of local resources and structures or just an imaginary representation of our physical space. Block VI will take up these issues and will thus also extend the study of identity. TV 10 showed how important the sense of place, in this case the sense of belonging to a nation, was for identity. After all, most of us, in describing ourselves, locate our identity not just in terms of social class and occupation but also physically, responding to the character of the place in the UK which we inhabit. First, however, Unit 22 will review Block V and discuss the role of methods in the social sciences.

=== AUDIO CASSETTE ===

Don't forget, before you move on to Unit 22, to listen to Part 3 of Audio Cassette 5 in which the unit authors explain the reasoning behind the choice of topics in Block V and the relationship between Block V and the remainder of D103.

ANSWERS TO ACTIVITIES

ACTIVITY 3

A disagreement for an assessment is dispreferred; there should be a short delay and probably softening of the disagreement with hedging and qualification. In the two other cases the second part is a preferred second and so responses will probably be brief and will occur with the minimum of delay.

ACTIVITY 4

It doesn't mean that every man will display this pattern all the time or that 51 per cent of men will display it all the time. The researchers would have measured the amount of time fifty men, say, took in their turns at talking in a particular context and worked out an average turn length for each man by dividing the total amount of time he spent talking by the number of his turns, thus giving fifty averages or fifty means (one for each man). These averages could then be compared with the averages obtained in the same way for fifty women. Eventually a grand mean or grand average could be calculated by adding all the means together for all the men and dividing by fifty and following the same procedure for the group of women, allowing one grand mean for men to be compared with the grand mean for women. It is worth noting that even if the grand mean for men was considerably larger than the grand mean for women you still couldn't conclude that there was a sex difference in speech style until some statistical test had been performed on all these data to check out the probability that the difference was merely due to chance and what we might expect from random effects. A statistical test allows you to judge if a difference is meaningful or likely to be due to chance. The important point to take from this example is that the term 'on average' in these cases refers to a *tendency* for the two groups to be different and doesn't indicate an absolute difference between the sexes.

APPENDIX: GUIDE TO TRANSCRIPTION SYMBOLS

// Indicates an overlap in speaking and the point in the conversation where the second person begins to speak simultaneously with the first person.

[ ] Square brackets serve the same function, indicating where two speakers are talking simultaneously in overlap.

= An equals sign indicates that words or lines are being run together with no gap between them.

... Indicates that speaking continues but the rest has been omitted from the transcript or extract.

(1.0) Numbers in brackets indicate pauses in conversation and the duration of the pause in tenths of seconds.

(.) A dot in brackets indicates a tiny gap in an utterance or conversation, probably less than one tenth of a second in duration.

:: Colons indicate prolongation of the immediately prior sound. The length of the colon row indicates length of the prolongation.

.hh A row of hh prefixed by a dot indicates an inbreath; without the dot, the h's indicate an outbreath.

heh Records laughter.

MUST Capital letters indicate especially loud sounds relative to the surrounding talk.

party Underlining marks changes in emphasis and intonation and points where stress is placed.

my Words in bold also indicate increased emphasis.

x-xxXXX This sign indicates clapping; the capital letters signal an increase in volume.

BE FORE A space in a word indicates an audible gap in the pronunciation of the word.

(Adapted from Heritage, 1984, and Atkinson, 1984)

REFERENCES

Atkinson, J.M. (1984) *Our Master's Voices: The Language and Body Language of Politics*, London, Methuen.

Atkinson, J.M. and Drew, P. (1979) *Order in Court: The Organization of Verbal Interaction in Judicial Settings*, London, Macmillan.

Berger, P., Berger, B. and Kellner, H. (1974) *The Homeless Mind*, Harmondsworth, Penguin.

Besag, V. (1989) *Bullies and Victims in Schools*, Milton Keynes, Open University Press.

Burnham, J. (1986) *Family Therapy*, London, Tavistock.

Cohen, S. and Taylor, L. (1978) *Escape Attempts: The Theory and Practice of Resistance to Everyday Life*, Harmondsworth, Penguin.

Collins, R. (1988) 'Theoretical continuities in Goffman's work', in Drew, P. and Wootton, A. (eds) *Erving Goffman: Exploring the Interaction Order*, Oxford, Polity.

Coupland, N., Coupland, J., Giles, H., and Wiemann, J. (1988) 'My life in your hands: processes of self-disclosure in inter-generational talk', in Coupland, N. (ed.) *Styles of Discourse*, London, Croom Helm.

Eibl-Eibesfeldt, I. (1972) 'Similarities and differences between cultures in expressive movements', in Hinde, R.A. (ed.) *Non-verbal Communication*, Cambridge, Cambridge University Press.

Ekman, P., Friesen, W. and Ellsworth, P. (1972) *Emotion in the Human Face*, New York, Pergamon.

Elias, N. (1978) *The Civilizing Process*, Oxford, Blackwell.

Freud, S. (1905) 'Fragments of an analysis of a case of hysteria', in Strachey, J. (ed.) (1953) *The Standard Edition of the Collected Works of Sigmund Freud*, vol.7, London, Hogarth Press.

Freud, S. (1966) *The Psychopathology of Everyday Life*, London, Ernest Benn.

Fontana, A. (1980) 'The mask and beyond: the enigmatic sociology of Erving Goffman', in Douglas, J. (ed.) *Introduction to the Sociologies of Everyday Life*, Boston, Allyn and Bacon.

Gahagan, J. (1984) *Social Interaction and its Management*, London, Methuen.

Garfinkel, H. (1984) *Studies in Ethnomethodology*, Cambridge and Oxford, Polity and Blackwell.

Giddens, A. (1988) 'Goffman as a systematic social theorist', in Drew, P. and Wootton, A. (eds) *Erving Goffman: Exploring the Interaction Order*, Oxford, Polity.

Giddens, A. (1989) *Sociology*, Cambridge and Oxford, Polity and Blackwell.

Goffman, E. (1959) *The Presentation of Self in Everyday Life*, New York, Doubleday Anchor.

Goffman, E. (1961) *Asylums*, New York, Doubleday Anchor.

Goffman, E. (1967) *Interaction Ritual: Essays on Face-to-Face Behaviour*, New York, Doubleday Anchor.

Goffman, E. (1971) *Relations in Public: Micro-Studies of the Public Order*, New York, Basic Books.

Goffman, E. (1974) *Frame Analysis*, New York, Harper and Row.

Goffman, E. (1981) *Forms of Talk*, Oxford, Blackwell.

Gumperz, J. (1982) *Discourse Strategies*, Cambridge, Cambridge University Press.

Henwood, K., Coupland, N., Coupland, J. and Giles, H. (1989) *Stereotyping and Problematicality in Talk about Elderly Painful Self-Disclosure*, unpublished manuscript, University of Bristol.

Heritage, J. (1984) *Garfinkel and Ethnomethodology*, Cambridge, Polity Press.

Heritage, J. (1988) 'Explanations as accounts: a conversation analytic perspective', in Antaki, C. (ed.) *Analysing Everyday Explanation*, London, Sage.

Heritage, J. and Greatbatch, D. (1986) 'Generating applause: a study of rhetoric and response at party political conferences', *American Sociological Review*, vol.92, pp.110–57.

Hinde, R. (1987) *Individuals, Relationships and Cultures*, Cambridge, Cambridge University Press.

Jupp, T.C., Roberts, C. and Cook-Gumperz, J. (1982) 'Language and disadvantage: the hidden process', in Gumperz, J. (ed.) *Language and Social Identity*, Cambridge, Cambridge University Press.

La Barre, W. (1947) 'The cultural basis of emotions and gestures' *Journal of Personality*, vol.16, pp.49–68.

Levinson, S. (1983) *Pragmatics*, Cambridge, Cambridge University Press.

Marsh, P., Rosser, E., and Harré, R. (1978) *The Rules of Disorder*, London, Routledge and Kegan Paul.

Milgram, S. (1977) *The Individual in a Social World*, Reading, Mass., Addison-Wesley.

Oakley, A. (1981) *From Here to Maternity*, Harmondsworth, Penguin.

Pomerantz, A. (1978) 'Compliment responses: notes on the operation of multiple constraints', in Schenkein, J. (ed.) *Studies in the Organization of Conversational Interaction*, London, Academic Press.

Pomerantz, A. (1984) 'Agreeing and disagreeing with assessments: some features of preferred/dispreferred turn shapes', in Atkinson, J.M. and Heritage, J. (eds) *Structures of Social Action: Studies in Conversation Analysis*, Cambridge, Cambridge University Press.

Potter, J. and Wetherell, M. (1987) *Discourse and Social Psychology*, London, Sage.

Sacks, H., Schegloff, E.A. and Jefferson, E.A. (1974) 'The simplest systematics for the organization of turn-taking in conversation', *Language*, vol.50, pp.697–735.

Schegloff, E.A. (1968) 'Sequencing in conversational openings', *American Anthropologist*, vol.70, pp.1075–95.

Schegloff, E.A. and Sacks, H. (1973) 'Opening up closings', *Semiotica*, vol.7, pp.289–327.

Smith, P. (1985) *Language, the Sexes and Society*, Oxford, Blackwell.

Spender, D. (1980) *Man Made Language*, London, Routledge and Kegan Paul.

Strong, P.M. (1988) 'Minor courtesies and macro structures', in Drew, P. and Wootton, A. (eds) *Erving Goffman: Exploring the Interaction Order*, Oxford, Polity Press.

Thorne, B., Kramarae, C. and Henley, N. (1983) *Language, Gender and Society*, Rowley, Newbury House.

Van Hooff, J.A.R.A.M. (1972) 'A comparative approach to the phylogeny of laughter and smiling', in Hinde, R.A. (ed.) *Non-Verbal Communication*, Cambridge, Cambridge University Press.

West, C. and Zimmerman, D. (1977) 'Women's place in everyday talk: reflections on parent–child interaction', *Social Problems*, vol.24, pp.521–9.

Wolfe, T. (1988) *Bonfire of the Vanities*, London, Picador.

Zimmerman, D. and West, C. (1975) 'Sex roles, interruptions and silences in conversations', in Thorne, B. and Henley, N. (eds) *Language and Sex: Difference and Dominance*, Rowley, Newbury House.

STUDY SKILLS SECTION: GOOD WRITING 2 — CONSOLIDATING THE SKILLS OF ESSAY WRITING

Prepared for the Course Team by Diane Watson

1   CONSOLIDATING THE SKILLS OF ESSAY WRITING

At a number of points in the course so far you have undertaken a variety of activities designed to help you develop the skills of reading, note-taking and essay writing. These skills have been dealt with step by step in the units, the study skills sections and *The Good Study Guide.* Your earlier assignments will have given you real experience of writing your own essays and of presenting arguments and discussions on paper. Now, before you conclude Block V and proceed to work on the essay associated with these units, I would like to help you consolidate some of the points that have been made about essay writing. One way of doing this is to take you through the process of making notes, selecting material and planning an answer on a specific Block V essay title. I want to do this using the material in the block, particularly that in Unit 21, and by using the study skills sections associated with Units 5 and 11 together with the ideas contained in Chapters 2, 5 and 6 of *The Good Study Guide,* most of which you have already been asked to read. It would be helpful to have this course material on hand as you work through this section.

You are now well over half-way through D103 and you will have observed that essays are becoming longer and are beginning to demand more of you. The essay titles may increasingly require close and careful analysis to determine precisely what your answer should cover, and how you may demonstrate your understanding of, and selectively make use of, the materials and ideas contained in the course. By taking you through the process of planning and structuring my own answer I hope to encourage you to reflect upon your progress with the 'craft' of essay writing and to give you confidence in the skills which you have acquired in your studies so far. A word of caution however! Do bear in mind that I have years of writing experience behind me and that inevitably this will be reflected in the essay which I have written. The essay is there as an aid to developing *your* writing skills further. It should not be seen as a 'model' to which you should aspire at this stage in your studies, nor should you be in any way intimidated by it. Regard it rather as my own personal and individual attempt at the essay. It is not the only way of proceeding and it certainly will not be perfect! In fact, as I sit here to write, I realize that I am feeling quite nervous. I find that getting those first few words down on paper is often the most difficult part of the task, and knowing that they are going to be read by other people makes me feel anxious and quite vulnerable. Experience with writing does not necessarily help one overcome such feelings. So if you are experiencing feelings similar to those I have described perhaps it will reassure you to know that you are not alone in this.

Like you, I have already read Units 19 to 21 of Block V and now have to write an essay on the following question:

Compare and contrast biological and macro-social analyses of social interaction.

I have been advised, as your student notes will generally advise you, that I should concentrate primarily on Unit 21 *Social Interaction*, and confine my discussion to approximately 1000 words. So, how shall I begin?

2   THE STAGES OF ESSAY WRITING

If you think back to the study skills sections of Units 5 and 11 and Chapter 6 of *The Good Study Guide* you will remember that the point is made that essay writing becomes far more manageable if it is broken down into separate stages. Your own experience will tell you that writing an essay is not accomplished at one sitting, but tends to be an active process taking place over a period of time. It can be a lengthy and uncomfortable experience filled with frustration and uncertainty. However, by taking it in stages we avoid the danger of overloading the mind, and we give ourselves time to experiment with ideas and explore various ways of handling the material.

3   THE 'CRAFT' OF WRITING

In the study skills section of Unit 5 Elaine Storkey discusses what is expected of you in a D103 essay and structures a plan for an answer to a Block I essay title. Chapter 6 of *The Good Study Guide* takes you through the stages of essay writing whilst warning you against seeing them as entirely separate and self-contained processes. I propose to build on this work by making use of the ideas contained in Section 2 of Chapter 6 to work on the present essay question. It would be useful at this stage to refer back to this section and remind yourself of its structure.

———————— ACTIVITY I ————————

Make a note of the main stages of essay writing and consider how closely they relate to your own experience so far.

The Block I study skills section and *The Good Study Guide* suggest that essay writing is likely to follow these main stages:
1   Thinking about the essay title
2   Gathering together relevant material
3   Generating ideas and getting them down on paper
4   Organizing the material into an outline plan
5   Writing the first draft
6   Reviewing the first draft
7   Writing the final essay.

Now I guess that when you think about this process you are likely to feel that it appears far more organized and logical than anything you have ever experienced! This is because, as a process, writing tends to move backwards and forwards between each of the stages, and is often experienced as a confused and disjointed activity. This is a very common experience. However, it is useful to attempt to separate out the different stages because each has a clear function in helping us arrive at the end product: a coherent and well argued response to the given essay question. So, let us now begin to move through these stages with the specific essay title in mind.

3.1   STAGE 1: THINKING ABOUT THE ESSAY TITLE

Although it might sound obvious that you should 'begin with the question' it is surprising how many essays appear to have been written with very little reference to the essay title. Reading the question carefully and deciding exactly what is required in an answer constitute the first stage in producing a coherent and well argued discussion which demonstrates your understanding of the issues involved. You are not being asked to tell your tutor everything you know about Unit 21 or Block V. What you are being asked to do is to think carefully about what you have read and to select from it that which is particularly relevant to arguing your case. The first step in doing this is to examine closely the *wording of the question* and to underline or highlight the key words or phrases you find there.

——————————— ACTIVITY 2 ———————————

Look closely at the essay title and underline the words which you think are likely to be particularly important. Can you see any difference in the nature of the words which you have underlined? For example, do some of the words tell you what you should do, while others indicate something about the kind of content which your essay should include?

In the case of this question there are two key words which feature frequently in social science essays and which tell us what we must do. Words of this kind are sometimes referred to as *process words*. They tell us how we should go about tackling the subject matter involved. In this particular case the process words are *compare* — which asks us to look for similarities and differences — and *contrast*, which requires us to highlight differences and dissimilarities. These two words instruct us to draw out the ways in which the things we are examining are both similar and different.

There are also words which refer to the things which we will be examining: the *content* to which we will apply the *process* words. The *content words* in this essay indicate the subject matter we are being asked to consider, namely, two particular ways of analysing *social interaction*: the *biological* and the *macro-social*.

Now, having 'taken in the question' and distinguished between the content and process words (and, in your case, having consulted the student notes for advice about how to approach the question and possible relevant content), we can begin to move towards the second stage of writing the essay: that of *gathering the material*.

3.2   STAGE 2: GATHERING TOGETHER RELEVANT MATERIAL

To see how the different stages of the essay-writing process merge with one another, consider how the 'thinking-about-the-essay question' stage merges with the 'gathering-the-material' stage. As *The Good Study Guide* suggests, having the title in mind as you progress through your reading (and before you get down to your essay in any concentrated way) will help you to ask relevant questions of the text and highlight and make notes of aspects of the course that are likely to be important. You might find that you have the question in the back of your mind over a period of several days and that ideas about possible ways of approaching the answer occur to you at strange and inappropriate times! You are likely to think over one possible way of approaching the task and then another, and to find yourself thinking about some piece of reading in quite a new light as you begin to formulate and firm up your ideas. In some senses then you will have already begun to think about the essay. However, there will come a point when you have to put time aside to begin to concentrate more formally on selecting and organizing the relevant course material, and to make notes and jottings with the aim of writing the essay.

For this part of this study section you should refer to Chapter 2 of *The Good Study Guide* on reading and note taking. In the 'key points' box at the end of Chapter 2 the author stresses that reading and note taking are a *'set of practices* which *you develop* to enable you to *engage* with the ideas in the text'. Through practice you should be aiming to develop a personal approach to note taking which best suits your own particular needs. For myself, I find that, by *highlighting key words and phrases* as I read through the units and Reader chapters, I am better able to concentrate on what I am reading. Perhaps of more importance though is the ease with which I am then able to review the broad structure and content of the things which I have read. I can then proceed to make my own notes, or structure an essay plan, without having to struggle through all of the text again.

Another way of gathering material and generating ideas, especially with a specific essay title in mind, is to make use of the *Introductions, Conclusions* and *Summaries* in the units. These have been incorporated into the text to help you map out the author's line of argument and provide 'breathing spaces' for you to check your understanding and consolidate your learning so far. These sections of Block V and Unit 21 are going to be invaluable to me as I review the material in the light of this essay title. Combined with the highlighting which I have already done, and the rough jottings I have made relating to my thoughts on this question, they will help me to focus on the main issues and to recall and select relevant material for my answer.

WHERE TO GO FOR MY MATERIAL?

Well, first of all I return to the *Introduction* to Block V which precedes Unit 19. This will remind me of the broad sweep of the block and set up some lines of enquiry for me to follow. Reading this Introduction, I then highlight the following points which seem relevant to this essay (note: for the moment please disregard the numbers in brackets on the right of the page in this section):

- That up to Block V the 'focus of the course has been on large scale trends affecting masses of people' (p.3). This focus is sometimes called the '*macro-social*' (p.4). (3)

- That Block V turns to the 'study of people as individuals and their relationships in daily life' (p.3). This focus is sometimes called the '*micro-social*' (p.4). (4)

- That a comprehensive discussion of identity needs to take account of the influence of 'physical characteristics, our bodies and biology' (p.4). One aspect of identity is, therefore, *biological*. (2)

- That social interaction is the study of '*the processes involved in acting jointly in social situations, in relating to other people, in mutual reaction and influence*' (p.3). (1)

- That Unit 21 extends the discussion of *biological* perspectives begun in Unit 19.(p.5). (2)
- That *social interaction* is concerned with 'the conversations, friendships and actions which constitute our experiences of everyday social life' (p.5) (1)

This is a very useful start and full of relevant ideas. Now I can move on to Unit 21 which is my main source for this essay. Relevant points from Section 1 seem to be:

- That Units 19 and 20 examine the influence of *biological* and *macro-social* processes on personal identity but that in order to obtain the complete story the individual must be located in the 'pattern of interaction with others' (p.100). (4)
- *Social interaction* involves relationships, converstions, mutual influence, impressions created, rituals and 'all the problems of generally getting on with others in the modern world' (p.100). (1)
- That Section 2 examines the contrasting influences of *biology* and *society* (p.100). (2) and (3)
- The definition of *social interaction is explored* through the use of examples (p.100). (1)
- That *social interaction* may be seen as 'the glue of social life' (p.103) and the place where social processes are brought to life (p.103). (1)
- For this reason social scientists are interested in studying social interaction (p.103). (1)
- The *Summary* of Section 1 emphasizes that the study of social interaction clarifies the interrelationship between the individual and the *macro-social* and examines the role of *human action* in this relationship (p.107). (4)
- Section 2 outlines the fact that *biology* and the *macro-social* have a vital influence on patterns of interaction. The section is the focus for this essay and contains examples of research into the role of *biology*. It emphasizes that 'biology can only tell us about the very broad possibilities for interaction and very little about the meaning and significance of any particular interaction' (p.112). It also examines the *macro-social* which, it is argued, provides the 'backcloth for everyday life' (p.113). (2) and (3)
- The Section 2 *Summary* suggests that research in these areas is limited in what it can tell us about the 'mechanics' of a given interaction or the variety of meanings which may be attributed to human action and social interaction (p.115). (4)

Finally, the *Conclusion* to the unit contains more relevant ideas:

- That *macro-social analyses* often give little attention to human agents (p.135). (3)
- That the *macro-social* context involves structures, institutions and social processes (p.136). (3)
- That the *micro-social* is an aspect of social life with its own order, norms and rules (p.136). (4)
- That both these levels are in 'complex interrelation' (p.136) and changes in one arena have an impact in the other. (4)
- That different levels of analysis have different characteristics and different assumptions (p.136). (4)
- That 'individuals have the property of agency' (p.136) and can create and shape their own lives. However, at the same time, they are constrained in their action by structures, processes and institutions operating at the macro-social level (p.136). (4)

I'm beginning to feel a little more confident now. That quick review of my highlighted notes has gathered together some key ideas which are going to provide me with the skeleton framework of my answer. Clearly the issues relating to the roles of *biology* and the *macro-social* in the study of *social interaction* are major ones. And as a student of D103 I am not going to be expected to arrive at some new and exciting conclusion! My short essay merely needs to demonstrate my understanding of the state of the debate as outlined in the course. However, I do have the scope to *select* and *illustrate* and to *structure the discussion* in my own preferred way.

So, I have a number of points and a range of material which might be useful in helping me formulate an answer. The question now is *how* am I going to get this material into some coherent and organized form and generate some ideas about the possible structure of an answer? This brings me to stage 3: generating ideas.

3.3   STAGE 3: GENERATING IDEAS

This stage of transforming relatively random thoughts and notes into some kind of ordered and coherent pattern is the one which I personally find the most difficult to demonstrate in written form. It is a culmination of a period of reflecting on the essay title, of reading and of making notes. And it's where scope for individuality and creativity comes in. I have read the course material, I have taken the essay title apart to decide what I must do and what I might include, and I have made a series of notes and jottings. Now I must decide what I am going to say, in what order and with what conclusions, and for this reason this is also a time of anxiety and uncertainty. So, how to proceed?

─────────────────── ACTIVITY 3 ───────────────────

Look over the points which I have listed above as being potentially relevant to answering this essay question. Can you group the points together so that you have a category relating to the concept of social interaction, a category for biological approaches, and a category for the macro-social? Are there other points which might be useful which do not come into these three categories? Might they form another category?

──

You may have noticed the numbers written alongside each of the listed points and wondered why they were there. Well, when I was looking over these points myself I decided that some of them related to *definitions* of 'social interaction' and issues related to the value of studying this area. Against these points I have placed the number (1).

A second set of points clearly related to those forms of analysis which focus upon the *role of biology* in social interaction. These are given number (2).

Thirdly, there are those parts of the material which explore the relevance of *macro-social* analysis and these are given the number (3).

Finally, there are the notes I have made relating to the *relationships* between the biological and the macro-social and the relevance of a further approach, the *micro-social*. These are given the number (4).

By grouping my ideas and notes into categories in this way I can begin to see a way forward in constructing the plan of an answer. Instead of having twenty-one different points I now have only four major categories to deal with. How might I arrange these in an answer?

Well, the first point to make in reply to that question is that there are a number of ways of handling the discussion (so if you decide to discuss the issue in a different way it is likely to be as valid as my own). In addition there is plenty of scope for selecting different ways to illustrate your answer and for choosing to emphasize different factors. However, the following is the plan which I settled on.

3.4   STAGE 4: PLANNING THE ANSWER

From your experience of writing essays so far you may have observed that short essays generally have a simple structure of three distinct parts: an introduction, a larger middle section, and a conclusion. My plan will follow this broad principle of organization.

THE PLAN

Compare and contrast biological and macro-social analyses of social interaction.

1   *Introduction:*

Define social interaction (points numbered 1).

Explain why social scientists are interested in the analysis of social interaction (points numbered 1).

Introduce the two approaches to social interaction: the biological and the macro-social (the 'content' part of the essay question and points numbered 2 and 3).

State what I intend to do; that is, compare and contrast the approaches (the 'process' part of the question).

2   *Middle section:*

Examine the features of biological analyses: focus of analysis, examples of research (points numbered 2).

Examine the features of macro-social analyses: focus of analysis, examples of research (points numbered 3).

Explore the ways in which these approaches differ: in their methods of analysis and in what they examine (points numbered 4).

Explore the ways they might be seen to be similar: in what they include, in what they leave out (points numbered 4).

3   *Conclusion:*

Broad summary of similarities and differences (points numbered 4).

Examine other forms of analysis more appropriate to the study of social interaction: what are they? Are they complementary to the biological or the macro-social or both? (points numbered 4).

3.5   STAGES 5, 6 AND 7: WRITING THE ESSAY

Unless you are working under the pressure of time, as in an exam or timed essay situation, it is always useful to write out the essay title. This helps to keep the focus of the essay in mind at all times and guards against the danger of failing to answer the question. I must assume that I am writing for an audience of interested but uninformed lay-readers and must, therefore, take care to communicate my argument logically and clearly using the 'tricks of the trade' outlined in Section 4 of Chapter 6 of *The Good Study Guide* and in the study skills section of Unit 11. These techniques of 'signposting', using 'link' words, paragraphing and careful sentence structure are not arbitrary but are the means whereby communication is enhanced. Now I can proceed to work on my plan, referring to my notes and back to the relevant sections of the course materials, and begin to write up my essay. As indicated in *The Good Study Guide*, this will take the form of a rough draft which will be followed by the final written version once I have reviewed what I have written and pruned, corrected and amended it. For now, though, I reproduce only the final version of my essay.

3.6   FINAL VERSION OF MY ESSAY

Compare and contrast biological and macro-social analyses of social interaction.

In Block V of D103 Margaret Wetherell defines *social interaction* as 'the processes involved in acting jointly in social situations, in relating to other people, in mutual reaction and influence' (Block V *Introduction*, p.3). The concept of social interaction focuses our attention on everyday, commonplace activities, such as our mutual conduct of conversations and social relationships. These everyday routines have been conceived of as 'the glue of social life' (Unit 21, p.103) holding societies together and are of interest to social scientists because of their capacity to tell us something about the way society is ordered and remains structured over time. Furthermore, the study of social interaction highlights the complex interrelationship between the *individual* and the *macro-social* and focuses attention on the capacity of individuals to shape social structures and the role of social structures in shaping individuals.

In this essay I intend to examine two particular ways of analysing social interaction. The first concentrates on the role of *biological factors* and the second examines the influence of the structures, institutions and social processes which make up the *macro-social context* in which individual social actors operate. In examining these two different and contrasting approaches to social interaction I shall draw out the ways in which they are similar and different in their focus and assumptions.

Biological analyses of social interaction have as their starting point the human individual. At the most basic level the physical presence of human beings is necessary for interaction to take place at all, but the question posed by this form of analysis concerns the extent to which the behaviour of people in social interaction is shaped or determined by inbuilt biological and genetic structures. Hinde, for example, has argued that there are certain stable, universal tendencies in human beings which 'arise from the very nature of our bodies' (Hinde, Unit 21, p.107) and work to 'pre-programme' and structure what occurs in social interaction. For example, the apparent universal human preference for the distinctive facial features of babies appears to elicit positive, nurturing responses from mature humans which, it may be argued, enhance babies' chances of survival. Hinde has noted that many expressions, such as smiling, crying, the 'eyebrow flash', or the expression of fear, appear universal and have their roots in biology. However, it is also clear that the meanings which people attribute to these expressions are culturally variable. Consequently it would be false to suggest that biology *determines* the structure of social interaction. Hinde would accept that biological 'pre-programming' merely provides a framework of possibilities within which particular forms of interaction are enacted (Unit 21, p.107).

In contrast, macro-social analyses of social interaction begin, not with the individual, but with those social, political and economic structures and institutions which make up the nature of the society in which the individual lives. However, again the question is raised as to the extent to which the specific dynamics of social interaction are shaped or *determined* by this macro-social context. Giddens, for example, contrasts the interaction patterns which occur in large-scale, modern, urban, technological, rational, bureaucratic societies like our own with those of small-scale, traditional, communal and intimate societies such as the !Kung of the Kalahari desert. In the case of the !Kung, interaction followed patterns of openness and close intimacy with 'familiar others'. However, in modern, industrial, urban contexts interaction patterns between 'familiar strangers' take on a 'diluted form' (Unit 21, p.113). This is not to imply that all interaction patterns are of the same form. Clearly, in modern, industrial societies there are a variety of types of relationship with appropriate forms of interaction associated with them. In the same way that biological structures provide only a framework for human interaction, the macro-social context creates a 'backcloth for everyday life' (Unit 21, p.113) — a context in which the dynamics of particular interactions take place.

Biological and macro-social forms of analysis differ both in their starting point for analysis and in the nature of the constraints they emphasize. However, both are important to the study of social interaction because, 'in their different ways they indicate some broad constraints guiding the who, where, what, why and how of interaction' (Unit 21, p.114). In addition, these different approaches share other common features. Both forms of analysis underplay the ways in which human social actors actively work to create their own lives and consciously choose to behave in particular ways within the framework set by biology or the macrosocial. There is a danger of assuming that patterns of social interaction are beyond the control of the individual and are determined by the constraints of biology or social structure. However, as Unit 21 argues, 'the *macro-social* context has a decisive effect on the actual patterns of daily life and the scope for interaction but, like *biological* research, it is uninformative about the mechanics of any particular interaction' (p.115).

Furthermore, as the introduction to this essay indicates, social interaction is about the ways in which individuals act and react to each other as they go about their daily lives, constructing and reconstructing their social worlds and relationships. By concentrating upon the influence of biology or social structure, these two perspectives are in danger of underplaying the importance of the *micro-social* with its order, norms, rules and regularities.

It must be acknowledged that the study of biology and social structure is vital to an understanding of social interaction. At the
same time, these approaches need to be complemented by the work of
social scientists using the *micro-social perspective*. Social
scientists working within this tradition, such as Goffman, would
agree that 'the study of interaction cannot be *reduced* [my
emphasis] to or collapsed into the study of biology or social
structure' (Unit 21, p.115). If we are concerned to understand the
dynamic processes involved in social interaction we must turn our
attention to the ways in which individuals interpret social situations and the methods they employ to create order and regularity
in their daily lives.

Bibliography

D103 Block V Introduction

D103 Unit 21

(Essay of 1015 words)

4   WHAT IS GOOD WRITING?: REVIEWING YOUR ESSAY

Well, that is my finished essay which I hope has 'answered the question' and
keeps to the word limit of 1000 words. What you see above is the product of a
process of working through several stages of essay writing. I found the 1000
word limit quite difficult to keep to but realized that it served to discipline me
in my choice of words and selection of illustrations. I usually find that before I
begin to write I am worried about not having enough to say but before long,
without realizing it, I have reached the word limit and more!

On several occasions, as I read through my work, I saw places where I had
effectively repeated myself, or included irrelevant material, and could cut back
on what I had written. On other occasions I realized that I had been making
assumptions about what my interested but uninformed *lay reader* already
knew and had to go back to include another illustration or explanation to
clarify my argument.

You will see that when I made my outline notes I was careful to reference the
pages and place quotations in quotation marks. It is so easy to return to your
notes, assume that the words are your own, and fall into the trap of *plagiarism*.
Plagiarism is the repetition of another person's words without credit. Most
students do this inadvertently at some point in the early stages of study so you
need to be alert to this and avoid it happening in your own work. As *The Good
Study Guide* says, plagiarism 'is, in effect, "stealing" other people's ideas'
(Northedge, Chapter 6, p.190). It follows, therefore, that it is regarded as a very
serious matter in academic work. I have also been careful to direct my reader to
the *sources* I have used for my essay by including *references* in the text and a
bibliography at the end. In this way the reader can be certain where I have
obtained my information from and, if necessary, can consult the same source to
check that he or she agrees with my interpretation.

5   ENHANCING YOUR ESSAY

Producing an answer to this essay question was a relatively concise and clearly defined task. I had to write to 1000 words and use the ideas in Unit 21. Had I had more space I could have chosen to enhance my writing by drawing upon a wider range of materials than I have been able to do here. For example, I could have explored the influence of the biological further by drawing on the discussion of Eysenck's theories of the *biological bases of personality* in Unit 19. I might have chosen to use the discussion of unemployment in Unit 20, or the piece on Phyllis Collins in Chapter 16.1 in the Reader, to illustrate my points about the effect of *social circumstances* on processes of social interaction. Or I may have decided to return to Block II, Unit 6 to use the illustration that smoking and dying have *physical and biological* characteristics but that *social factors* are crucial in their distribution throughout the population. Whatever I had decided to do I must be sure to make it clear to my reader where I have obtained my material and when I am using another person's ideas. Finally, in the last paragraph of the essay, I touched on the issue of how we begin to choose between *competing theories*. This is something we shall be dealing with in Unit 22.

At a number of points in this study skills section I have made reference to the need to produce a coherent and well argued discussion and for you to argue your case in a convincing way. Now you have followed through the processes involved in producing my essay, you might find it helpful to think about what I have written in the light of the points made in Chapter 5 (Section 3) and Chapter 6 (Section 5) of *The Good Study Guide*. If you have time, refer to these sections now and remind yourself of what is said about drawing on course material, using evidence and quotations, citing references, and avoiding plagiarism. Reflect on the analytical style which I have adopted and the means whereby I have grouped and sorted my points in a relatively logical structure. And finally, remember that my essay is here to help you to consider some of the technical aspects involved in writing an answer to an essay question. If you can follow what I am doing, criticize it, or feel that you would have approached the answer in a different way, then you are well on the way to consolidating your own essay-writing skills.

6   RECEIVING CRITICISM

As I said at the beginning of this study skills section, writing is not a comfortable and easy task, however experienced one is at doing it. It is made all the more difficult by the fact that, sooner or later, what we have written is going to become 'public'. Other people are going to read your work and they are going to look at it critically. You may have spent many hours working through the material and writing out your drafts of an answer. You may feel well and truly sick of the whole thing and just hope for a good grade to make it all seem worthwhile. I know how you feel! In spite of these emotions, it is worth thinking about the final stage in the process of writing a good essay — that of taking advantage of your tutor's comments and criticism.

One of the advantages which you have as an Open University student is that the system of teaching and learning through correspondence should ensure that your essay is returned to you with detailed comments and feedback. It would be unfortunate therefore if your *feelings* about your essay prevented you from gaining maximum benefit from your tutor's comments. By all means look at the grade and put the essay away until you have sufficient time available to consider the feedback carefully. But don't wait too long. Once you have accustomed yourself to your grade, make yourself read through your essay and your tutor's advice, both on the PT3 and on the script itself. Make a note on your essay (perhaps in a different coloured pen) of your responses to your tutor's comments. On reflection, if you are unclear about any of the comments or puzzled about the grade, make a note to ask your tutor about it, either at your study centre or by telephone. And finally, note down one or two items of advice which you can bear in mind for the next essay which you write. Most of us have some difficulty with this process of receiving criticism. We feel misunderstood, annoyed at the seemingly critical tone of the comments, aggrieved that the tutor doesn't appreciate how difficult the task was, or irritated that the course team didn't set a more clearly worded essay title. These feelings are difficult to avoid and they are very common. Even when we tell ourselves that our work is not very good and we don't really mind, we still can't help feeling a little hurt. Try not to let such feelings interfere with the learning process. Think how your tutor would feel if he or she knew that you hadn't bothered to read the comments on your essay!

You might find it helpful to talk through these issues with your tutor and fellow-students at your study centre. In the meantime, good luck with your next essay.

===== GOOD STUDY GUIDE =====

This would be an appropriate point to read Chapter 6, Sections 6 and 7 of *The Good Study Guide* where this aspect of essay writing is discussed further.

ACKNOWLEDGEMENTS

Grateful acknowledgement is made to the following sources for permission to reproduce material in this unit:

Tables

p.119: Heritage, J. *Garfinkel and Ethnomethodology*, Basil Blackwell, 1984.

Photographs

p.112: Brenda Prince/Format; *p.114:* Joanne O'Brien/Format; *p.125:* Maggie Murray/Format.

UNIT 22   INVESTIGATIVE METHODS

Prepared for the Course Team by Richard Stevens

CONTENTS

1   INTRODUCTION

Like the other half-units at the end of each block, the main purpose of this unit is to continue our reflections on the nature of social science. These were begun in Units 4 and 5, which provided a broad overview of how social scientists go about their work of making sense of society. You may remember, for example, the discussion of the use of concepts to classify, abstract from and conceptualize different aspects of society; also of the way explanations are developed through the interplay of theory and evidence.

Each of the subsequent half-units then takes up and explores in greater depth a different aspect of the process of social science investigation and understanding. The significance and nature of *concepts* was discussed in more detail in Unit 9. Unit 13 then took up the issue of the role of *models and metaphors* in helping us to understand what is going on in economics and in society. Unit 18 at the end of the last block followed up by discussing further the intrinsic *interrelationship between theories and evidence*. Now, in this unit, we go on to look at *how* social scientists investigate the questions and subject matter they are interested in—in other words, the nature of the *methods* they use.

You may have noticed that in each of the preceding three units of this block, the methods used to underpin each theory or piece of research considered have been highlighted and some of the implications and problems involved have been discussed. Looking back over this ground will provide a very useful starting point to more direct examination of the topic of methods and the issues these raise. It is also part of the second aim of this unit, which is to *review* the material in the block.

Plan of the unit. Section 2 provides a brief *review* of the content of the three units of Block V. This will include a set of Activities so that you can check out how well you have understood and assimilated it.

Section 3 will be focused on *methods* though it will also continue to serve a review function. By drawing on examples from the Block V units, it will contrast and discuss the different kinds of investigative methods which social psychologists use. It will also raise core issues about the nature of understanding in social science and the relevance of this to the different kinds of methods.

Section 4 then broadens the discussion of methods in social science to draw on examples from the course as a whole.

Finally, Section 5 briefly takes up a key feature of Block V and social science in general—the use of *different perspectives* to make sense of its subject matter. How do the different investigative methods relate to such different perspectives? Are they best regarded as complementary or are they essentially irreconcilable?

2   REVIEW

Block V has been concerned with two broad topics: identity (Units 19 and 20) and social interaction (Unit 21). A feature of the block was to explore these topics from four different perspectives. These were, as you will no doubt remember, phenomenological, psychoanalytic, biological and social.

Let us recap first on *identity*.

Unit 19 Personal identity. We began in Unit 19 with a *phenomenological* perspective by exploring the experience of self and its characteristics of self-awareness, agency and continuity. We discussed the question of whether a sense of self-direction and the capacity to create one's own identity is a universally experienced reality or a socially created illusion. We also considered how far identity is unitary and the idea of multiple identity.

The unit then moved on to look at identity from the perspective of *psychoanalysis*. We considered Freud's ideas about (1) *psychosexual development* and the idea of transference; (2) *psychodynamics*—the conflict that arises between the id, ego and superego, and the defence processes which deal with the anxiety this arouses; and (3) the significance of *unconscious* meanings and desires. Psychoanalytic theory suggests that the phenomenological perspective with its focus on conscious experience cannot provide adequate understanding of identity, for much of what constitutes identity is influenced by unconscious memories from childhood and is underpinned by unconscious intrapsychic conflict. By briefly examining two transitional phases, adolescence and midlife, we went on to consider how identity develops and changes in adult life. This is a theme taken up in TV11.

The third perspective, the *biological*, explored some of the different ways in which the body and physiology can influence identity. Bodily characteristics affect self-image, for example, and our ability to act on the world. They can make us vulnerable and open us up to feelings of ecstasy or pain. We considered two main approaches which claim more specific links between biology and identity—*Eysenck's theory of personality* and (in the article in Chapter 15 of the Reader) *sociobiology*.

By statistical analysis of questionnaire answers and other responses from a large number of subjects, Eysenck claims to have established core dimensions which underlie personality. Two of these dimensions are Extraversion–Introversion (E) and Emotionality or Neuroticism(N). Eysenck relates these to the physiological processes in the part of the brain which controls arousal level (in the case of E), and the autonomic nervous system (in the case of N).

Sociobiology, in contrast, as described in the Reader article works from principles of evolution. It assumes that genes can influence social behaviour as well as physiological processes, and that those social behaviours will have been selected for in the past which facilitate individual and group survival and/or increase the chances of producing offspring who will grow to sexual maturity.

——————————————— ACTIVITY 1 ———————————————

These self-assessment questions are designed to test out how well you have understood and remembered the more detailed content of the units and the associated Reader articles. You may find it necessary to refer back to a unit to answer some of the more difficult ones. Answering each question in this way should be a very useful revision strategy. Answers are given at the back with an indication of the section of the unit to which the particular question refers but try to answer for yourself before referring to these.

1   Three 'existential issues' were described as arising from our capacity to reflect on the experience of being a person. Can you remember what these were?

2   What are the three stages of psychosexual development during the first five years of life which Freud describes?

3   Name three defence mechanisms?

4   What is meant by the 'ideal self'?

5   In terms of Eysenck's theory, what is it that extraverts require that underlies their behaviour and style of responding?

6   What kind of research study is the primary basis for his assertion that E and N are genetically influenced?

7   How does Eysenck explain the evidence that extraverts are more likely to become involved in crime?

8   How has the evolution of personal identity been related to the evolution of altruism?

9   What evolutionary advantages might consciousness have endowed?

10 What explanation would sociobiologists give for the greater physical size and strength, on average, of men in comparison with women?

(Answers at the back)

Unit 20 Social identity. Analysis of the *social* perspective on identity occupied the whole of Unit 20. It first considered the effects which immediate social circumstances (such as the work you do or whether you are unemployed) may have on identity.

The unit then extended the argument originally developed in Block II that the major categories of social identity, such as gender or ethnic background, arise from social conditions under which people live rather than from any essential, in-built differences between them. It demonstrated this argument by examining psychological differences between women and men and indicating how a social analysis of categories such as homosexuality and educational 'subnormality' would proceed by looking at stereotypes and images, history and culture.

A third way in which social forces influence identity was explored by noting ethnographic claims that aspects of identity seem to vary in different cultures. Such variation would seem to demonstrate the plasticity of human behaviour and the point that identity is related to the organization of a society.

The focus of the unit then turned to explaining how society can influence individual identity and the work of Mead was introduced to show how representations bridge between individual experience and the social situation. Representations of identity, it was argued, reflect current ideologies. This process was demonstrated by reference to advertisements and a story in a girls' comic.

———————————— ACTIVITY 2 ————————————

1   What was the the main finding from the Zimbardo experiment described in Chapter 17 of the Reader?

2   Give an example of the problems involved in ethnography?

3   What is meant by the 'looking glass self'?

4   What is meant by the word 'interpellation'?

[*Note*. The shorter list of questions here compared to Activity 1 reflects the fact that only one perspective was covered in Unit 20 compared with three in Unit 19.]

(Answers at the back)

Unit 21 Social interaction. The third unit of the block, Unit 21, took up the topic of *social interaction*. A multi-perspective approach was applied as it had been for identity in Units 19 and 20. This focused in particular on the complex way in which the wider context of society (macro-social aspects), particular rules and conventions (micro-social aspects) and biological predispositions inter-relate in the way people communicate and interact with each other.

Biology clearly plays a part in determining the form which communicative behaviour takes, but the wider social context sets the scene and is crucial for determining how such communications will be interpreted. The particular patterns of communication and interactions, and the implicit rules which govern them, are only revealed by close analysis of specific situations (e.g. conversation analysis and the work of Garfinkel and Goffman).

The unit concluded with consideration of how research in social interaction might be applied in every day life: for example, by improving people's social and communication skills at work and in relationships, or with children at school to decrease bullying and prejudice.

——————————————— ACTIVITY 3 ———————————————

1 What do Garfinkel's studies which involve deliberate breaking of social conventions tell us about the nature of interaction?

2 Give two examples of communicative behaviours which would appear to be biologically based.

3 Give an example from the unit of how miscommunication can result from the different communication conventions of different ethnic groups.

4 Give two examples of the kind of regularities in conversations which conversation analysts have discovered.

5 Give an example of the strategies used by dominant individuals identified by conversation analysts' studies of interactions between men and women.

6 Give two examples of effective rhetorical strategies as shown by research analyses of political speakers.

7 In terms of Goffman's ideas about self-presentation, distinguish betwen 'giving' and 'giving off'.

(Answers at the back)

If you have understood this review of the three preceding units and have successfully worked through the questions, you should have a good idea of the material of Block V.

An issue raised in the block is: how is it possible to inter-relate the different perspectives on identity which have been presented? Do they fit together in some way or should they be seen as offering alternative kinds of understanding? This issue will be briefly taken up in Section 5.1 at the end of this unit.

In relation to this unit's focus on methods, one advantage of taking a multi-perspective approach in Block V is that you have now had a chance to sample a range of varied research strategies and techniques used in social psychology, and have seen something of their respective advantages and limitations. You will have noticed that these have been noted and discussed in the unit texts. So, in order to focus the discussion, we will begin our consideration of social science methods in the next section by looking a little more closely at the methods mentioned in Block V and considering what implications the differences between them may have for the nature of understanding and explanation in social science. The following section (4) will then broaden the discussion to look more generally at methods in social science in the context of the course as a whole.

3   METHODS

The first and important point to make about social science research methods is that they are not a means to look at the social world about us and just 'see what is there'. They are not simple objective tools of discovery and investigation. Right from the start and all along the way, the research process will be guided, constructed you might say, by the researcher in question and the context in which the research is carried out. Why in the first place are these particular questions being asked, this particular issue being studied and these particular methods being used? How is the research being funded and why? What is its ultimate purpose? By asking such questions, it becomes clear how the process of research is actively constructed and directed.

A major starting point is the researcher her- or himself. Reflection on their own experience may well generate the line they will take. That experience itself will have been nourished by the observations and experiences of daily life, and perhaps their own introspections in the case of some psychologists. By his own account, Freud, for example, spent four years in intensive self analysis (1892–6) and this proved to be a major and fertile source of his ideas. Research and therapy are influenced also by the values and even the temperament and personality of the theorist (is she or he anxious to have black and white results, for example, or can they tolerate ambiguity?). And, as we have seen in discussing the traditions of social thought, the kinds of question asked, as well as the way they are pursued will depend on the model of the person and society, the political and social values with which the researcher is aligned.

3.1   QUALITATIVE METHODS

Given this background, what *kinds of method* do social scientists use in their research? Throughout the course you have had numerous examples of these methods. For social psychologists studying identity and interaction, a basic method is *observation*. This may be carried out in a systematic, formal way, as in Strong's recording of doctor-patient interactions, communications between Asian serving staff and customers in a work's canteen, or Couplands' study of how old and young women interact together (all of these are described in Unit 21).

Recording and observation, however, do not occur in a vacuum. It would be quite wrong to suppose that we can just see or hear objectively what is there. It all has to be made sense of. This reiterates the point made in each of the review units so far: that *what we observe is structured by the concepts we use, guided by the models and metaphors we bring to bear, and made sense of in terms of the theoretical frameworks we employ*. And this applies whatever the investigative method we use.

Because we are all participants in social life, all of us engage in observation as a matter of course. What the researcher or theorist provides is a set of concepts, or a model, which directs our attention to particular aspects or ways of looking at what is going on around us, and thus gets us to structure our observations afresh. In Goffman's fascinating analysis of the ways in which we interact (Unit 21), for example, he offers us the analogy and metaphor of the theatre with its roles, scripts and improvization. Thinking of social behaviour in this way can transform how we make sense of it. On your next holiday after reading Goffman, no longer will you merely see men and women parading on the beach but you may well be noting the manner of their presentation of self. Are their displays just 'given' or are they being 'given off'? In this way, his concepts can help to structure your perception of the social world about you. If the theory is a good one, in doing this it will deepen our understanding or heighten our awareness of what is going on. It will illuminate the factors which influence social behaviour or particular social processes and the ways in which they work.

All this, however, is not meant to imply that observations are entirely created by the observer. Research is a two-way process. Our concepts and way of framing may enable us to make sense of what we see but this understanding is grounded too in what is there. We may find that the particular way we are looking at our subject matter yields few insights, so that we may be forced to modify our concepts or models or invent new ones accordingly in a dialectical (or two-way) development of understanding.

Such analysis may not only be directed at the world we can immediately observe and record. Goffman, for example, used 'social records' of various kinds—such as clippings from newspapers, extracts from novels and letters to lonely-heart columns, as the material of social life to be analysed and understood. As we saw in Unit 20, even children's comics can provide a medium to allow us to begin to see how ideologies may structure personal identity. *Historical records* such as Greek or Roman accounts of their sexual conventions (Unit 20, Section 3.3) or *autobiographical accounts* like those of Phyllis Collins in the Reader (Chapter 16.2) about her experience of work, are all grist to the mill. But the same point emphasized above applies. All require selection, interpretation and analysis and this in turn will be guided by the concepts and ideas of the researcher or writer.

A lot of what the social science researcher is interested in is not lying around waiting to be studied. It may need to be *elicited*. One way of doing this is to *interview* people, to find out what they think about a particular topic or how they see their world. Thus, Plummer's study (Unit 20, Section 3.3) involved interviewing a selection of homosexuals about their life and experiences. Here, there is even more danger of finding what you want to find. That is why training in interviewing skills emphasizes the need for open, non-directive questions which, as far as possible, do not bias or influence the respondent to answer in a particular way. Inevitably, however, the assumptions of the researcher will influence the kinds of questions asked and how they are interpreted. (Plummer's study, for example, was grounded in symbolic interactionist theory involving notions of role-taking and the 'looking-glass self'—see Unit 20, Sections 6.1–6.2.)

Attempts to elicit the meanings underlying social life may require the development of special techniques. So Freud used *free association* and developed a method of *interpreting dreams* as a way of trying to get at unconscious meanings that could not be elicited by interview because they were not

Well now, to get back to my original reason
for accosting you . . . "

available even to the patient's conscious mind (see Unit 19, Section 3.3). Such techniques, however, to an even greater degree place weight on interpretation and produce analyses which are open to dispute.

The same kind of situation or behaviour may be observed or the same person interviewed, at different points in time. Such *longitudinal studies* can produce useful information about change or the effect of different kinds of situation such as being in and out of work. Or we may apply observations and interviews in the study of people in other cultures. Section 4 in Unit 20 introduced the *ethnographic method* where the researcher spends time in another society observing, learning the language so that he or she can live and talk with the people being studied. The discussion warned though that, although fascinating material can be obtained in this way, there are formidable difficulties, such as deciding how much significance to place on the metaphors and forms of language which the members of that society use to describe their social world. Do they really reflect the way that people think or are they better regarded as just particular modes of expression?

A more extreme way of eliciting the meanings that underpin social behaviour and interaction is the *interventions* practised by Garfinkel and his colleagues (described in Unit 21) which involve the deliberate breaking of normal social conventions. These might involve, for example, going home to your parents and behaving as a lodger: or trying to knock 50 per cent off the price of goods in a posh shop. They can be a useful way of highlighting the expectations and conventions which govern social behaviour but which we normally take for granted. They do, however, pose *ethical questions*. Is it right to risk upsetting people and interfering in this way for the sake of whatever benefits the research may yield?

So far, then, we have reviewed a range of methods referred to in Block V: from observation and interview to ethnography, dream analysis and deliberate interventions by violating conventions. All these are *qualitative methods* in that they produce verbal accounts and analyses of the subject matter in question. They are concerned with unpacking and exploring the *meanings* which underlie social life. None of them, as has been stressed, are passive indicators. They are all guided by concepts and models (even though this may sometimes be unacknowledged by the researcher). Research findings then are essentially *representations* which have been generated by the interplay between the subject matter being investigated and the way of studying or investigating it imposed by the researcher. Looking at social scientific methods, we see, provides further elaboration of the point stressed in Unit 18, that social science understanding emerges from the interplay of theory and evidence. There is a continuum here in the degree to which the emphasis is on the subject matter studied or on the concepts which are being brought to bear to make sense of it. At one extreme, for example, *conversation analysis* (see Unit 21) requires detailed and precise analysis of the transcripts of conversations and spoken utterances. At the other extreme, Goffman does not give a detailed analysis of specific observations but provides concepts for us to use in interpreting and making sense of the social interactions that we observe in everyday life.

A lot of stimulating ideas in social science involve heightening our consciousness and directing attention in this way rather than providing a detailed record of what might be going on. There is an important role for what might be termed *rational speculation*. Thus, Luckmann (Unit 19, Section 2.2) invites us to consider that we live in multiple worlds and the likely impact this may have on our experience of personal identity. Sometimes, such rational speculation is grounded in established principles. Thus sociobiology's speculations about the likely origins and nature of different aspects of social behaviour work from the principles of evolution and natural and sexual selection. There is a place also for *introspection*, turning the focus on our own thoughts and feelings and reflecting on what these tell us about the nature of both subjective experience and the social world.

The big theories in social science rarely emerge from tightly focused re-search strategies, but as *personal syntheses*—an integration of ideas and understanding from a variety of sources in theorists' lives. Often the basis of their assertions is indirect. Thus both Mead and Freud produce theories of socialization and childhood development with little or no attempt to observe or investigate systematically the experience of children themselves. The rich quality of Freud's theorizing, it could be argued, does not depend so much on specific observations or research but on the variety of his intellectual apprenticeship— wide learning in the classics, in literature and history as well as a scientific and medical training. Not only did he have the experience of his patients to draw on but also his own systematic and prolonged self-analysis. It is as if Freud's wide array of intellectual and personal experiences were transmuted into some rich compost mould that provided a fertile source for the growth of his ideas.

Qualitative methods and approaches have yielded rich insights. However, as we have seen, they are always open to question. It is always possible to come at the same subject matter from a different angle, to define it differently, to produce a different interpretation or to deny one already made. Can we not be more objective, you may well ask? Is not the role of a science to clarify such ambiguities and uncertainties, to free us from the subjectivity of personal interpretations and disputes? Can we not learn from natural science and introduce more rigorous methods like measurement and experiment to make the study of society and social life a more objective affair? We will take up such questions in the following sections.

SUMMARY

- Research is a two-way process, constructed by the researcher but grounded too in what is being studied.

- Qualitative methods include observation, analysis of social and historical records and autobiographical accounts.

- They may involve interviews or ethnographic studies of other cultures.

- The results of qualitative methods have to be interpreted. In the case of some special techniques like free association or dream analysis, interpretation may play a major role.

- Research which involves interventions may raise ethical questions.

- Qualitative methods vary in approach from detailed analysis of small specific samples of the subject matter (e.g. conversation analysis) to broad speculations and the provision of concepts to structure our perceptions of the social world.

3.2 QUANTITATIVE METHODS

You have already encountered the distinction between qualitative and quantitative approaches (see, for example, Units 4 and 8, Audiocassette 2 for Block II and Unit 20, Section 2.1). Essentially, a quantitative method yields results in the form of numbers—it involves measures or statistics of some kind. Sometimes, these are generated by a 'head count' of people or items which come within a certain category. Official (HMSO) statistics for 1986, for example, tell us that in England and Wales 87.4 thousand men and 5.7 thousand women received custodial sentences. Another kind of method which yields quantitative data is a psychological test, like the spatial ability or aptitude test referrred to in Unit 20 (Figure 2 in Section 3.2).

'Personally I'd stand up and be counted tomorrow, except that everyone else is innumerate."

Qualitative material can also be converted to numerical form. In conversation analysis, for example, we can count up the amount of time each participant spends talking or interrupts the other, or the number of times a particular speech form is used in a conversation (see Unit 21, Section 3.2). Again, if instead of using open-ended questions in an interview, we devise a set of questions which permit only a limited choice of answers, we end up with a multi-response questionnaire. Then we can compare the number of times people in different categories respond positively (or negatively) to particular questions—quantitative results.

The great advantage of quantitative findings is that they allow us to compare in a fairly precise way one set of data with another. By working out statistics like the average or mean, or the 'standard deviation' (roughly, the average amount by which each score deviates, either above or below, the mean), we can quickly and efficiently describe the pattern of a set of data and give meaning to each item in relation to the set. The only real meaning a score on an ability or intelligence test has is to tell us how that score compares with the average and pattern of scores for the general (or a specified, particular) population. An IQ of 100 means only that the score achieved on that particular intelligence test is exactly average for the population as a whole. Other IQs, above or below this, tell us what proportion of people are likely to achieve a score on this test at or below this level. On a standard intelligence test, for example, an IQ of 115 usually (though it does depend on the test) indicates that a person's score is just at the level for the top 16 per cent of the population.

(Although this is not the place to elaborate on the nature of numbers, it may be worth noting, at least for the mathematically inclined, that such comparative or relative scores are of a different nature to ratio scales like height and weight which have a true zero. Although it is perfectly valid to talk of a fourteen-stone person being twice as heavy as one of seven stone, it makes no sense to say a person with an IQ of 140 is twice as intelligent as a person with an IQ of seventy.)

Statistics not only provide a means of describing and comparing data but also enable a researcher to analyse the patterning of results. In the discussion in Unit 19 of Eysenck's research, we saw how he used statistical procedures based on correlating together large numbers of results from questionnaire items and other kinds of test to see how they cluster together. It is by such statistical analysis that he claims to have established his core personality factors or dimensions, such as Extraversion and Neuroticism. On the basis of this analysis, he was also able to devise the Eysenck Personality Inventory—a set of questions designed to measure how a person rates on these dimensions.

In spite of the advantages which quantitative methods offer of precise comparison and statistical analysis, it is necessary to recognize their limitations. The major issue of how far it is possible to capture the meanings intrinsic to social processes and social life in the form of numerical data will be taken up later. Suffice it for the moment to note that there is an inevitable loss of detail and information in the reduction of the qualitative to the quantitative—a 'trade off', if you like, of richness for rigour. How far can, for example, an extraversion score contain the complexity and nuances of feelings and thought which might be conveyed in an autobiographical account?

A further issue is that quantitative results must usually be labelled at some point: in other words, they are still tied ultimately to some form of qualitative verbal description. This is a fact that has bedevilled the history of personality and intelligence testing. It is simply not sufficient to define intelligence (as some have tried to do) as 'what intelligence tests measure'. At some point, it is necessary to describe the qualities that it denotes.

3.3   A METHOD FOR TESTING HYPOTHESES

It is worth noting that quantitative measures and descriptive statistics in themselves do not enable us to determine relationships of cause and effect: in other words to explain why something comes about. We cannot conclude that, because there is a correlation between measures on two separate items, that either one causes the other. This may be the case but, equally, it may be some third, as yet unobserved, factor which is causing them both to fluctuate in this co-related way.

--- ACTIVITY 4 ---

1   Several studies have found a low but significant correlation between aggressive behaviour and level of male hormone testosterone.

2   The highest peak for offenders is males in their late teens when testosterone levels are at their highest.

Can we conclude, therefore, that testosterone causes aggression and increases the likelihood of antisocial behaviour?

(Answers at the back)

The most effective method for confirming whether one event causes another is an *experiment*. Although experiments are much used in mainstream psychology, they are difficult to apply in investigating the complexities of social life and society and so do not figure a great deal in this course. There have though been one or two examples in Block V. Eysenck has relied heavily on experiments to establish particular aspects of his theory: for example, to try to show that extraverts condition less well than introverts (Unit 19). The most detailed account of an experiment is given in the article by Zimbardo (Chapter 17 of the Reader).

======= READER =======

You might like to look again at this article. In re-reading it quickly, focus this time on the methodology rather than the content. This is not stated very clearly in the article but see if you can work out the design of the experiment: what was being investigated and how? You might also like to glance again at the discussion of the experiment in Unit 20 (Section 2.2).

An experiment starts with a hypothesis about a causal (i.e. cause-effect) relationship. In the Zimbardo experiment (although it is not immediately obvious from the article), this was about the effects that playing the role of either prisoner or guard would have on the behaviour and experience of the people concerned. The experimenters then proceed to test their hypothesis. A common way to do this is to assign subjects randomly to one or more groups. In the Zimbardo study, subjects were randomly allocated to be either guards or prisoners. By comparing the responses to different experimental conditions given by the subjects (in the Zimbardo study being either a 'prisoner' or a 'guard'), the experimenters can begin to determine their causal effect. A feature of an experiment is to try, as far as possible, to 'control for' (avoid the influence of) any other factor that might bias the results. This is one reason for conducting experiments in a 'laboratory' rather than out in the real world where all sorts of things which the experimenters could not predict might influence what is going on.

The effects of the two conditions are usually recorded as quantitative measures of some kind (note the reference in the Zimbardo paper to 'tests' of the subjects at various points during the course of the experiment). An advantage of this is that statistical procedures can be used in yet another way: to assess the probability that any differences found between the results from the two conditions are due to the experimental manipulation (e.g. being either a prisoner or guard) or merely to chance variations in the subjects' responses. Such quantitative comparisons are often fleshed out with qualitative descriptions gained from interviews and observations. (These, in fact, make up the bulk of the Zimbardo article.)

To sum up, the essential features of a *psychological experiment* are:

1   A clearly defined *experimental hypothesis*.

2   Allocation of subjects to *two or more conditions* which are different or varied only in respect of the experimental hypothesis being tested.

3   *Control* to ensure the elimination as far as possible of any extraneous influences which might affect results.

4   Some *quantitative* measure of the subjects' responses so that the statistical significance (the probability that they are not due to chance) can be assessed.

Although they do offer the potential for exploring precisely relationships between causes and their effects, experiments have many limitations. Not many social issues can be brought effectively into the laboratory. The requirements of control and quantification often create a very artificial situation and the findings, therefore, may not be applicable to the complexities of the real world.

Experiments on social behaviour can also pose ethical problems. Subjects may have to be deceived, for example, as to the real purpose of an experiment in case knowing it could influence the ways in which they behave. A few studies such as the one by Zimbardo (as also the Milgram experiment to which the paper refers) may even impose distressing experiences on the people who take part.

A form of experiment which circumvents both kinds of concern (though, in consequence, it loses out on control) is the 'natural experiment'. This is a study in a natural setting where the comparison made is between the effects of the different conditions created (e.g. before and after) by a naturally occurring event. Reference to a study of this kind by Warr was made in Unit 20 (Section 2.1) The anxiety level of nurses was recorded as they moved from one type of ward to another in the normal course of their work. The different type of wards, in other words, represented the different experimental conditions whose effects were measured.

There may be limits to the extent to which experiments can be used to investigate the kinds of question which concern social scientists. But given the advantage of rigour and precision which experiments and quantitative methods in general offer, why is not more use made of them in social science? This is a question we shall take up in the next section.

SUMMARY

(Sections 3.2 and 3.3)

- Quantitative methods include descriptive statistics, questionnaires and tests.

- The advantage of quantitative methods is that they make possible precise comparisons.

- The patterns formed by data (e.g. the way they intercorrelate) can be explored.

- Quantitative methods are limited because they do not capture the richness and detail of meanings which is possible with qualitative methods.

- Cause-effect relationships can only be properly ascertained by means of experiments.

3.4   THE SIGNIFICANCE OF MEANING

The answer to the question as to why more use is not made in social science of experiments and quantitative methods, lies in the nature of the subject matter with which social scientists deal. It was suggested in Unit 4 that this is essentially constituted by *representations* and this has been amply illustrated in the course material so far. In Block V, for example, we have noted that identity and social interactions are made up of 'meanings'—how people interpret and make sense of themselves, other people and the nature of the situation. When two people interact, we cannot understand effectively what is going on unless we know something about their thoughts and feelings and the social conventions and strategies which are implicit in the relationship concerned.

Natural scientists such as physicists and chemists study a material world of objects and energies, the vast majority of which are, potentially at least, measurable with some precision. The social world, in contrast, is essentially a representational reality. It is made up of ideas, feelings, concepts and expectations. There are physical aspects (such as products, weapons, being hungry, pollution) which help make society what it is, but even these are made sense of and responded to in terms of the representations people have of them. Relationships, encounters, a sense of identity are not things which exist 'out there'. Our only access to them is by inference and by trying to reconstruct what the meanings which make up a particular experience or situation may be. The major, perhaps only, way we can represent these reconstructions in their subtlety and richness is in some form of language or qualitative account. (It is interesting that Levinson in Chapter 15 of the Reader even resorts to poetry as the most effective way of conveying the elusive quality of life experience.) This is true even of observable behaviour. Although in some sense it exists in tangible form, the real significance which behaviour has for the social scientist are the intentions and meanings which underlie it. To push someone under a bus by accident or by design may involve the same physical movements and have the same terrible effect, but, as a court of law would recognize, they are entirely different kinds of action because of the different meanings and intentions involved.

——————————————————— ACTIVITY 5 ———————————————————

Try observing two people in conversation. Think how you could describe this. How much of the interaction do you think it would it be possible to capture and convey in quantitative form (i.e. as a set of numbers of some kind)?

For much of this century, psychologists have tried to invent ways of measuring meanings. Attitude scales have been designed, rather along the lines of the personality scale you encountered in the discussion of Eysenck's work, so that people's positive or negative feelings about different aspects of their world can be rated. But although these, like personality test scores, may have some value for general research and for providing basic indicators of what a person is like, they tell us little of the complex ways in which people represent and experience themselves and the world about them.

A subject matter which consists of meanings and representations is inevitably somewhat elusive. We have no alternative but to interpret and reconstruct it. The more precisely we manage to measure it, the less of it we are likely to encompass.

Not only are meanings elusive and not amenable to measurement, they are also 'reactive'. What is meant by this is that the way in which people see and make sense of different aspects of their world itself may change as a result of the feedback they receive and the new interpretation which they can then put upon them. In this way, when we encounter a particular theory, it may change the ways in which we represent the world. As a result of the theories and ideas you have encountered in the course, perhaps you have begun to make sense of society and the people in it a little differently from the way you made sense of it before you started.

The constructed nature of the representations and meanings which are the core subject matter of social science creates other methodological problems. Applying the methods of natural science requires not only measurement but also the precise testing of causal hypotheses. In order that we may do this, the hypothesis must be formulated in such a way that the observable results of an experiment can potentially invalidate or 'falsify' it, as well as be consistent with it. In this way, the hypothesis is *tested* by the experiment: i.e. it will be confirmed or invalidated, depending on the results. As we noted in the discussion of the nature of psychoanalytic theory (Unit 19, Section 3.3), one of the problems with psychoanalysis is that it is very difficult to formulate its theoretical ideas in such a form that they can be tested in this way.

What kinds of reasons were given for this difficulty in Section 3.3 of Unit 19?

One reason is that its explanations of behaviour are expressed in terms of theoretical concepts (such as repression) which are not directly observable but which can only be inferred. Another reason is that the same effect may arise from different causes (e.g. frustration *and* gratification may lead to fixation).

The crucial point here is not that psychoanalysis is necessarily wrong (or necessarily right), but that it is impossible to firmly establish or undermine its validity. An advocate of the positivist methodology of natural science, such as Eysenck, would argue that therefore it is 'unscientific' and, by implication, of no value. I would suggest, however, that this is to ignore the nature of the subject matter with which we, as psychologists and social scientists, deal. Psychoanalysis is used here only as an example. The same considerations apply to most theorizing in social science. As we saw in Chapter 15 of the Reader, 'The evolutionary origins of identity', even a theory like sociobiology, supposedly grounded in the natural science theory of evolution, also produces hypotheses which are not open to precise testing.

What psychoanalysis and most other social science theories do offer are, in Erikson's phrase, 'tools to think with'. They give us concepts and models to interpret and give new meanings to the phenomena of social behaviour and society. We may not be able to test precisely whether or not they hold up, but we can get some impression of how plausible and consistent such interpretations are. We can judge whether using the theory and concepts in question enable us to make sense of the world in a deeper and more convincing way. We can also use evidence, if not to test the theory, at least to see how consistent with it this may be.

A positivist natural science approach should not, therefore, necessarily be regarded as the ideal methodology for social science. The precision and clarity which it offers may be attractive, but the critical issue remains of how far is such an approach applicable to a subject matter constituted by meanings. The positivist approach of measurement and experiment should also not be regarded as the only form of science. Although its subject matter may often preclude scientific investigation of a positivist kind, social science is scientific too in the broader sense of the word, of engaging in enquiry of a systematic and rational kind.

Most social scientists accept the need to pursue this broader form of enquiry though there are some (particularly within psychology) who believe, along with Eysenck, that the best way forward is to restrict investigation to that which is possible with rigorous methods of measurement and experiment. More rarely, perhaps, are the two approaches used to complement each other in an attempt to get the best of both worlds. An example of this kind is the large-scale study of prejudice by Adorno *et al.* (1950) mentioned in Unit 19 (Section 3). In this investigation of the nature of the authoritarian personality, the team of researchers used scales for measuring the attitudes and personality of their subjects as well as intensive psychoanalytically-oriented interviewing to form a more detailed psychological picture of samples of subjects selected with the scales.

3.5   KINDS OF UNDERSTANDING

Two methodological approaches, then, have been contrasted. The positivist's approach asserts that effective understanding depends on developing methods for measuring the subject matter in question and for testing precisely the explanatory hypotheses of the theory concerned. The other approach questions the possibility of both these procedures, given that the subject matter of social science consists of representations or meanings of different kinds. Inference and qualitative reconstruction are essential and quantitative data can represent these only in grossly simplified form. We might call this second position 'hermeneutic', a word (taken from the study of ancient scriptures) meaning to do with interpretation.

As we have seen, the two approaches not only use different methods but produce somewhat different kinds of understanding. *Positivist understanding* comes, ideally, as precise, testable, causal laws and these are inevitably of restricted scope. *Hermeneutic understanding* (i.e. interpretative understanding), in contrast, is more broadly applicable and is provided by concepts to help us interpret rather than precisely predict.

There is a third distinction which should be made. Unit 19 (Section 2) discusses the nature of personal agency: that people have some capacity to direct their lives and create, at least partially, their own identities. If this is the case, it is not sufficient for social science to account for society and social behaviour only in terms of explanations or interpretations of a determinist kind. It should fulfill a further function of enhancing this capacity for agency and self-direction. Social science methods should be directed at emancipation and *self-empowerment* as well as explanation and interpretation. An example of social science used for increasing our awareness and (hence our self-empowerment) is presented by Section 7 of Unit 20. Here, it was demonstrated how advertisements (and other kinds of media representations) may contain ideological themes which can structure the ways in which we come to think about ourselves. Such analyses may help to heighten our awareness of such influences and, in so doing, dilute their power to affect our lives.

Analyses or research which emphasize our capacity for choice and the importance of perceived self-efficacy (Unit 19, Section 2), or explore the kinds of changes in experience which may come as we grow older (Unit 19, Section 3 and TV11), are also examples of ways of encouraging self-direction and heightening our awareness of different facets of our lives.

SUMMARY

(Sections 3.4 and 3.5)

- One approach to social science is provided by *positivism*. This models itself on the approach of natural science in studying the material world and emphasizes measurement, expressing theories in terms of what can be observed and the precise testing of hypotheses by means of experiment.

- The *hermeneutic* approach argues that the core subject matter of social science is constituted by meanings and representations. These are not amenable to positivist methods because they can only be investigated and understood by means of interpretation and reconstruction.

- A further goal of social science is to give us more understanding and control by *heightening our awareness* of different forms of social influence and facets of our lives.

- Although, in practice, one or other approach tends to be followed or focused on, they should not be regarded as necessarily mutually exclusive.

---

4   THE METHODOLOGY OF SOCIAL SCIENCE

Most of what has been said so far in this discussion of methodology is intended to apply to social science in general. Our examples, though, have been drawn largely from Block V and the discussion focused on the kinds of methodological problems which confront social scientists such as psychologists interested in understanding the behaviour and experience of others in society. Other disciplines within the social sciences are concerned with different kinds of topic and issue. Their focus, as you have seen, is on macro-social aspects of society like social divisions, the economy and the nature and exercise of power. So it is also worth looking more specifically at the way methods have been used in other parts of the course.

———————————————— ACTIVITY 6 ————————————————

Jot down some examples of the *methods* used or drawn on in earlier blocks of the course.

How did you get on? Here are some examples that I noted.

Throughout the first three blocks of the course, in particular, much use was made of descriptive *statistical data*. In other words, statistics were used to describe different aspects on the economy and society. To name but a few examples, there were data on population growth and distribution of wealth and income in the UK, consumer expenditure and car ownership, imports/exports, EEC surplus build-up of cereals, and the percentage of the market held by different supermarkets and by types of fast food. As was noted, such data vary considerably in reliability. Data on food production are suspect, for example, because so much of such production goes unrecorded (see Unit 2). Another problem can be the difficulty of finding data recorded in the right way (for example, it may have been recorded both whether or not a person is black or a woman, but it may not be possible to put these together and tell how many black women there are in any particular population: see Unit 8). One common way of using such descriptive data is to draw comparisons between those from different sources. Thus, infant mortality rates in the EEC were compared with those in commonwealth countries; and indices of comparative economic performance like GDP per capita, unemployment or inflation rates were compared between EEC countries and the UK. Other comparisons made were longitudinal, showing how the same statistic (e.g. unemployment) rate has varied over a specified period of time.

As was strongly stressed in Units 2 and 6, however, such data have to be treated with care. Statistics of this kind cannot be regarded simply as representing existing objective facts. We have noted above the problems of reliability but there are other problems too. Data often have to be selected—a sample taken from a wide array of possibilities, and how this is done can make a world of difference. As was pointed out in Unit 6 (Section 1.1), unemployment data can be selected in such a way (e.g. from a period which shows a temporary rise) as to mask a more long-term trend. Even where statistics seem straightforward, there may be biases in recording which invalidate comparison between data from different sources. A notorious example of this is suicide statistics. In a country where social and religious attitudes towards suicide are negative (Ireland or Austria, for example), such an act is only likely to be recorded officially if it is beyond all doubt. In other countries, the balance of probability that there was suicidal intention may be sufficient. Finally, even where data are reliable, they still have to be interpreted, and that leaves much room for controversy and speculation.

Much of the data and information drawn on in the course and in social science is referred to in terms of the method used to collect it. It may be generated, for example by opinion *questionnaires* (e.g. 'do you think there is a class struggle?') or by *surveys* (comparing, for example, the class background of people at university or in professional as opposed to blue collar jobs, or the incidence of anorexia nervosa among girls). There have also been *qualitative accounts*: for example, narratives about the history of tea, and reactions in the UK to EEC policy decisions relating to the UK economy, and a personal note from Harold Wilson. Some use was made as well of what we might call *'formal information'*, such as details of the constitutional structure and institutions of the EEC.

Would you say that the development of the theme in the final movement of Beethoven's Third Symphony is (a) too long, (b) too complex, or (c) just right?"

What we have been considering so far constitutes the *evidence* for social scientists; the outward measurable or observable manifestations of society. Much of the methodology you encountered in the course though was not about recording or collecting data. Considerable effort was expended, for example, in *conceptual analysis*. The meaning of different concepts was unpacked and explored: what do we mean by 'famine', 'democracy', 'sovereignty' or 'work'. Although there was some attempt (as in the definition of power, for example) to find ways of measuring the category concerned, such definitions were largely conceptual, rather than 'operational' (i.e. expressed in terms of measurable, observable effects).

One approach is to use concepts (such as class, gender and race) to help categorize and organize our understanding of, say, the different kinds of social division and groupings within society (see Block II). Another approach, which depends on inter-relating data with conceptual analysis, is the development of *models*. Block III provided several examples of this where models, say of the market and capitalism, were elaborated to show how the economy works.

It is perhaps worth distinguishing here between specific methodological techniques (such as data collection, interviewing and experiments), which have been largely the focus of this discussion, and a more general sense of *social science enquiry* concerned with developing understanding of the way society works. The essence of this broader notion of social science method, as the last review unit (Unit 18) made clear, is the interplay between conceptual analysis or theorizing and evidence. Data may be brought to bear to test an explanation (for example, why famine occurs). Or a pattern, formed by say the statistics and policy decisions relating to the UK economy, may be established and then examined from the standpoint of different theories (e.g. Keynesianism, or monetarism).

The basic steps of this research process in social science were set out explicitly in Unit 6, Section 1 Summary. They involve identifying a social problem, collecting or consulting information about it, classifying the data to draw out significant patterns or trends, using social science concepts and theorizing to define and explain them, and setting the problem in a wider social framework. Here, then, we are looking for patterns and consistencies and interpreting them in terms of concepts and theories. We have seen these procedures in action in Unit 2, for one example, in trying to understand famine and what causes it.

A point worth noting in relation to this broader notion of social scientific enquiry is that, while the degree of fit between theory and evidence may serve to confirm or raise questions about the theory, rarely, it should be noted, does it serve to *test* it precisely in the way that the positivist position would require. This may sometimes be due, as we have seen in the analysis of the causes of famine, to the complexity of the factors involved. But a major reason for this limitation, as was argued in Section 3.2, is the nature of the subject matter. It is inevitable because society and social behaviour are constituted and organized by meanings and these are rarely, if ever, open to precise measurement and the kind of experimental test which will be sufficient to falsify or completely disconfirm the hypothesis or theory concerned. Although the kind of evidence, then, we can obtain in social science may not enable us to dismiss a particular theory, perspective or tradition of thought, nevertheless, as Unit 18 pointed out, it does enable us to make some evaluation of specific hypotheses and get some idea of a theory's limitations.

As can be detected by comparing Blocks III to V, particular social science disciplines emphasize somewhat different methodological strategies. So, for example, economics has a variety of data (about economic performance, production and consumption for example) from which to draw, and there is an emphasis on model building to explain relationships in the pattern of data. In politics and sociology, there is, perhaps, less emphasis on data and models, and conceptual analysis and grand theorizing tend to play a more major role. Psychology, as we have seen in this unit, employs a range of methods. In mainstream psychology (as compared with Block V where the scope was restricted to psychology in relation to identity and interaction) the dominant method has been use of *experiments*.

This different emphasis on methods in different social sciences is, in part due to the special nature of their subject matter (i.e. the particular aspects of society and/or social behaviour with which they are concerned). But it has also been influenced by the traditions of intellectual thought which have prevailed in the different disciplines. (This aspect and the emergence and development of the disciplines of social science are discussed further in Section 3 of Chapter 22 of the Reader.)

SUMMARY

- A core method in social science is a gathering of descriptive statistics and the comparison of data from different sources.

- Such data are not to be regarded as 'objective facts'. They are open to problems of reliability, selection, potential bias and interpretation.

- Other sources of information include opinion questionnaires, surveys, qualitative accounts and, occasionally, statements of a formal or constitutional kind.

- Research involves not only collecting evidence but conceptual analysis. Concepts, models and theories are used to help define the subject matter in question and to organize our understanding about it.

- In addition to specific investigative techniques, there is a broader sense of social scientific enquiry into aspects of society.

- While it is possible to use evidence to confirm or lose confidence in more general theorizing of this kind, because the subject matter of social science is essentially constituted by meanings, rarely is it open to precise and definitive test.

- Different social science disciplines emphasize somewhat different methodological strategies partly due to the particular nature of their subject-matter and partly to their particular historical and intellectual origins.

5 METHODS AND PERSPECTIVES

When we look back over what we have covered in this half-unit, we see a variety of investigative methods and procedures (see Table 1).

Table 1   Social science methods

A. SPECIFIC METHODS

Qualitative
- observation
- analysis of social documents and historical records
- interviews
- introspection
- free association
- dream analysis
- ethnographic methods (involving observation and interviewing)
- accounts and narratives
- interventions violating conventions

Quantitative
- descriptive statistics
- multi-response questionnaires
- psychological tests
- behavioural responses

Both or either qualitative and quantitative (see Note 1 below)
- content analysis
- conversation analysis
- surveys
- opinion questionnaires
- longitudinal studies

For precise testing of specific hypotheses about cause-effect relationships
- experiment (see Note 2 below)

B. GENERAL METHODS FOR SOCIAL ENQUIRY

- conceptual analysis
- rational speculation
- personal syntheses
- model building

A strategy for social science enquiry
1   Identify, conceptualize and define the problem.
2   Collect information about it.
3   Classify this data to draw out patterns.
4   Further apply social science concepts/explanatory framework.
5   Set problem in wider social framework.

NOTES ON TABLE 1

1   Note that some specific methods are not easily classified as either qualitative or quantitative. As mentioned earlier, it is sometimes possible, for example, to convert qualitative information into quantitative form. One way (as in the case of content analysis) would be to analyse the qualitative content in terms of the number of times a particular category of response, characteristic or utterance occurs. Thus we could compare newspapers (qualitative accounts) in terms of the amount of content concerned with sport or news etc. (giving a quantitative measure).

2   Note also that, while experiments provide a means of **precisely** testing a specific hypothesis, hypotheses can also be supported or undermined by using other forms of social science method.

5.1 WHICH METHOD?

Which particular method is used will depend on a number of factors. In part, it clearly depends on the kind of subject matter being investigated and the kind of questions being asked. As we mentioned above, different social science disciplines may tend to emphasize one kind of method rather than other.

But there is more to it than that. Choice of method will also depend on assumptions about the nature of people and society. The major traditions of thought in the social sciences, and what they assume about people and society, have been distinguished and discussed both in Chapter 22 of the Reader and in the course as a whole.

In terms of choice of methods, it is also crucially important what assumptions are made about the goals of social science as well as about the nature of its subject matter. In Section 3.4, we distinguished three broad approaches. If you take a *positivist* line, you will be looking for 'hard data' and trying to establish laws of cause and effect, and you will favour methods designed to yield these. If you are *hermeneutically* inclined and concerned to interpret and unpack the meanings underlying the social world, then qualitative methods and conceptual analysis are more likely to be your forte. If your goal is emancipation and empowerment through *heightened awareness*, it is likely you may draw on both approaches but may well be disinclined to accept determinist assumptions that people and society are fixed by factors outside their control. You will be more concerned to 'give social science away' and present it in such a way as to help people gain fuller understanding of themselves and the society in which they live.

These different approaches, with their assumptions about both the nature of people in society and also about the goals of social science, are found co-existing *within* disciplines and are reflected in the different perspectives which may be encountered there. Block V has sought to exemplify this theme by presenting four very different perspectives (phenomenological, psychoanalytic, biological and social). Actually, one of the key thrusts in the development of psychology was the attempt to get away from the influence of traditional modes of thinking and 'armchair theorizing', and substitute for this the supposedly objective empiricism of natural science. The aims of early academic psychology have been described as being to apply the methods of physiology to the problems of philosophy. But, in effect, this has had only limited influence. It is true that the positivist tradition in the concern with measurement and experiment has been strong. But, as we have seen, other approaches like psychoanalysis and the social perspective are essentially hermeneutic in their focus on meanings. And even the determinism explicit in positivism (and more implicit in hermeneutic approaches) has been challenged by the phenomenological perspective's concern with personal agency.

As the comment on psychology in Chapter 22, Section 3, of the Reader indicates, many issues similar to those which divide the major traditions of thought in social science are still being actively explored by psychologists. What helps to distinguish the different approaches contained within psychology is their different position on questions such as the degree to which human behaviour is shaped by socialization or genetic predisposition, or whether conscious or unconscious thought is the directing force in human affairs. These questions stem from the varied intellectual ancestors which gave birth to the subject, including philosophy with its emphasis on conscious reasoning, biology with its use of natural science methods and psychotherapy where the full complexity of personal problems has to be confronted and made sense of in some way.

Another reason for differences in methodological emphasis between psychological perspectives is that the aspects of the person which each approach regards as of central interest varies. For the phenomenological approach, as we have seen, it is conscious awareness; for psychoanalysis, unconscious motivations; for a biological perspective, it is the body and physiological processes; and, for the social perspective, it is the meanings assimilated from the social context in which the person lives. It is not surprising, given this, that their methods differ. Biological approaches can deal with the more tangible world of hormones and physiological processes. (The one exception is sociobiology which is inevitably forced into speculation when its focus turns to humans because of the need to reconstruct the distant past.) Even for the behaviourist, behaviour is assumed to be out there to be observed and measured. The major thrust both in biological approaches and in behaviourism is to use the positivist methods of natural science. Turning the focus on our own experience, though, as the phenomenological approach does, inevitably requires a totally different methodological approach—that of introspection and reflection on how we experience our lives. The social approach, in turn, goes beyond immediate awareness, seeking to explore its origins in, and dependence on the representations and beliefs we assimilate from society. The methods for this, as we have seen, are also primarily hermeneutic, aimed at interpreting the structures that underlie the social phenomena which we can observe. Psychoanalysis similarly seeks to penetrate beneath surface forms, though the techniques it has developed for trying to uncover unconscious meanings are more directed at their origins in childhood than in society.

To some extent different methods can be used together in a complementary way. (The study of prejudice by Adorno *et al.* which combined positivist measurement of attitudes with hermeneutic in-depth interviewing is an example of this already mentioned.) In effect, the degree to which this is done is very limited. It is likely to depend also on whether different perspectives themselves are seen as compatible or in opposition. Methods which analyse at the level of an individual's intentions or actions are likely to be of limited interest, for example, to someone who has adopted a strongly social position which does not acknowledge individual agency.

When we compare the four perspectives presented in this block and the different kinds of understanding and explanation they produce, they may appear irreconcilable. For, their methods are different, as also are their focus and the concepts which they use. If they *are* incompatible, this would suggest that we need some way of evaluating them, of choosing between the different accounts of identity and interaction they put forward. Ways in which we might compare and evaluate theories will be the theme of the next half-unit, Unit 26. But are they necessarily irreconcilable? Is not the focus of each perspective on a different aspect of the human condition? We are all biological beings, all live in society, have a long personal past of childhood experience, and are capable of conscious reflection on the ways we experience our lives. Would it not be better to regard the perspectives and their methods as offering different kinds of insight into who we are?

I'm taking the day off from abstract concepts today ...

ANSWERS TO ACTIVITIES

ACTIVITY 1

1 (i) Mortality, (ii) choice, and (iii) search for meaning. (Sections 2.1 and 2.2)

2 Oral, anal and phallic stages. (Section 3.1)

3 Any three of repression, projection, displacement, sublimation. (Section 3.1)

4 An unrealistic, idealized self image of what we should be like or should do, often assimilated from the attitudes and values of our parents. (Section 3.2)

5 Stimulating activities and experiences (due to extraverts' low arousal level). (Section 4.5)

6 Twin studies, especially comparisons of separated fraternal and identical twins. (Section 4.5)

7 Crime offers stimulation: also, because of the poorer conditionability of extraverts. (Section 4.6)

8 The evolution of reciprocal altruism would have depended on a clear sense of identity so that a favour given could be returned later to the person who originally gave it. (See the section on 'Consciousness and a sense of self' in the article on Sociobiology in Chapter 15 of the Reader.)

9 Greater capacity to infer what others may be feeling and thinking, and thus greater ability to predict their behaviour. (Reader, Chapter 15.2.)

10 Males, because of the genetic advantages to them of mating with as many partners as possible, would have been in competition for mates. Bigger and stronger males would probably have been advantaged in such competition. Therefore, they were more likely to mate and thus more likely to pass on these characteristics to offspring, thereby increasing their incidence in future generations. (Reader, Chapter 15.2)

ACTIVITY 2

1   Being assigned to the role of guard or prisoner and being placed in a prison-like situation can have a profound effect on behaviour and attitudes. (See the article by Zimbardo in Chapter 17 of the Reader.)

2   Either of

(i)   Can a researcher be sure that he/she has correctly identified the way that the people they are studying view the world? Could what they say be merely a metaphor or joke rather than actually how they see things?

(ii)   Is the informant representative of his/her culture?

(Section 4.2)

3   This is Cooley's idea that the ways in which other people see us act as a 'mirror' and influence the way we see ourselves. (Section 6.2)

4   This is Althusser's term for when something we see or read 'strikes a cord'; i.e. it seems to relate to the kind of person we feel we are. (Section 7.2, also Unit 17)

ACTIVITY 3

1   They reveal the implicit rules which underlie and govern the ways in which we interact. (Section 1.4)

2   The eyebrow flash and the basic patterns of smiling, laughing and crying all appear to biologically based (though not the situations which elicit them). (Section 2.1)

3   *Either*

(i)   Gumperz's observation of the way in which serving staff at a work's cafeteria said the word 'gravy'. Falling intonation is the normal style for questions for Indian women though it could be perceived as rudeness or indifference by native English listeners.

or

(ii)   Jupp *et al.'s* account of interactions between Mrs K and the Asian worker under her supervision. (Both in Section 2.2)

4   Examples include patterns for turn-taking, changing the topic or closing down a conversation, adjacency pairs (e.g. questions and answers, offering and accepting greetings and returning the greetings). (Section 3.2)

5   They talk longer, interrupt more often and overlapping conversation. (Section 3.2)

6   Three point lists, contrast structures. (Section 3.3)

7   'Giving' is expressing information about oneself and self-presenting consciously and deliberately. 'Giving off' information in self-presentation refers to those cues which others use to infer what we are like, over which we do not usually have conscious control (though we may in fact be capable sometimes of 'managing' these surreptitiously). (Section 4.5)

ACTIVITY 4

It may do but, from this evidence, we cannot be sure. Both are open to alternative explanations. In (1), engaging in aggressive behaviour may have increased testosterone level rather than the other way round. In (2), the two observations may both be characteristics of teenage males but not necessarily be a result of each other: for example, it is possible that they may both stem from a further cause such as culturally encouraged competitiveness among teenage boys.

REFERENCES

Adorno, T.W., Frenkel-Brunswik, E., Levinson, D.J. and Sanford, R.N. (1950) *The Authoritarian Personality*, New York, Harper and Row.

ACKNOWLEDGEMENTS

Grateful acknowledgment is made to the following sources for permission to reproduce material in this unit:

p. 7: Punch; *p. 10*: London Express News and Features; *p 18*: Copyright Sidney Harris; *p 22* Mel Calman.

FURTHER READING FOR BLOCK V

UNIT 19

(Please note that the following works are ordered according to their relevance to Unit 19.)

Glover, J.(1988) *I:The Philosophy and Psychology of Personal Identity*, Harmondsworth, Penguin.

Stevens, R.(1983) *Freud and Psychoanalysis*, Milton Keynes, The Open University Press.

Fromm, E.(1960) *The Fear of Freedom*, London, Routledge and Kegan Paul.

Levinson, D.J. et al. (1978) *The Seasons of a Man's Life*, New York, Knopf.

UNIT 20

Hewitt, J.(1984) *Self and Society: A Symbolic Interactionist Social Psychology* (3rd edn), London, Allyn and Bacon.

Hirst, P. and Woolley, P. (1982) *Social Relations and Human Attributes*, London, Tavistock.

UNIT 21

Gahagan, J. (1984) *Social Interaction and its Management*, London, Methuen.

Goffman, E.(1959) *The Presentation of Self in Everyday Life*, New York, Doubleday.